"In what other land save this one
is the commonest form of greeting
not 'Good day,' nor 'How d'ye do,'
but 'Love'?
That greeting is 'Aloha' —
love, I love you, my love to you."
— Jack London

KAUAI TRAILBLAZER
Where to Hike, Snorkel, Bike, Paddle, Surf

Fifth edition
text by Jerry Sprout
photographs, art direction, production by Janine Sprout
technical consultant, Michael Sagues

For Cynthia, Deanne and Roger

ISBN 10: 0-9786371-4-3
ISBN 13: 978-0-9786371-4-9
Library of Congress Catalog Card Number: 99-091787

Diamond Valley Company, Publishers
89 Lower Manzanita Drive, Markleeville, CA 96120
P.O. Box 422, Kilauea, HI 96754

Find us online at: www.trailblazertravelbooks.com
www.trailblazerhawaii.com (blog)

e-mail: trailblazertravelbooks@gmail.com
Published in the U.S.A. on recycled paper.

Mahalo to: Donald Bodine and Bob Keane, Suite Paradise; Gordon and Roberta Haas, Heather H. Giugni
at Juniroa Productions; Kapu Kinimaka Alquiza at Kamanawa Foundation; Phil Silva and Janet Leopold at
Allerton Gardens; Susan Kanoho, Kaua'i Visitors Bureau; Hero Dave Allred; Walter (Freckles) and Kamika
Smith; Lani Kawahara; Kenny Gibbs, Happy Hour Productions; Melila Purcell at Kauai Beach Resort; Jess and
Sky at Kayak Kauai; Nalani Ka'auawai Brun, Office of Economic Development; Kaleo Ho'okano, Water Safety
Supervisor; Mary A. Requilman, Kaua'i Historical Society; Keith Nitta, County Planning Department; Fred and
Carol Tangalin; Kalani Kali; Tarey W. Low and Sam Lee, Department of Land and Natural Resources; Frederick
Wichman, Kaua'i Place Names; Beth Tokioka, Public Information Officer, Mayor's Office; Keala Senkus, Hula-
room; Jodi Esaki; Rudival and Jamie Niere; Edwin Hagstrom; Tebo Booth, Na Hula O Kaohikakapulani Hula
Halau; Koke'e State Park staff; Jessica and Tracy at KKCR; Lilian de Mello; Kapa'a Camera Club; Phyllis Crain,
Limahuli Tropical Garden; Judy Drosd, Kaua'i Film Commission; Paulette Burtner, Koke'e Natural History
Museum; Darrell Aquino, Hyatt Resorts; the crew at Holoholo Charters; Jo Evans, Outfitters Kauai; Capt. Rick
Brown; Doug and Sandy McMaster at Ki Hoalu; Denise Carswell and all at Princeville Ranch; Amy Vander-
hoop; Dawn M. Traina; Joe and Lihue Kinimaka-Lopez; Aunty Rose; Margaret and Dennis Daniels; Tiane,
David, and Cole Cleveland at Wailua River Kayak; Darla, Kauai Coffee; Leilani Rivera Bond, Halau Hula O
Leilani & Leilani Records; Chris Porter at Kaua'i Adventure Activities; Titus Kinimaka; Joanne Smith and Ed
and Joyce Doty at Na Aina Kai; John Cruz; Jack Johnson; Melinda Morey; Tom Ziemer and family; Diane
Tilley at Kilauea Refuge; James the Jumper; Adventure Amy Smith and Adam; Ruth and Jim Cassel; Charlie
Cobb-Adams; (the late) Andy and Bruce Irons; Aletha Kaohi at West Kauai Center; (the late) David Boynton;
Mark and Tina at Java Kai Hanalei; Spark and Melissa at Coconut Coasters; Cynde at Jungle Girl; Julie and Ehu
at Ehu Kai Shells; Saa Tamba Ginlack; John Pia at Taro Patch; Prime Minister Henry Noa; and to everyone else
who shared their Kaua'i with us. Aloha!

Proofreader: Greg Hayes
cover: Kalalau Valley

Napali Coast

Waipo'o Falls

KAUAI

WHERE TO
HIKE SNORKEL BIKE PADDLE SURF

JERRY & JANINE SPROUT

A TRAILBLAZER TRAVEL BOOK

DIAMOND VALLEY COMPANY
PUBLISHERS
MARKLEEVILLE, CALIFORNIA
KILAUEA, HAWAII
© COPYRIGHT 2012

Table Of Contents

Introducing Kaua'i

Covering an area of 65 million square miles, the Pacific Ocean is by far the biggest single feature on Earth—as big as the other oceans combined and easily larger than the world's land masses put together. A satellite photo over the Pacific shows nothing but blue.

In the center of these waters is the Hawaiian Archipelago, some 132 islands strung in a line for about 1,600 miles, all part of the State of Hawaii. If territorial waters are considered, Hawaii is a far larger area than Alaska, but in terms of landmass, the state is the 47th smallest, larger only than Connecticut, Rhode Island or Delaware. The islands and waters from Kaua'i north to Midway Island comprise the Northwestern Hawaiian Islands Marine National Monument.

The archipelago is the top of the Hawaiian Ridge, a mountain range standing in seawater about 5 miles deep. Snow gathers on its 13,000-foot peaks, though situated well south of the Tropic of Cancer.

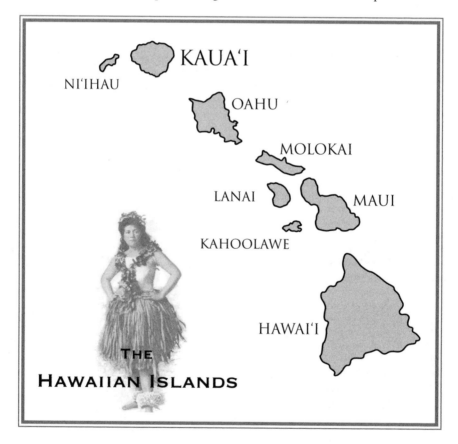

NI'IHAU

KAUA'I

OAHU

MOLOKAI

LANAI

MAUI

KAHOOLAWE

HAWAI'I

THE
HAWAIIAN ISLANDS

Considering its entirety, the Hawaiian Ridge is the tallest mountain range on Earth.

Almost all of the islands in the archipelago are sea-washed atolls, barely above a foaming surface and home to only birds and aquatic life. Ninety-nine percent of Hawai'i's 6,415 square miles is shared among its eight most southerly islands, and two-thirds of that area is allotted to just the Big Island of Hawai'i.

In terms of people, three-quarters of the state's 1.5 million live on Oahu, about 100 miles southeast of Kaua'i. Maui and the Big Island each have more than twice Kaua'i's 65,000 resident and visitor population.

These are the most isolated populations in the world—about 2,500 miles from San Francisco, Los Angeles and Seattle to the northeast, and the same distance from Alaska, which is due north. (Although the archipelago extends west of the Bering Sea, the principal islands of the state do not take most-westerly honors from Alaska.) Japan is almost 4,000 miles to the northwest. To the south, southeast and southwest, 2,500 miles of open sea lie between Hawai'i and other Polynesian islands of Tahiti, Tonga and the Marquesas. The largest chunk of land southward is Antarctica.

Kaua'i (pronounced like "Hawaii") is the northernmost of the populated Hawaiian Islands and by far the most ancient—volcanic origins date back millions of years whereas the lava has not stopped bubbling on the Big Island 400 miles to the south.

At the center of Kaua'i is 5,148-foot Mount Waialeale—Wey-ahlee-ahlee—forming the rim of an ancient volcanic caldera that, at 60 square miles, is the largest in the Pacific. Waialeale, located nearly at the center of the world's largest body of saltwater, receives the most rainfall in the world—an average of 430 inches per year. Over the eons, the island's caldera has evolved into Alakai Swamp—lying 4,000 feet above sea-level, the highest of any swamp environment in the world. As one Kauaian saying is translated, "At the birthplace of all waters, it rains and rains, and then it pours."

Rainfall on other parts of the island is radically less. Kaua'i's arid, leeward west shore gets 15 to 30 inches per year, its windward north shore gets 60 to 90 inches on average, and parts of eastern portions of the island get 40 to 60 inches of rain per year. The rain comes in buckets, both in storms and quick showers, followed by intense tropical sunshine that extends for days. The average temperature on Kaua'i is 75 degrees, around the clock, around the calendar. The average high varies just 8 degrees from the average low, and temperatures rarely break 90 degrees and never 100.

Although weather conditions cycle over a year—primarily winter's northerly trade winds and rains give way to summer's southerly Kona winds and drier conditions—on Kaua'i it is eternal summer. Something is always in bloom. These climatic conditions led to Kaua'i's nickname of the Garden Island. Virtually everything that can grow and doesn't require a cold snap is growing here, from redwoods to pineapples. Three of the country's five National Tropical Botanical Gardens are here.

The profusion of plant life that blankets Kaua'i in many shades of green also accents its startling topography: Rain, plus millennia of trade winds and pounding surf have turned what was once a volcanic dome into a series of towering ridges radiating out from the center of the island to the sea, ridges above valleys and canyons 3- to 4-thousand-feet deep and made of red volcanic earth held together by a tremendous root mass of tropical greenery.

Anahola

These valleys yield more than a dozen rivers and large streams, the only navigable fresh water in Hawai'i. The origins of these waterways are a capillary system of streams and brooks that seep from the swamp or spring from cliff walls. Many of these contributing streams are obscured by jungle foliage, only becoming apparent after a rainstorm when dark green ridges are streaked with silvery waterfalls. Where rivers and streams meet the sea are wide slack-water lagoons extending inland from a mile to several miles before disappearing into riverbank flora or giving way to rapids and cascades. At the beach, these rivers are most often shallow, almost dammed by surf-born yellow sand. During storm conditions, the slack waters can become debris-filled torrents of destruction.

Along Kaua'i's 110-mile coast, in between the rivers and streams, are grassy, open bluffs fringed by sand and coral reef beaches. The notable exception to this landscape is Napali—The Cliffs—a 25-mile quadrant of the northwest coastline. Here ridges end in wave-battered cliffs, inaccessible by car and only partially accessible by foot. Even in Napali, however, there are little beaches with valleys that supported Hawaiian communities for centuries.

Kaua'i has the longest sand beach in the islands, as well as the longest coral reef. Many of its dozens of beaches and coves are accessible only by hikes. Generally speaking, in the winter, north side beaches near Hanalei are pounded by the trade wind's swells and the south beaches of Poipu are relatively calm. In the summer, the opposite is true, as southerly Kona winds bring bigger surf to the south and the north shore's coves become aquamarine pools. Beaches on the west and east are variable in terms of water conditions—but beach conditions everywhere can vary greatly from day to day.

Kaua'i's physical features—while perhaps beyond the scope of any engineer's or animator's imagination—are perfectly designed for recreational exploration. Roads go inland at numerous places and ancient trails rim the coast and follow ridges to dizzying heights, inviting hikers and mountain bikers. Surfing beaches are too numerous to be crowded, although on any given day the local boarders may flock to the hottest spot. Coral reefs and coves create saltwater pools—home to some 650 species of fish—made for snorkeling and swimming. River lagoons and protected bays invite kayaks and outrigger canoes. These activities combined are the only way to fully appreciate this complex island.

While ecotourism may be part of Kaua'i's future economic health, it is only a recent development. The island's powerful beauty is just a backdrop for the story of the world's least understood and perhaps most interesting human migrations. The first Polynesians, from the Marquesas, sailed here in 200 AD, followed by a second migration from Tahiti that ended in the 1400s. Polynesian life was undisturbed by any other cultural influence until Europeans and Americans arrived in the late 1700s.

Alakai Swamp, Hanalei Bay

GETTING TO & DRIVING AROUND KAUA'I

AIR TRAVEL
Lihue Airport, 808-246-1440.
Most flights to Kauai include a stopover and change of terminals in Honolulu. Most international airlines service Honolulu. Some airlines have non-stop flights to Kauai: From Los Angeles, check with United. Hawaiian Airlines offers lower rates for stays of more than 30 days, and is equipped to handle surfboards and bicycles.

CAR RENTALS
All major car rental agencies are available at Lihue Airport.

PUBLIC TRANSPORTATION
A public bus with limited schedules is available on most parts the island. For routes and timetables call County of Kaua'i Transportation, 808-241-6410.

DRIVE TIMES
From road's end at one end of the island to road's end at the other is about a two-hour drive—part of the island's coastline is roadless. All roads are scenic, with traffic only at junctions around Lihue and Kapa'a in the morning and evening. There are no freeways; maximum speed is 50 mph.

FROM LIHUE TO:

Nawiliwili Harbor, 2 mi., 5 min.
Kalaheo, 14 mi., 20 min.
Koloa, 11 mi., 20 min.
Poipu, 15 mi., 25 min.
Hanapepe, 19 mi., 35min.
Waimea Town, 23 mi., 40 min.
Kekaha, 27 mi., 45 min.
Barking Sands Beach, 36 mi., 60 min.
Waimea Canyon, 34 mi., 60 min.
Koke'e State Park, 38 mi., 70 min.

FROM LIHUE TO:

Wailua, 6 mi., 15 min.
Kapa'a, 9 mi., 20 min.
Anahola, 14 mi., 25 min.
Kilauea, 24 mi., 35 min.
Princeville, 27 mi., 40 min.
Hanalei, 31 mi., 50 min.
Haena, 38 mi., 60 min.

THE ISLAND OF

KAUA'I

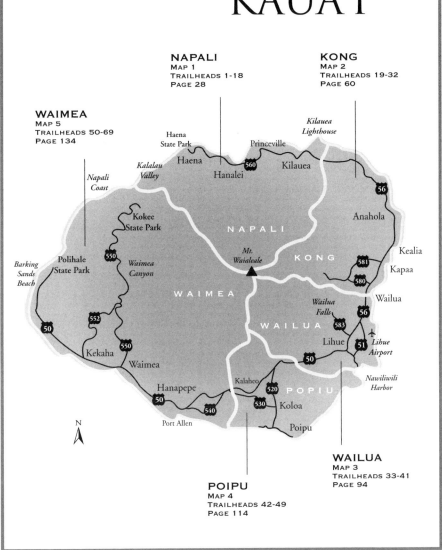

NAPALI
MAP 1
TRAILHEADS 1-18
PAGE 28

KONG
MAP 2
TRAILHEADS 19-32
PAGE 60

WAIMEA
MAP 5
TRAILHEADS 50-69
PAGE 134

Kilauea
Lighthouse

Haena
State Park

Princeville

Napali
Coast

Kalalau
Valley

Haena

560

Hanalei

Kilauea

56

Kokee
State Park

NAPALI

Anahola

Barking
Sands
Beach

Polihale
State Park

550

Waimea
Canyon

Mt.
Waialeale

KONG

581

Kealia

Kapaa

580

552

WAIMEA

Wailua
Falls

WAILUA

56

Wailua

50

550

Kekaha

Waimea

583

Lihue

51

Lihue
Airport

50

Nawiliwili
Harbor

Hanapepe

Kalaheo

520

POPIU

50

540

530

Koloa

Port Allen

Poipu

N

WAILUA
MAP 3
TRAILHEADS 33-41
PAGE 94

POIPU
MAP 4
TRAILHEADS 42-49
PAGE 114

KEY TO READING TRAILHEAD DESCRIPTIONS

23. TRAILHEAD NAME   ACTIVITIES BANNER
    What's Best:
    Parking:
    HIKE: (S A M P L E)
    SNORKEL, BIKE, PADDLE, SURF

"23." **Trailhead Number:** These correspond to the numbers shown on the five Trailhead Maps. There are 69 trailheads. Numbering begins on Map 1, Napali Trailheads, and numbers get bigger as you go clockwise around the island. Trailhead 69 is at the top of Waimea Canyon, on Trailhead Map 5. Within the text of the Trailhead Descriptions, numbering starts at "1." and continues sequentially.

Trailhead name: This is where you park for hiking, snorkeling and the other activities originating at this trailhead.

Activities Banner: This shows which of the five recreational activities are possible at this trailhead. Activities include one or more of the following, always listed in this order:

HIKE:	Trail treks, beach walks, and around-town strolls.
SNORKEL:	Both fish viewing and swimming in areas that are not in breaking surf.
BIKE:	Trails, dirt roads, rural roads, and touring around town.
PADDLE:	Kayaking and canoeing in rivers and streams, lagoons and bays.
SURF:	Surfing, boogie boarding, and body surfing.

What's Best: Tells you, in a nutshell, what's best about this trailhead.

Parking: Gives specific directions to the trailhead and where to park. A single trailhead may include additional parking instructions to nearby activities within the same general locale.

Abbreviations used in parking directions:

Since Kaua'i is circular, with highways around its coast, compass directions change as you drive. "Toward the mountain" and "toward the ocean" are a traditional way of giving directions in the islands.

Makai = Turn toward the ocean

Mauka = Turn toward the mountains, inland

mm. = Mile Marker. All island highways are marked at each mile, beginning at "0" where they originate. Marker signs show the miles from the beginning and the highway you are on. Both Hwy. 50 and Hwy. 56 originate in Lihue. Hwy. 56 goes toward Hanalei, with numbers ascending in that direction. Hwy. 50 goes toward Polihale, with numbers ascending in that direction. Driving directions are usually given heading away from Lihue, toward the higher mile marker numbers. Use your odometer to determine fractions of miles.

HIKE: The first paragraph after the **HIKE:** symbol gives the destination of each hike for this trailhead (followed by the roundtrip distance and elevation gain of 100 or more feet for that destination in parentheses).

NOTE: ALL HIKING DISTANCES IN PARENTHESES ARE ROUNDTRIP.

The second and following paragraphs after the **HIKE:** symbol give details about the hike's destination, including trail descriptions and junctions. The first mention of a **Hike Destination** is boldfaced. Hike destinations are described in the same order in which they are listed in the first hiking paragraph.

SNORKEL, BIKE, PADDLE, SURF: Following the hiking descriptions are the letter symbols for the other activities that are available at this trailhead. Descriptions and details about each activity follow its symbols. The **Location** at which the activity takes place is boldfaced. Each trailhead, for example, may have several places to surf or ride a mountain bike. Directions to each activity are either the parking directions, or otherwise noted in the text.

Activities are always listed in the same order, i.e., hiking, followed by snorkeling, mountain biking, paddling and surfing. If an activity is not available at a particular trailhead, its symbol is not listed.

More Stuff: Lists secondary activities, often less popular (and less crowded), harder to get to, or with questionable access.

Be Aware: Notes hazards and gives safety tips that give an idea of hike difficulty.

TRAILHEAD DIRECTORY
A list of trailheads and their activities.

HIKE: HIKES & WALKS
SNORKEL: SNORKELING & SWIMMING
BIKE: MOUNTAIN AND ROAD BIKING

PADDLE: KAYAKING & CANOEING
SURF: SURFING & BOOGIE BOARDING

NAPALI
Map 1, Trailheads 1 through 18

KONG
Map 2, Trailheads 19 through 32

Awaʻawapuhi Trail, Secret Beach

THE BEST OF KAUA'I

WHAT DO YOU WANT TO DO TODAY?

Best For Hikers—

MOUNTAIN VISTA HIKES

COASTAL BLUFFS

SHORT WALKS TO BIG VIEWS

BIRDWATCHER HIKES

FALLS AND RIVERS

GARDEN STROLLS

Kuilau Ridge Trail

Best For Hikers, cont'd—

TREES AND JUNGLE
Bamboo Forest, TH8, page 40
Sleeping Giant, TH30, page 81
Kuilau Ridge Trail, TH32, page 85
Haele'ele Ridge, TH60, page 153
Kumuwela Lookout, TH63, page 159
Nualolo Trail, TH66, page 162
Halemanu-Kokee Trail, TH67, page 164

TOWN WALKABOUTS
Hanalei, TH7, page 38
Kapa'a, TH28, page 77
Hanapepe, TH51, page 137
Waimea, TH54, page 143
Koloa, DT1, page 183

LONG-AND-SCENIC BEACHES
Kepuhi Point, TH3, page 33
Lumahai Beach, TH5, page 35
Hanalei Bay, TH7, page 37
Secret Beach, TH16, page 52
Larsens Beach, TH20, page 62
Nukoli'i Beach, TH35, page 100
Kekaha, TH55, page 146
Polihale, TH57, page 148

PEOPLE-WATCHING BEACHES
Hanalei Bay, TH7, page 37
Kalapaki Bay, TH41, page 106
Poipu Beach, TH44, page 120

COASTAL WILDLIFE
Kilauea Refuge, TH 17, page 53
Waiakalua Beaches, TH19, page 61
Larsen's Beach, TH20, page 62
Seabird Point, TH21, page 64
Heritage Trail, TH43, page 118

HIKE-TO ONLY BEACHES
Hideaways and Kenomene Beach,
  TH9, page 43
Queens Baths and Kaweonui Beach,
  TH10, page 45
Wyllies Beach, TH11, page 46
Secret Beach, TH16, page 52
Waiakalua Beach, TH19, page 61
Larsens Beach, TH20, page 62
Donkey Beach, TH26, page 71
Haula Beach, TH42, page 115
Pakala Beaches, TH53, page 141

PORTS, PIERS, JETTYS & MARINAS
Hanalei Pier, TH7, page 37
Wailua Marina, TH33, page 95
Ahukini Landing, TH39, page 104
Nawiliwili, TH41, page 106
Waimea Pier, TH54, page 144

Poipu Beach

Best For Snorkelers—

BEST OVERALL
Keʻe Beach, TH1, page 32
Tunnels Beach, TH2, page 32
Kenomene and Hideaways,
    TH9, page 43
Lydgate Park, TH34, page 100
Prince Kuhio, TH45, page 122
Niʻihau-Lehua, TH50, page 136

HIKE-TO SNORKELING SPOTS
Pilaʻa Beaches, TH19, page 62
Papaʻa Bay, Aliomanu Beach,
    TH22, page 67
House Beach, TH26, page 73
Wahiawa Bay, TH50, page 136

A QUIET DAY AT THE BEACH
Waikoko Beach, TH6, page 36
Anini Beach, TH13, page 49
Secret Beach, TH16, TH17, page 52
Kilauea Bay, TH18, page 54
Larsens Beach, TH20, page 62
Moloaʻa Bay, TH21, page 65
Papaʻa Bay, TH22, page 66
Queens Pond, Barking Sands,
    TH57, page 149

LOCAL-STYLE BEACHES
Kalihiwai Bay, TH14, page 51
Anahola Beach Park, TH24, page 69
Kealia Beach, TH27, page 73
Hanamaulu Bay, TH38, page 103
Salt Pond Beach, TH52, page 139

Best For Mountain Bikers—

MOUNTAIN AND RIDGE VISTA
Powerline North, TH12, page 47
Waipaheʻe Falls, TH25, page 71
Alexander Reservoir, TH49, page 129
Haeleʻele Ridge, TH60, page 154
Polihale Ridge, TH61, page 155
Kaʻaweiki Ridge, TH62, page 158

TROPICAL FOREST
Waialeale Basin, TH32, page 89
Halemanu Valley, TH63, page 160
Kumuwela Road, TH67, page 167
Mohihi Road, TH67, page 167

COASTAL
Kealia Beach, TH27, page 75
Kapaʻa Town, TH28, page 78
Coconut Coast, TH29, page 81
Ahukini Coast, TH40, page 105

RIDEABOUT TOWN
Hanalei, TH7, page 39
Princeville, TH11, page 46
Kapaʻa and Coconut
    Coast, TH28-29, pages 78, 80

Tunnels Beach

Best For Paddlers—

BEST OVERALL
Hanalei River, TH7, page 39
Kilauea Stream, TH18, page 55
Wailua River, TH33-34, pages 96
Huleia Stream, TH41, page 108
Hanapepe River, TH51, page 138

PADDLE IN PRIVACY
Wainiha River, TH4, page 35
Lumahai River, TH5, page 35
Kalihiwai Stream, TH14, page 51
Kealia Stream, TH27, page 76
Waimea River, TH54, page 147

Kalihiwai Bay

SEA VENTURES
Hanalei Bay, TH7, page 39
Anini Beach, TH13, page 50
Hanamaulu Bay, TH38, page 104
Kipu Kai Beach, TH42, page 117
Hanapepe Bay, TH51, page 138
Waimea Bay, TH54, page 147

Best For Surfers—

WINTER SURF
Cannons, TH2, page 33
Tunnels, TH2, page 33
Pohakuopio, TH6, page 37
Black Pot Beach, TH7, page 39
Hideaways, TH9, page 44

SUMMER SURF
Poipu Beaches, TH44, page 122
Prince Kuhio Beaches, TH45, page 123
Pakala Beaches, TH53, page 143

ALL-YEAR POSSIBILITIES
Kalihiwai Bay, TH14, page 51
Quarry Beach, TH18, page 55
Kealia Beach, TH27, page 76
Kalapaki Bay, TH41, page 109
Shipwreck Beach, TH43, page 119
Kekaha Beach, TH55, page 147
Polihale, TH57, page 150

PLACES TO WATCH SURFERS
Hanalei Pier, TH7, page 39
Kalihiwai Bay, TH14, page 51
Quarry Beach, TH18, page 55
Kealia Beach, TH27, page 76
Kalapaki Bay, TH41, page 109
Brenneckes, TH44, page 119
Longhouse Beach, TH45, page 123

Best Free Hula Shows—
Poipu Beach, TH44, page 119
St. Regis Princeville Hotel,
   DT3, page 201
Coconut Marketplace,
   DT3, page 197
Kaua'i Marriott, DT1, page 181
Kukui Grove Shopping Center,
   DT1, page 180
Poipu Village, DT1, page 185

Best For A Rainy Day—

MUSEUMS AND ATTRACTIONS
Waioli Mission, DT3, page 203
Kaua'i Museum, DT1, page 180
Grove Farm, DT1, page 180
Kilohana Plantation, DT1, page 188
West Kauai Visitors Center,
   DT4, page 211
Kokee Natural History
   Museum, DT4, page 213
See Museums in Resource Links, page 242

**HOTELS WITH
HAWAIIANA ON DISPLAY**
Courtyard Marriott, TH29, page 80
Kaua'i Marriott, DT1, page 181
Grand Hyatt Kaua'i, DT1, page 183
Sheraton Kaua'i Resort, DT1, page 185

**WALK-AROUND
SOUVENIR SHOPPING**
Hanalei Town, DT3, page 203
Kapa'a Town, TH28, page 77
Kukui Grove, DT1, page 180
Kukuiula Village, DT1, page 184
Koloa, DT1, page 183
Hanapepe, DT4, page 209

Best Local Style Eats—
see Resource Links, page 244

Bubba's
Dani's,
Duane's Ono-Char Burger
Garden Island BBQ
Hanamura Saimin Stand
Kauai Pasta
Koloa Snack Shop

Best Pacific Rim Gourmet—
Cafe Coco
Duke's Canoe Club
Gaylord's Kilohana
Grand Hyatt Ilima Terrace
Keoki's Paradise
Lighthouse Bistro
Plantation Garden Poipu
St. Regis Princeville

St. Regis Princeville

Kalalau Trail

When the Academy Award-winning movie *South Pacific* was released in 1958, Americans were left wondering where the film's magical paradise existed in real life. They discovered that this "South Pacific" was actually on the north shore of the northern-most Hawaiian island in the north Pacific—and Kaua'i became a premier destination.

With fancifully sculpted ridges, spewing waterfalls, exotic beaches and several river valleys, the north side of Kaua'i fits the image for most people's fantasy of what tropical splendor should be.

At road's end on the north shore is where Napali—or The Cliffs—begin. From here the notorious Kalalau Trail takes hikers on an arduous 11-mile trek along Napali to the Kalalau Valley, ducking into and out of other valleys along the way. Kalalau remains a remote and mysterious place with stone terraces echoing an ancient Hawaiian village long since vanished, and inaccessible inlets, where many a bandito or recluse has successfully hidden out. The most famous desperado was Ko'olau the Leper, who, with his wife and young son, was able to evade a military assault by authorities trying to deport the afflicted man to Molokai. After three years, the disease finally overcame both Ko'olau and his son, leaving his courageous and loving wife to make the trek alone back to her village.

Near the Kalalau trailhead are Ke'e and Tunnels beaches, whose reef-protected waters are home to schools of colorful fish and a lure for snorkelers. Surfers ride the reef break at several places offshore of these beaches, near Haena Beach Park.

Just inland from Ke'e Beach is Limahuli, one of Kaua'i's three National Tropical Botanical Gardens—Eden realized. Just around the point from Ke'e, where Bali Hai Ridge meets the ocean, is perhaps the most sacred spot in all the islands, a heiau and hula platform where cultural tradition was enacted for centuries in the form of dance and chanting. These ancient arts are still practiced there today.

Heading down the highway from Napali, several rivers and streams intersect the coast, originating in deep, steep valleys that cleave the island to its center. The Wainiha, Lumahai and Hanalei rivers are all navigable for kayakers, with a mile to several miles of still-water lagoons where fresh water meets the sea.

Wainiha River—the closest of the three to road's end—is noted for its rickety one-lane bridges. The river is framed by Wainiha Pali, a 4,000-foot high rippling green cliff that curls inland, serving as a high-altitude dam for the Alakai Swamp, which is on its other side. Wainiha Valley was home to the last of Kaua'i's original inhabitants, the Menehune people, 65 of whom were recorded as residents here by the U.S. Census in the late 1800s. Paddling the river here is one way to catch a view of this valley.

Lumahai, the next valley over from Wainiha, ends at Lumahai Beach, the poster shot for *South Pacific*. Lumahai is a huge sand beach with spectacular wave action.

The third river fanning out from Napali is the north shore's longest, the Hanalei. The river comes into Hanalei Bay through a National Wildlife Refuge, parts of which are open to hikers and cyclists. The river is also a major attraction for kayakers. The agricultural lands of Hanalei Valley are reminiscent of bygone days, when all Kauaian lands were divided into self-sufficient communities—called ahupua'a.

Hanalei Bay is a deep scoop out of the coast which today is known for several surfing beaches. The Hanalei Pier, now considered picturesque, was not all that long ago a structure vital to keeping the north shore supplied. Bowl-shaped Waioli Valley, known as the birthplace of rainbows, rises above Hanalei Town, often streaked with a half-dozen waterfalls. Joggers, hikers and cyclists will have as much fun as surfers in Hanalei, exploring not only the beach, but also the beachside neighborhood, historic church and mission, and laid-back shops.

The river-and-valley theme is less pronounced after Hanalei, as the road climbs up to the Princeville bluff. Adventure-seeking visitors may tend to overlook Princeville, with its condos and luxury hotel, but several hike-to snorkeling and surfing beaches here are among the best on the island. And inland from Princeville is Kaua'i's only trans-island trail, the Powerline, a five-star route for hikers and mountain bikers.

The bluff at Princeville gives way to Anini Beach, boasting the longest coral reef in the islands. Anini is also known for its tiny seashells, as well as its snorkeling and windsurfing. A polo field and campground, set on the lawn under spreading heliotrope trees, add to the scenery that makes this beach a favorite among many visitors.

Anini Beach

Just around the point from Anini Beach, is Kalihiwai Bay. Kalihiwai Stream— which turns heads of drivers who pass overhead on a highway bridge—is a secret among kayakers. The beach at Kalihiwai Bay is usually a safe swimming spot and also a choice for local-boy surfers and body boarders. The offshore break at Kalihiwai Bay is a sleeper surfing spot, overshadowed by nearby Hanalei Bay.

As you leave Kalihiwai, heading toward Kilauea, the river jungle lands of Kaua'i transition into open, sloping agricultural lands, fanning out above the coast and abutting ridges running parallel to the road in the distance inland. Cyclists can ride upland, through a variety of huge spreading trees, with guava, banana and papaya mixed in to add a tropical accent. Much of Kaua'i's fruit and produce is grown here.

The highway turns inland from the coast along this segment of the island, but hikers will find a number of short trails to some huge sandy beaches, known for vistas and wave action. Secret Beach runs for two miles, ending at Kilauea Point under its historic lighthouse. On the other side of the point is Kilauea Bay, another mile-plus

arc of fine sand. Kilauea Bay also receives Kilauea Stream, a wide lagoon sweeping inland through an open valley. Secluded Kilauea Falls is a show-stopper.

Kilauea Lighthouse, on the massive bluff between these two beaches, is the northernmost spot in Hawai'i. The lighthouse grounds are now part of the Kilauea Point National Wildlife Refuge, and home to Laysan albatrosses, tropicbirds, boobies and a number of other exotic winged creatures. Crater Hill, above the lighthouse, is a spot not only to view birds but also a place to take in a vista of the north coast.

Hanalei

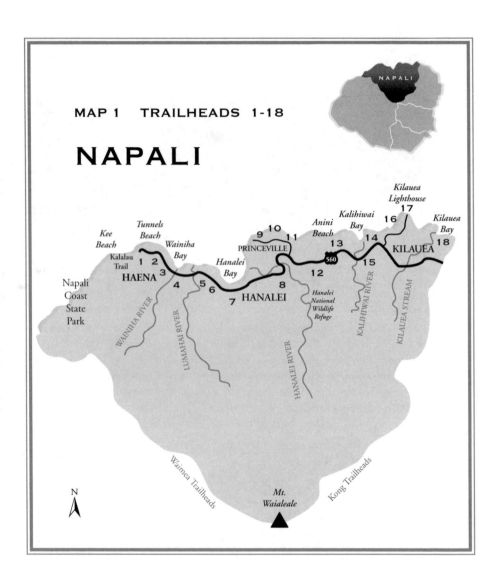

MAP 1   TRAILHEADS 1-18

NAPALI

NAPALI

Kilauea
Lighthouse

Kalihiwai
Bay

17
16

Kilauea
Bay

Kee
Beach

Tunnels
Beach

9 10

Anini
Beach

14

18

Waimiha
Bay

11

13

KILAUEA

Kalalau
Trail   1 2

PRINCEVILLE

15

HAENA 3

Hanalei
Bay

12

Napali
Coast
State
Park

4

5
6

8

7   HANALEI

Hanalei
National
Wildlife
Refuge

560

WAINIHA RIVER

LUMAHAI RIVER

HANALEI RIVER

KALIHIWAI RIVER

KILAUEA STREAM

Waimea Trailheads

Kong Trailheads

N

Mt.
Waialeale

NAPALI

T R A I L H E A D S
1-18

HIKE   HIKING
SNORKEL   SNORKELING AND SWIMMING
BIKE   MOUNTAIN OR ROAD BIKING
PADDLE   KAYAKING, CANOEING
SURF   SURFING, BOOGIE BOARDING

TH   TRAILHEAD
Makai   TOWARD OCEAN
Mauka   TOWARD THE MOUNTAIN, INLAND
mm.   MILE MARKER, CORRESPONDS TO HIGHWAY SIGNS.
       USE CAR ODOMETER FOR FRACTIONS.

*Note: All hiking
distances are roundtrip
unless otherwise noted.*

1.   KALALAU TRAIL-KEʻE BEACH   HIKE, SNORKEL

WHAT'S BEST: Take a hike along the fabulous Napali Coast, snorkel at a picture-perfect beach, or saunter through one of the world's best botanical gardens. This is one of Kauaʻi's headliners; get here early to avoid crowds.

PARKING: Take Hwy. 560 from Hanalei and continue past mm9. *For Limahuli Garden:* At mm9.6, turn left up a signed driveway. *For Kalalau Trail, Hula Heiau, and Keʻe Beach:* Continue to road's end at mm10. On busy days, retreat and use the overflow parking lot, which is on the right at mm9.8—you'll save a big hassle by making a short walk.

HIKE: *Kalalau Trail hikes:* Napali view (1 mi., 375 ft.), Hanakapiai Beach (2 mi., 825 ft.), Hanakapiai Falls (8 mi., 1,575 ft.), or Napali high point (6 mi., 1,625 ft.); *Other hikes:* Kauluolaka Hula Heiau (.5-mi., 150 ft.); Keʻe to Haena Beach (up to 2.5 mi.); Limahuli Garden loop (1.25 mi., 225 ft.)

The 11-mile **Kalalau Trail** along the Napali Coast begins at the trailhead kiosk on your left at road's end. The entire Kalalau is a tough trail, and even seasoned hikers should not attempt a round-trip dayhike to the end. Start on a sunny day, the earlier the better. Sturdy shoes and a hiking pole will help, even though a major rennovation in 2011 added steps, diverted water, and cut back flora to make the going fast for the first 2 miles. The **Napali viewpoint** comes after just .5-mile, as the trail levels out in a garden of ti and pandanus. Wave-battered cliffs can be seen down the coast.

On the way from the viewpoint to **Hanakapiai Beach**, you'll get another good view down Napali, before dropping about 400 feet through lush foliage to the beach. You need to cross the stream at beach level, over rocks, which is not usually possible without getting your feet wet. *Be Aware:* Drownings occur at Hanakapiai—avoid the water except on the calmest days. Also, stream crossings are dangerous during rains.

Hanakapiai Falls

To **Hanakapiai Falls**, look for the trail heading inland about 30 feet after the streamcrossing. The first mile is the easiest, although often mucky. You'll pass a rain shelter and a helicopter landing site, and then enter a jungle garden of bamboo, ti, ferns, and huge mangos. The tangle of greenery hides ancient rock agricultural terraces. About halfway to the falls you cross the stream again. The trail weaves over rocks and crosses the stream two additonal times, the last one about .25-mile from the falls. (Might as well wade in your boots.) After scaling a hands-on rocky section, you reach the steep-walled amphitheater that frames Hanakapiai—a 200-foot white ribbon falling into a pool. *Be Aware:* Hanakapiai Falls is a fatiguing 8-mile hike. Be sure to note stream crossings going in to be able to find them on your return.

To **Napali high point**—800 feet above sea level—continue past the trail to the falls, beginning switchbacks immediately. After a mile of climbing, affording some spectacular seaward and inland views toward the falls, you reach the high point. *Way More Stuff:* The trail doesn't come back down to sea level until reaching the Kalalau Valley, another 8 miles distant. *Be Aware:* Be careful not to step off the trail: what looks solid is often matted greenery over steep cliffs.

To the sublime **Kauluolaka Hula Heiau**, begin at Ke'e Beach and pick up a stepping-stones trail that skirts the shoreline to your left as you face the beach. Curl around at the edge of the black rocks, losing sight of Ke'e. Near the point, climb left up the rugged stone steps. Stay just to the right of the greenery all the way up to the cliff base. You reach the top of a series of grassy terraces, about 80 feet above the sea. This spot today, as it was in antiquity, is where the ancient hula and chants are performed. *Be Aware:* At times this sacred Hawaiian spot is closed to give the place a rest.

Ke'e to Haena Beach is the shortcut to a long view of the Napali Coast. Head down the sand at Ke'e Beach. In a minute or two, look back to see the Napali Coast buttresses receding in the distance. About midway on this walk is Limahuli Stream. Inland from here is the site of Taylor Camp, which in the hippie days was a well-known commune, with more than 100 flower kids, hosted by a generous landowner. After crossing the stream, you need to negotiate the black-rock shoreline around the point.

Limahuli Garden

Limahuli Garden is a National Tropical Botanical Garden, and some say it's as close to heaven as you can get on earth. The grounds are beneath the spires of Makana ("Bali Hai") Ridge and extend up lava rock terraces built by the valley's ancient dwellers. Both native Hawaiian plants and those brought by the voyaging Polynesians thrive here. The walking path skirts a stream and then winds upward, shaded by larger mango, autograph, and other trees. You'll reach a grassy, panoramic viewpoint, affording photo ops both seaward and up the Edenlike valley. *Note:* Admission is charged for self-guided tours, which includes a booklet—one of the best plant books available.

SNORKEL: Though fish are not copious, **Keʻe Beach**, when surf is breaking gently on its reef, is an ideal saltwater pool, one of Hawaii's all-around best. Keep to your right as you enter a sandy shore, swimming out along the reef. The view from the water back toward the cliffs is a keeper. *Be Aware:* Water escapes this cove on the cliff side, so be mindful of the current. Avoid swimming here when surf is high, though a new lifeguard station has increased swimmer safety.

2.   HAENA BEACH-TUNNELS   HIKE, SNORKEL, SURF

WHAT'S BEST: Surfing, beach strolling, and superlative snorkeling with drop-dead views of Makana Ridge. This Kauaʻi classic demands an encore.
PARKING: At Haena Beach Park, mm8.75, about 7 mi. from Hanalei Bay.
Note: Different parking noted below for the Tunnels snorkeling.

HIKE: Haena Point (2 mi.)

To rounded **Haena Point**, start up the beach to your right as you face the surf. You'll pass Tunnels Beach, a popular snorkeling and surfing spot. Just beyond Tunnels is sandy Haena Point. When the surf is fairly calm, you can walk a hundred yards or so offshore in ankle-deep water; a good vantage point for photography buffs. *More Stuff:* Walk to the left from the beach park for the more-secluded stroll of Cannons Beach.

SNORKEL: The real action is a 15-minute walk up the beach to Tunnels, one of Hawaii's best snorkeling venues. **Tunnels Beach parking** can be difficult (try late afternoon to beat the crowd and enjoy sunset). For the closest parking, look makai for a dirt drive at mm8.5, past Haena Street and at telephone pole #144R; it's next to a home with the address 57670. A second Tunnels Beach parking spot is .2-mile beyond the first—a dirt drive with a green chain-link fence running along both sides. It's across from telephone pole #14 and along a driveway marked by the address 57777; walk right when you hit the beach. A third, little-used public beach access is off a private road, at mm8.25 and telephone pole #19R, just after Haena Place. The access is .25-mile in from the highway, and Tunnels is a 10-minute walk to your left at the beach. Tunnels has a generous swath of sand and a deep-water coral reef near shore that attracts a multitude of fish, as well as tourists. A bonus for Tunnels is the perfect view of Bali Hai—the name for Makana Ridge that originated from the movie, *South Pacific.* Large ironwoods at the shore cast welcome shade. *Be Aware:* Haena lifeguards normally post hazard signs, but any time the surf is high you can count on rip current.

SURF: Surfers paddle the channel at **Tunnels Beach** to the reef break. This is a shallow break with tricky currents; ask the locals. **Cannons Beach** is on the other end of Haena City Beach Park. Scope the break—usually a left slide—from the unimproved turnouts as you leave the park headed for Keʻe. Like Tunnels, this is a reef break; watch the locals. When surf is low, Cannons will be a quiet getaway from Haena, ideal for family wading and snorkeling.

3. KEPUHI POINT
HIKE, SURF

WHAT'S BEST: A beach walk with Bali Hai views and solitude, even on busy days along this popular stretch of coast.
PARKING: Take the Hwy. 560 through Hanalei and continue past Wainiha to mm7.5. Patrons and shoppers may park in the lot for the Hanalei Colony and Napali Coast Art Gallery. Parking also just past the lot; turn makai on dirt Oneone Rd. *Alternate access for a shorter hike:* Continue to almost mm8, turn makai on Alealea Pl., and take a short path along a white fence at the YMCA camp.

Haena Beach and Makana Ridge (Bali Hai)

HIKE: **Kepuhi Point to Haena Point (2.5 mi.)**

Haena Point is a sure-thing scenic getaway for beachcombers, even on busy weekends. Take a short access path between the restaurant and the resort and head to your left when you get on the sand, which is Kaonohi Beach. Palms mingle with ironwoods among a few low-key vacation homes inland. After about .5-mile, the homes give way to open space, part of a YMCA camp, and the reef encroaches on the sandy shore. *Be Aware:* Surf and reef here can combine for dangerous swimming.

As you continue, the reef protrudes from the water, just as you reach a wide cove, noted by the half-dozen black rocks at its shore. Keen eyes will find tiny Ni'ihau-type shells here. At the far end of this cove is Haena Point, where, if conditions permit, you can walk a surprisingly far distance on a shoal. A Bali Hai view draws you along the last part of the walk. Rainbows seem to favor this beach. *More Stuff:* More energetic hikers can continue along the beach to Tunnels and Haena Beach Park.

SURF: Too reefy for the board boys, but intrepid kite-boarders and windsurfers have taken to the waters between Kepuhi and Haena points. The kite-boarders are usually nearer **Haena Point.**

Lumahai Beach

4. WAINIHA HIKE, BIKE, PADDLE

WHAT'S BEST: A non-tourist short hike, bike ride, drive, or paddle up one of Hawai'i's most mysterious valleys, home to the last of the Menehune people.
PARKING: Wainiha is small outpost just beyond Lumahai Beach on Hwy. 560, after mm6. *For the beach hike*, park at bedraggled Wainiha City Beach Park: Look right for a tournout after Powerhouse Road—when the the highway turns right and goes uphill.

HIKE: Waihina Beach (.5-mi.)

For **Waihina Beach**, make your way from the parking area, passing rustic beach camps and entering the wide spit of sand that separates the ocean from Wainiha Stream. At the far end is the stream's mouth and a fabulous view inland of the valley walls rising above the village and river. Virtually zero tourists find this spot.

BIKE: Start in town and head toward Haena. You immediately come to the first of two wooden, one-lane bridges, slung low across the Wainiha River. Between the first and second bridge is a dirt road upriver that you can bike about a mile, giving you a look at tropical gardens and old homestead cottages. This neighborhood has been home to the same families for three centuries. Then backtrack and cross the second bridge and head up paved Powerhouse Road, on your left. It's two miles and about a 500-foot climb to the end of the road. Jungle flora and birds are at hand.

The road opens to ridge views after about one mile. The pavement ends and the dirt road is blocked by a locked gate and an assortment of "keep out" signs. As you look up the mountain, toward your right, is Wainiha Pali, the 4,000-foot cliffs which are the border of the Alakai Swamp, sitting on a plateau behind the pali. Up this river valley until the late 1800s lived a 65-person colony, the descendents of the folkloric Menehune.

PADDLE: Put in at Wainiha, in town, where the river parallels the road and a shoal separates it from the bay. The **Wainiha River** forks upstream from the bay, at the two bridges, and comes together again about a mile upstream, making a narrow island. Both forks can be paddled along a short stretch of navigable water.

5.   LUMAHAI BEACH   HIKE, SNORKEL, PADDLE, SURF

WHAT'S BEST: Relax where the river meets the sea, or take a walk along the crashing surf of Kaua'i's most glamorous beach. On hot days, try a dip in the river pool.
PARKING: At Lumahai City Beach Park, around the point from Hanalei Bay, .75-mi. past mm5. Unimproved parking is before the bridge. *Alternate parking:* To access the far end of Lumahai (Kahalahala Beach), park at a paved turnout on your right at mm4.6, where the highway curves left. Walk a short distance up to the unpaved turnout and take a trail on the left. The beach is down stairsteps, through a pretty pandanus grove.

HIKE: Lumahai Beach (2 mi.)

From the parking area at **Lumahai Beach**, which is amid an ironwood grove on the bank of the Lumahai River, walk away from the river, heading onto a mass of fine sand up to two hundred yards deep. A little over halfway down the beach, the cliff draws nearer, and black rocks emerge from the sand, taking on the surf and creating bursts of spray. You may spot a coveted sunrise shell. The far end of Lumahai is called Kahala-hala Beach. Lumahai is the cover girl among Kauaian beaches, a reputation that began during the filming of *South Pacific*. *Be Aware:* Stay well back from the shore break.

SNORKEL: Lumahai is a dangerous swimming beach, site of many drowings and rogue waves that sweep people from the shoreline. But ... during dry periods when **Lumahai River** is slack, a large, inviting freshwater swimming area forms near the shore. Still waters are clear and green, reflecting the embankment that rises on the other shore.

PADDLE: The **Lumahai River** is a short stretch of navigable water upon which commercial outfitters are not permitted. Encroaching foliage blocks passage less than a mile up from the beach. Easy access is from the sandy shore. The Lumahai River valley, some 3,200 feet deep and 10 miles long, lies between the Hanalei and Wainiha rivers. *Be Aware:* Be mindful of getting lost in tree-shrouded passageways with no exits.

SURF: Across the stream is a left-break that peels off a black-rock ledge toward the beach. This is spot for experienced surfers, who use a ballsy entry from the rocks.

6.   WAIKOKO BEACH   HIKE, SNORKEL, SURF

WHAT'S BEST: A quiet beach stop on a busy road for a picnic. Float in warm water and enjoy jaw-dropping views of the Hanalei ridges.

Waikoko Beach

PARKING: Pass through Hanalei on Hwy. 560, cross two bridges, and park at turnout at mm4. *Alternate (surfer beach) parking:* Continue uphill to near mm4.5 and park at a paved turnout before a curving-arrow traffic sign. A steep trail leads down the embankment.

HIKE: Waikoko Beach (1 mi.)

Waikoko Beach is the continuation of Hanalei Bay beyond Waioli Stream at the edge of town. You can walk back toward town from the parking area along the beach. This beach is the homestretch for joggers who regularly run the length on Hanalei Bay, which is a little more than two miles. Smaller Waipa Stream, enters the bay up the beach from Waioli, and the sand in between is called Waipa Beach. Rocks and reef end the beach walk at the mouth of the bay, which is Makahoa Point. Inland across the road, is Waipa, an agricultural community that hosts a farmer's market. *Be Aware:* The streams can be hard to cross after rains.

SNORKEL: **Waikoko Beach** is a good place to take a swim with fins and mask, although fish are not usually abundant. The entrance is sandy, into deep water, with a smaller onshore break than the rest of the bay. The view inshore from the water is portrait quality. Waikoko is protected by a coral reef, called Pohakuopio, which juts into the bay from Makahoa Point. Use *alternate parking* above to locate the most-private beach, which has more coral and good snorkeling. *Be Aware:* No lifeguards serve these beaches. Watch for currents farther out.

SURF: **Pohakuopio** reef creates an offshore break at the mouth of Hanalei Bay, especially during the winter. Locals check out the break—a left-slide that is best when wind is offshore—from turnouts along the highway as the road climbs to the bluffs toward Lumahai. Break is shallow upon the reef in places. Observe the locals and don't surf this tricky spot if no one else is out there.

7.   HANALEI BAY   HIKE, SNORKEL, PADDLE, SURF

WHAT'S BEST: Hanalei may be the best walk-around beach town in Hawaii—an old-style town fringed by skyscraper ridges that are laced with waterfalls, and bordered by taro fields, a sandy bay, and wide river.
PARKING: Take Hwy. 56 into Hanalei Valley, where it becomes Hwy. 560. Continue to the center of town near mm2.6 and turn makai on Aku Rd. Continue on Aku to the stop sign, turn right on Weke Rd., and go about .5-mi. to parking at Black Pot City Beach Park. *Additonal Parking:* Near the Aku-Weke stop sign is the Hanalei City Pavilion. Continuing on Weke (away from Black Pot) are beach access paths at telephone pole #19 and at He'e Road, both within .4-mi. of the pavilion. Pine Trees Beach is at Ama'ama Rd., .5-mi. from the pavilion, and Weke Rd. ends not far after that at Waioli City Beach Park.

HIKE: Hanalei Beach (2.5 mi.)

The **Hanalei Beach** walk begins at **Black Pot Beach**, the center of life for surfers, kayakers, and beach lovers. Hanalei Pier, a set for a number of Hollywood movies, extends from the park. Its covered dock house is a cozy spot to make a dash for on a rainy day, watch sunset, or get close to surfers. Local kids take a leap and fishermen try their luck. To the right of the pier, as you face the water, is where surfers park for the long paddle out to the offshore breaks and where the Hanalei River enters the bay—a contemplative spot.

Continuing around the bay, you'll see shore-break surfers and joggers, and pass a number of beachfront homes, some of which are historical landmarks, and bed-and-breakfast cottages—all set among palm trees and gardens. After about .5-mile on packed sand you come to the **Hanalei City Pavilion**, the main station for the Hanalei lifeguards, who are among the best-trained in the world. From the pavilion, it's about .75-mile to **Waioli Beach Park**, which ends at Waioli Stream. (You pass the picnic tables and ironwoods of Pine Trees Beach along the way.) Across the stream is called Waipa Beach, which leads to the stream of the same name. Cross Waipa Stream and you're headed for Waikoko, at the far end of the bay. This walk has numerous options built in, starting at any of the access points described in the parking instructions, and popping out from the beach to quiet roads to take in beach life, Hanalei style. *Be Aware:* Steep soft sand in the middle of the bay gives way to riptide channels during high surf; watch out when wading. The streams can be difficult to cross after rains.

Walkers will also enjoy tooling around **Hanalei Town**, where exposed feet outnumber lace-ups ten-to-one. Don't miss the green church and grounds of the Waioli Mission House on the mountain-side at the far end of town as you head toward Haena. Behind

the church are rich agricultural lands of the Waioli Valley, "the birthplace of the rainbows." After a rain, the 3,500-foot ridge above Hanalei reveals scores of ribbon waterfalls. Most of the inland is private property, but landowners usually don't mind tourists, if you ask permission. The town features two quaint shopping areas, set off the highway on either side—plate lunches, sporting goods, surf duds, tiki-torch dining and high-end giftware.

SNORKEL: With its sandy bottom and shore break, **Hanalei Bay** is not known for snorkeling. But in calm conditions swimming is good around the pier at **Black Pot Beach**, where you'll see a few fish. Stay clear of fishing lines and surfers.

PADDLE: At **Black Pot Beach** is a boat ramp to put in for upriver paddles or soirees into the bay and around toward Pu'u Poa Beach at St. Regis Princeville Resort. To get to the ramp, go straight through the parking lot as the paved road ends. The **Hanalei River** may also be accessed at one or two openings observable along the grassy bank as you drive into Hanalei after crossing the bridge. Local outfitters also provide access, including Kayak Kauai Outbound, which has its own dock. The Hanalei River runs miles into the Hanalei Valley Wildlife Refuge, below 3,500-foot tropical ridges.

Adventure Amy Smith of Kayak Hanalei, Hanalei Bay

SURF: For beginners and kahunas alike, the breaks at **Black Pot B** to make it one of the best and most popular spots in Hawaii. Learners board heads like the break at the pier. Stand-up paddlers (SUPs) roam the bay. The big boys and girls go for the tiers of swells rolling in a couple hundred yards offshore, beyond the mouth of the Hanalei River—called **Queens. Kings**, several hundred yards farther out, only breaks with winter surf of 40 feet and up. Legendary surfer Titus Kinimaka in the 1990s was the first to ride Kings. The end of the pier is where to be for watching surfers. Bring your binoculars.

Pine Trees (look for the stand of ironwoods) has long tiers close to shore, a hangout for lots of locals, including pro champs Bruce Irons and the late Andy Irons. The Irons brothers put on a kids' competition, normally held in late February. For a mellow onshore break, better for boogie boarding and in view of lifeguards, try **Hanalei City Pavilion** in the middle of the bay. **Waioli Beach Park** is similar to Pine Trees, a closer-in break for mid-level or better surfers. *Be Aware:* Keep a lookout for flat, frothy spots in the breaking waves, which indicate channels where rip currents are going out.

8. HANALEI WILDLIFE REFUGE   HIKE, BIKE

WHAT'S BEST: Climb for a bird's-eye view of Hanalei Valley, or stay grounded on a hike through bamboo forest to a wild spot up the river without a paddle.
PARKING: Take Hwy. 56 toward Hanalei from Princeville and after crossing the river on the one-lane bridge, turn left immediately on unsigned Ohiki Rd. You enter the Hanalei National Wildlife Refuge, most of which is off-limits to humans.
Okolehao Trail parking: Proceed .6-mi., passing the historic Haraguchi Rice Mill (un-signed, now refuge offices), and park on left at the improved, signed parking lot.
Hanalei River Trail: Continue until the pavement ends, 2 mi. in. You'll see a cable across the road and a stop sign. Park as near as you can, step over the cable and walk in straight, past the house about .1-mile—not taking the drive that goes up to the right. You im-mediately come to the Halelea Forest Reserve checking station. *Note:* Despite the cable, this is access to the forest reserve designated by state officials. Some of the residents are not welcoming of hikers. Use your own judgment.

HIKE: Okolehao Trail (4.5 mi., 1,325 feet); Hanalei River Trail-bamboo forest (2 mi., 200 ft.)

The splendid **Okolehao Trail** rises to the best vantage point of the Hanalei coast and valley. The route was hewn during prohibition, when the Hawaiian liquor okolehao was being distilled from ti plants that grew along the trail. To begin, cross the road to the little footbridge at the trailhead and jog to your right on the red-dirt trail. Walk 40 or so yards on the road and turn left, uphill, on a rutted road in front of another chained road—which leads to the historic Japanese cemetery above the old rice mill. You leave wildlife refuge lands and enter the Halelea Forest Reserve. After about .75-mile and a long switchback, the road becomes a trail and footing becomes more difficult. This key juncture is marked by a huge steel power pole; cut left and head up the ridgeline. *Be Aware:* Stay back from drop-offs as you climb the ridge. A hiking pole will help, especially coming down when the trail is wet and slippery.

You'll penetrate a forest of Norfolk pine, strawberry guava, and pandanus as the trail heads inland on a series of ramps and benches. Several view knobs will entice shutter-bugs to stop for a shot. Then press on. After one hands-on steep section and the 1.75 mile marker, you reach an "end of trail" sign. But *make sure* to take the final hairpin left and walk about 150 overgrown yards (dropping a little at first) to the top, which is called Kaukaopua. The summit is a flat oval adorned by ti plants that partially obscure the 360-degree view of the Hanalei region. Wow. *Note:* Before taking the Okolehao Trail, you may wish to stop at the scenic turnout across from the shopping center in Princeville: Kaukaopua is the peak above the river, down from the double-tipped peak, that looks like Batman but is called Hihimanu. Named for a manta ray, this peak seems close enough to touch from the end of the maintained trail—but only fit hikers with local guides should even think about it.

The **Hanalei River Trail-bamboo forest** hike is a stomp through pig mud that is best done on a sunny day, not during rain. The trail is easy to follow, but is ingrown and dark to the point of eliciting claustrophobia. After passing the house at the uninviting trailhead, you begin in a tunnel of ferns and bamboo on a wide swath that it is not driveable, even by the Kauaian hunters. After about .5-mile within the bamboo, the sky appears, as well as a hillock of spongy grasses too deep to trod. Then you drop down again, hearing a stream before you see it, and finally crossing it, under overhanging branches and roots. After this thicket—all the while the trail is plainly observable—you cross a rocky streambed, veering left, and entering the bamboo again.

After about .25-mile in this last, dark bamboo cave, you reach the riverbank. From the riverbank, you are able to walk through ferns to a better viewpoint of a sweeping turn of the river, a few hundred feet upstream. *Be Aware:* Make sure you know how to get back to the first river sighting, as the trail through the ferns is sketchy.

BIKE: Park at the start of the road into the wildlife refuge, called Ohiki Road, and take the paved road on a flat, 4-mile roundtrip cycle. Near the end of the road you will also see 4WD tracts that lead into the Waioli Valley inland from Hanalei town. Some of this area is private property, and other portions are difficult.

9.   PRINCEVILLE   HIKE, SNORKEL, SURF

WHAT'S BEST: Behind vacation homes and resort condominiums are showy sunset views and some of Kaua'i's best hike-to beaches with snorkeling and surfing.
PARKING: Take Hwy. 56 several miles past Kilauea to near mm28. Turn makai at Princeville on Ka Haku Road, passing a large fountain, and continue 2 mi. to St. Regis Princeville Resort. Public parking is on the right, just outside resort entrance station, or in designated rows of the resort lot. Hotel valets will park your car.

Taro fields of Hanalei

Okolehao Trail vista point

HIKE: Fort Alexander site-St. Regis Princeville Resort (.25-mi.); Puʻu Poa Beach to Hanalei River (1.5 mi., 125 ft.); Hideaways-Kenomene Beach (.75-mi., 250 ft.)

Fort Alexander is a stroll across the resort lawn next to the parking lot, hugging the ocean side of the grassy bluff. A pavilion on the point commemorates the Russian traders' failed attempt to gain a foothold on Kauaʻi in the early 1800s. This is an excellent sunset spot, also used by surfers to check out the combers in Hanalei Bay. You'll also want to wander down to check out the views and sample the menu at the fabulous St. Regis Princeville Resort, which was rennovated in 2009. From the opulent lounge, a wall of towering plate glass shows off an unreal panormana of Hanaleii.

To **Puʻu Poa Beach**, which is used by the St. Regis and Hanalei Bay Resort, look for a beach access sign just to the left of the kiosk as you enter the resort parking lot. Access is via a concrete ramp and stairs that run behind the hotel, skirting the drainage that separates it from the Hanalei Bay Resort. At the beach, go left under spreading heliotrope trees along the shoreline. You reach black rocks, over which you scramble briefly, until getting a close-up view of Black Pot Beach across the river. On the point above river mouth are the terraces of the old Hanalei Plantation Hotel, the estate where *South Pacific* was filmed. The land is private property. *Note:* You can reach Puʻu Poa Beach by using the hotel elevators near the balcony doors: Descend to the fourth floor, walk the hallway, and then take another elevator down to the first floor.

The trail to **Hideaways-Kenomene Beach** is on the right, just before the resort entrance station. Look for a corridor between two chain-link fences parallel to the tennis courts. You walk the corridor for a couple hundred feet, and then descend steeply, on dirt-and-wood stairs, aided initially by a weathered pipe railing. One short section below the stairs is slick after it rains. Hideaways is a cozy swath of sand, pocketed by jungled cliffs. From the far end of the beach, a hands-on trail leads over black rock and through pandanus—a 10-minute, fairly rough scramble—to adjacent Kenomene Beach. Don't be surprised to see a monk seal on the sand; stay well back. At low tide you can walk around the point to Kenomene, but see *Snorkel* for a more civilized route to this beach.

SNORKEL: Although small, **Pu'u Poa Beach** is one of the island's better snorkeling beaches. Expect to mingle with hotel guests on this strip of reef-protected sand. Look for a sand entry and a coral section that is perpendicular to the shoreline. For the King-Kong view (nine stories above), head to the balcony of the resort where you can scope out the coral and take in one of the signature views in Hawaii. *Be Aware:* Water is shallow at low tide. Avoid stepping on coral.

Hideaways Beach, a small sand cove cupped into the bluffs, has very good snorkeling—sandy entry with clear water, coral and ample fish. And, although Hideways is on the tourist

Stairs to Hideaways-Kenomene Beach

radar among Kaua'i's best beaches, the pesky hike down tends to keep crowds away. *Be Aware:* Be wary of high surf offshore, especially during the winter, which can cause unsafe currents, normally flowing from right to left.

Kenomene Beach is straight down from the guardrail at the scenic overlook about .25-mile from St. Regis Princeville. See *Hike* above for access. But an easier access is via a concrete walkway that begins to the left of the parking lot for the Pali Ke Kua condominiums next to the overlook. It's near unit 106. The path zigzags steeply through a lush tropical gardenscape. Once at Kenomene Beach, head to the far end for sandy entry points among the black rocks. Snorkeling is excellent—among the best on Kauai—during lower surf conditions. *Be Aware:* A sign at the start of the walkway declares that access is for residents only. Use your own judgment and proceed at your own risk. Avoid swimming here during high surf, though moderate surf is safe.

SURF: **Hideaways** is a locals' surfing spot, with consistent offshore rollers. Driving in to the beach, park near a scenic overlook to observe conditions—a guardrail marks the overlook. On the trail down to the beach (not and easy board carry) you'll also come to a viewing spot, about 30 feet above the water.

Surfers also lug boards down the public access to **Pu'u Poa Beach**; under some conditions, it's a shorter paddle out the channel from there to catch the river mouth break off of Hanalei Bay.

10. QUEEN EMMAS BATHS   HIKE, SNORKEL

WHAT'S BEST: A hike-to beach and a shoreline pocketed with volcanic swimming pools, both giving a faraway feel at close-by places.
PARKING: Two different spots. For both, take Hwy. 56 past mm27 and turn into Princeville on Ka Haku Rd.
For Kaweonui (Sea Lodge) Beach, go about 1 mi. and turn makai on Pepelani Loop, at a sign for Sandpiper Village. Take a right off Pepelani onto Kaweonui Rd. Follow it about .3-mi., and turn right on *second* Keoniana. Park at end of cul-de-sac (address 3577), being careful not to intrude on residential parking. *Alternate Parking:* A more-used and less-scenic path leads from the Sea Lodge Condominums: Coming in on Ka Haku, turn right on Kamehameha (two streets befor Pepelani Lp.) and continue to the end, bearing left. Take a path between C and B buildings and bear left across a lawn at the bluff.
For Queen Emmas Baths, continue on Ka Haku past Pepelani Loop, and turn makai on Punahele Rd., about .5-mi. before reaching the Princeville Hotel. Go down Punahele about .25-mile and look for a designated, 12-car grass parking area. *Be Aware:* During prime conditions, this lot fills up early. Public officials may close the baths at times due to beach safety concerns. (You can look down on the baths from a vacant lot at the end of the cul-de-sac.)

HIKE: Queen Emmas Baths (.5 mi. to 1.5 mi., 175 ft.); Kaweonui (Sea Lodge) Beach (1 mi., 175 ft.)

Queen Emmas Baths are a series of black-rock tidal pools and intricate reef openings named for King Kamehameha IV's Queen Emma, who soaked here too. Steps aid on the first part of the .25-mile walk down a lush, steep trail. At one spot near the bottom, hands may be required. Watch your footing all the way. You pass a small, photo-worthy waterfall and pool near the bottom. Continue around to your left, walking the rocky bluffs and shoreline for about .5-mile. *Be Aware:* Observe wave action before venturing out on rocks. Use routes farther from the shoreline and avoid this area during in surf. People have drowned at these baths, so be extra careful.

The path to secluded **Kaweonui (Sea Lodge) Beach**, begins down a driveway shared by a residence. From the street, go to the left of the gate (as a beach access arrow indicates) and cross a chain about 50 feet away. The first part is steeply down a wide concrete path, coming to a pump installation at the bottom, enclosed by a chain-link fence. The beach trail is behind this enclosure. It's flat for the first part, then drops down through pandanus trees on dirt-and-wood steps to the coast at a grove of ironwoods. The trail continues to your left, over roots and finally rocks before hooking into Kaweonui—a sandy nook in a black-rock cove. *Be Aware:* This trail can be slippery. You'll see the other trail, from the Sea Lodge condos, on the right about halfway down.

SNORKEL: On calms days the tide pools and rocky inlets of **Queen Emmas Baths** are good places to relax and enjoy a view of the endless swells rolling in from the vast Pacific. You can gear up with mask and fins, or just swim around and play in the bubbling warm water. The best pool is about .25-mile from where the trail meets the coast. *Be Aware:* Observe wave action for ten minutes before entering; people have been swept away during high surf. Don't swim if surf comes over the rocks.

The reef offshore of **Kaweonui (Sea Lodge) Beach** limits shore break, often making for good snorkeling among a fair number of fish and maybe a turtle or two. You will usually find privacy at this little known cove. *Be Aware:* Privacy means you are on your own. The sand slopes into deep water.

A swimmer barely avoids drowning on an unsafe day at Queen Emmas Bath

ST: The 'back way' to Anini Beach will be high on the beach-hike list
endent travelers. Leisure cyclists can take a spin through the green bluffs
and of Princeville, or along the shores of the beach.
Take Hwy. 56 to Princeville, just beyond mm27. Enter on the main entrance
on Ka Haku Rd.
For the bike rides: Park on the right at a turnout just .1-mi. in, at the fountain, and just
before a sign for Queen Emmas Dr.
For the hike or snorkel at Wyllies Beach: Continue for about .25-mi. and turn right on
Wyllie Rd., also marked by a sign for the Pahia-Kaeo Kai condos. Go about .4-mi. park
in the public lot to the right of the entrance to the Westin Villas.

HIKE: Wyllies-Anini Beach (.5-mi. to 3 mi., 225 ft.)

To **Wyllies Beach**—which is actually at the far end of **Anini Beach**—walk the tree-
lined path between the Westin resort development and the golf course. The wide trail
descends into a shaded canopy of trees, alongside a stream. It's steep, but not hazardous, especially since the road was widened and graded in recent years. You pop out to
the beach from an umbrella of heliotrope and ironwood trees. As you begin the beach
walk, look back to memorize the spot to pop back in when the time comes.

At the beach, head right and cross shallow Anini Stream, which is often blocked by
a sand dam at the shoreline, and continue along the shore to Anini Beach. At one
point, about .75-mile into the stroll, you need to leave the beach at a black-rock point,
hopping up to the quiet road for a short distance and then back down to the beach.
Anini Beach campground will be in view after the point. Windsurfers, campers, kite-
boarders, and (guess what) polo players spice up the beachscape.

SNORKEL: The fresh water from the stream, in which coral cannot live, makes **Wyllies** a sandy-bottomed snorkeling area, protected by a reef farther out. Water clarity is
only fair near the stream. Wyllies is a very good spot to take a swim, which is not that
easy to find during winter surf. The best snorkeling is by a pool formed by black rocks,
a couple hundred yards down the road. *Be Aware:* During higher surf, an extremely
dangerous rip current develops farther out, where surf breaks and water escapes through
an opening in the reef. Use caution. Stay closer to shore.

BIKE: The **Mea Ho'ona Nea** bike trail, taking off behind the gate across the road
from the fountain, is a 3-mile roundtrip, rolling ride to the Princeville Golf Club. The
paved path, with blue-water views, is also a good walking and jogging path. To continue
any farther on a bike from the golf club, you need to turn right out to Hwy. 56, which
does have an adequate paved shoulder. *More Stuff:* As the Mea Ho'ona Nea bike path
leaves the golf course, and just before it becomes a path on a frontage road, look for
a gate on your right; the road here, at the Church of the Pacific, is directly across the
highway from the road leading up past the stables to Powerline Trail north, TH12.

Mountain bikers can also ride an 8-mile loop to **Anini Beach** from the parking area via the Wyllies Beach trailhead. Walk your bike down the steep part of the trail. From Wyllies Beach, you need to push the wheels across a short stretch of sand to the paved road that runs 2 miles along Anini Beach. From the far end of Anini, hardcore riders can also continue, taking Kalihiwai Road up to Highway 56, turning right, and riding about a mile to the golf club. At the entrance to the golf club, duck in and pick up the Mea Hoʻona Nea bike trail back to the parking area.

12. POWERLINE TRAIL NORTH
HIKE, BIKE

WHAT'S BEST: Hike or pedal past the peaks and streams at the heart of Kauaʻi. You begin overlooking Hanalei Valley and skirt the shoulders of Waialeale on the only cross-island trail.

Powerline Trail

PARKING: Take Hwy. 56 past the Princeville Airport. Turn mauka about .4-mi. past mm27 on Kapaka St.—look for a yellow intersection sign and a horse-shaped sign for Princeville Ranch Stables. Go 1.8 mi. up to the end of the street, behind a huge concrete water tank at a signed trailhead. *Note:* Different parking for heiau hike.

HIKE, BIKE: Powerline Trail (13 mi., 1,900 ft., one-way to Keahua Arboretum, TH33. In-and-out hikes of shorter lengths and elevations, as described below; Poʻoku Heiau (.5-mi.); Princeville Ranch Adventures (see *More Stuff*)

The **Powerline Trail North** is an all-day hike best attempted by prepared hikers on dry days. Cyclists and hikers alike may enjoy the route most by going in partway and seeing the other half of the trail another day from the Keahua Arboretum, TH33. In spite of its dreary name and a route following a utility easement through Kauaʻi's interior, the wide trail offers open vistas and lush greenery that makes the power poles all but unnoticeable. Most bikers will be dismounting for ruts and puddles at numerous spots. A trans-Kauaʻi bike race often is held on the the Fourth of July, and you'll find single-track trails looping from the main road at various spots.

Kualapa Ridge, the great divide for this route, is about 7 miles in to an elevation of almost 2,000 feet—or about half as high as the other ridges of the island's interior. You encounter a number of ups and downs along the way. Just into the hike, look for a falls to the right on a shoulder jutting out from the trail. Then, about .5-mile from

Princeville Ranch, Kalihiwai swimming hole

the trailhead, a short spur road leads to the right through ferns and trees to a good vantage point of the Hanalei Valley—river rapids below and waterfalls across the way. (The number of falls visible depends on recent rains.). The middle segment of the Powerline Trail, after about 2.5 miles, is a long, open ascent through swampy ferns and a dwarf ohia forest. All the dead tree spires are remnants of Hurricane Iniki of 1992. The best look back toward the Pacific comes near the top of Kualapa Ridge. All the while you are traveling above the Hanalei Valley, and you get good looks at the 3,800-foot ridge of the Halelea Forest Reserve as it rises, draped with greenery.

The short walk to the **Po'oku Heiau** site serves up an exquisite view of Hanalei Wildlife Refuge. Park on your right after a downhill stretch about .3-mile from the highway, at the last heiau sign. Walk a grassy two-track to your right, which becomes a path that eventually peters out at some wicked stickers. The overgrown heiau site is atop the hill.

More Stuff: The Powerline Trail starts out along the border of the 2,500-acre Princeville Ranch, on which the Carswell family—stewards of this natural treasure for many generations—now operates **Princeville Ranch Adventures**. (See *Outfitters* in *Resource Links,* page 238.) You can see this stunning place on foot, swimming, by kayak, or zinging through the air on a zipline cable that spans jungled valleys.

13.   ANINI BEACH   HIKE, SNORKEL, PADDLE, SURF

WHAT'S BEST: Leisurely hikes along the longest coral reef in Hawai'i, and taking a dip with the fishes. Anini has the total package for a tropical vacation, and some people never want to leave.
PARKING: Turn makai on Kalihiwai Rd. (second), which is past mm25, about 2 mi. beyond Kilauea—on an uphill grade after crossing the highway bridge over the river. *For Hanapai Beach:* Bear left downhill on Anini Dr., continue for .5-mi.to the coastline, and park at a dirt turnout on the right under trees where the road turns left.

For Anini: Continue along Anini Dr. You'll come to beach homes, where there are several access paths: at address 3530, across from address 3611 (the better), and at address 3650. The main parking is 1.5 mi. in from the highway at the large lot at Anini Beach Park.

HIKE: **Anini Beach (up to 2.75 mi.)**

The road to **Anini Beach** reaches sea level after about .5-mile from the highway, and then runs about 2 miles along the shore before ending at Anini Stream. The beach park area covers a .75-mile segment in the middle. Use one of the beach access paths noted above for a longer beach walk or start at the beach park, where windsurfers and high-flying kite-boarders provide entertainment at Kaua'i's best spot for these sports.

The coral reef, hundreds of feet offshore, makes for a wave-free coast, and trees provide pockets of shade. You leave the park after about .5-mile and walk the road a bit, around Honono Point, which is marked by a telephone pole on the ocean side of the road. After the point, you enter a tropical nook and sandy cove where Anini Stream enters the sea. This trail connects with Wyllies Beach, TH11.

SNORKEL: With its fabled reef, the snorkeling at **Anini Beach** is good, but shallow water, strong current, and coarse sand keep it from getting the highest marks. Even so, many claim this golden beach with big turquoise views as their favorite. Good snorkeling is at the camping section of the beach park, just after crossing a little bridge. For more private beachgoing, use the beach access paths noted in the parking section; better snorkeling is at address 3530. *Be Aware:* Surf surge escapes through a channel between the windsurfing area and the camping area at the beach park. A series of pipes leading from near the shore out to the reef mark the channel. You want to enter the water to the left of that. Currents can be swift in the shallow waters near the channel.

Anini Beach

Anini Beach rescue

For a quick snorkeling getaway try **Hanapai Beach**. Water can be choppy, amid black rocks, but under the right conditions, this beach scores big points among families and couples seeking a day at the shore. Also, at the other end of Anini—around Honono Point—is a safe swimming spot. Look for **Baby Beach**, a sandy pool near the road, protected by its own small crescent of black rocks, which attract fish.

PADDLE: The reef far offshore of **Anini Beach** makes for a safe and scenic lagoon for salt-water paddling—the best on Kaua'i—especially beyond the beach park at road's end. Put in near the campground and work your way inside the reef. *For stream kayaking:* Keep right on Kalihiwai Rd. and drive down about .75-mi. to unimproved parking on left just before road's end.

SURF: **Anini Beach** is not known for surfing; but during winter, good board-heads try the reef break, which slides both right and left. Windsurfing and kite-boarding are the things to do at Anini. These sports are limited to certains locations, as noted by signs. Board surfers also like **Hanapai Beach** for its rocky left-break called **Wires**.

14. KALIHIWAI BAY   SNORKEL, PADDLE, SURF

WHAT'S BEST: Surfing a deep-water break (and watching surfers!) taking a paddle up a lesser-known exotic river, and playing in the waves at a locals' beach. Get out of the car and hang around for a while.
PARKING: Take Hwy. 56 past Kilauea. At about .75-mi. past mm23, turn makai on Kalihiwai Rd. (first). It's before the highway bridge. Go 1 mi. down to the beach park.

SNORKEL: No real snorkeling here, during dry periods, slack green waters of the **Kalihiwai River** form a pretty swimming pool near the shore, very similar to the one at Lumahai. The rest of the beach is also excellent for family wave play and a day at the beach. Kalihiwai is a winner for tourists looking for a local-style beach.

PADDLE: The .75-mile slack waters of **Kalihiwai River**, with bananas and other fruits in the small river valley, might remind you of Southeast Asia. Commercial trips are not permitted here, but locals dip their paddles. The navigable part extends about one-quarter mile inland from the bridge, to below thundering Kalihiwai Falls. Access is in the ironwood grove at the far end of the bay (or across the river, as noted in the previous trailhead for stream paddling).

SURF: **Kalihiwai Bay** is a consistent and popular surfing spot. To be a spectator, stop on the way down, .75-mile from the highway, at an unimproved two-car turnout before the guardrail. When conditions are right, this is one of Hawaii's best viewing. spots. A four-tier right-break extends from the mouth of the bay inland, usually breaking close to the cliff. Entry is to the right as you reach the beach park. Body boarders like the shore break by the river. *Be Aware:* Get friendly with locals before paddling out. They protect their surf turf.

15.   KALIHIWAI RIDGE   BIKE

> **WHAT'S BEST:** Tropical trees and gardens galore adorn a paved ride through the "Beverly Hills of Kaua'i". Private property borders Kalihiwai Ridge, but you can get a darned good look at it.
> **PARKING:** Take Hwy. 56 past Kilauea and turn mauka on Kahiliholo Rd. .4-mi. after mm24. You'll see yellow sign noting a left-hand turn. Park at highway.

BIKE: Paved **Kahiliholo Road** is a 7- to 10-mile ride, roundtrip, to the top, depending on whether you take one of the side-road options. Your route is lined with ferns, palms and monkeypod trees, winding steadily upward, passing grand estates with gardens, and other, more modest homes. Living here, and in the general area, are (or were) Pierce Brosnon, Bette Milder, Sylvester Stallone, Ben Stiller, and other refugees from Tinseltown. At this part of the island, the dense tropical valleys typical of the north shore transition to the sloping moist-forest uplands of the northeast Kaua'i.

On the left side of the road, about 2.5-miles up, is Haulauani Road, a dead end which gives you the best tree-filtered view toward Mount Namahana in the foreground, and the Makaleha Mountains in the distance. Another side jaunt is to ride left on Kamo'okoa road toward Silver Falls Ranch, an abundantly scenic area with ridge views. They offer some of Hawaii's best trail rides; see *Resource Links*.

16.   SECRET BEACH   HIKE, SURF

> **WHAT'S BEST:** A hike-to, beach-lover's beach, with a long sand-and-surf walk and dramatic view of Kilauea Lighthouse on the cliffs above. Hike down and find a spot to lose your sense of time.

Secret Beach

PARKING: Take Hwy. 56 to past Kilauea. Just before mm24 and a guardrail, turn makai on Kalihiwai Rd (first). Pass the first driveway to the school bus yard, and then turn right, just .1-mile from the highway, on a dirt road cut through a 15-foot-high embankment. Continue .4-mi. to unimproved parking by recently built homes.

HIKE: Secret Beach (.5-mi. to 2.25 mi, 175 ft., depending on beach walk.)

Secret Beach, officially Kauapea Beach, might be renamed Not-So-Secret Beach, since this access is widely known. The beach is a long and deep deposit of fine sand, running from below the lighthouse at Kilauea Point. The trailhead is between newer homesites, a dirt path in the shade of broadleaf kamani trees and bananas. You then steeply descend wood-and-dirt steps, roots, and rocks—all of which can be slippery after rains. You walk the last hundred yards or so through a flourishing pandanus grove.

Secret is divided into three segments: "First" Secret Beach is the part you first access from this trail; "Second" Secret is the middle part that has black rocks poking up along it surf line; and "Third" Secret is the last beach which is nestled up to the cliffs that lead out to the lighthouse. Keep your eyes peeled seaward for spinner dolphins. *More Stuff:* Go to the left as you get to the sand for a scenic short walk onto a low bluff with tide pools (though winter surf can fill them with sand). *Be Aware:* Be alert for rogue waves, which can be lethal. High surf and tide sometimes closes off access to the far end of Secret Beach.

SURF: **Secret Beach** commonly has an onshore break that is dangerous, especially during winter months. During calmer periods of onshore break, Secret is good for body boards, and during some winter storms the locals ride the offshore swells at Third Secret, nearest the lighthouse *Be aware:* Get advice on hazards from locals.

17. KILAUEA POINT REFUGE AND LIGHTHOUSE   HIKE

WHAT'S BEST: Take a gander at magnificent shorebirds and crashing surf at the lighthouse and national wildlife refuge on Hawaiʻi's most northerly point. Nearby is a locals' walk to a "movie star" falls. Both places are among Hawaii's top attractions.
PARKING: From Hwy. 56, turn makai toward Kilauea on Kolo Rd., near mm23. Jog right to behind the gas station and then left on Kilauea Rd. *For Kilauea Point National Wildlife Refuge:* Continue makai for 2 mi. Pass a first lighthouse parking lot and go down a steep road to the paved lot. *For Crater Hill:* About .25-mile before the entrance to the lighthouse, park at Iwalani Road, the entrance to Seacliff Plantation, a gated residential development. *For Kilauea Falls (and Kahili Beach):* Well before the lighthouse on Kilauea Rd.(about .3-mile past Kong Lung store) turn right at a paved Kilauea Quarry Road, marked by a green gate and poles near telephone pole #21X. Drive in .3-mi. and park near the end of pavement. (Locals drive the dirt road, since it was improved in 2010.)

HIKE: Kilauea Point Refuge and Lighthouse (.5-mi.); Crater Hill (2.5 mi., 350 ft); Kilauea Falls (3.25 mi., 425 ft.)

Kilauea Point Wildlife Refuge and Lighthouse, although drawing many tourists, will still give you a faraway feel, located on the most northerly part of the main Hawaiian Islands. From the tip, you look down 200 hundred feet to seas crashing on tiny Mokuaeae Island. Dotting the Pacific north from here are the 100-plus small islands that comprise the Nortwestern Hawaiian Islands Marine National Monument. Tropicbirds, Laysan albatrosses, great frigatebirds and other seabirds soar about, while waddling the grasses are nene, or Hawaiian goose, the state bird. Shearwaters and red-footed boobies nest on steep hillsides. In the seas, whales, monk seals, and spinner dolphin vie to steal the show. Binoculars are provided for free. You'll want to step inside the visitors center, both for brightly presented exhibits and nature-themed gifts. *Notes:* A small fee is charged. Normal hours are 10 to 4 daily.

Crater Hill, the grassy knob above the lighthouse gives you a decent view of the the north coast. (This walk is on residential streets, and does not include the fenced area at the very top.) Us-

Kilauea Lighthouse

Kilauea Falls

ing the pedestrian access, walk up through the upscale neighborhood, bearing left on Makanaʻano Place. At a cul-de-sac, go through an opening provided in the fence and walk a short distance out to a viewing area.

Kilauea Falls is a beautiful baby Niagara, a fifty-foot high, 150-foot wide white curtain falling into a swimming oval nearly 200-feet across—where Harrison Ford watched Anne Heche get goosed by somehing in the water in the 1998 schmaltzy adventure comedy, *Six Days, Seven Nights. Be Aware:* In 2004, The Kilauea Point National Wildlife Refuge Expansion Act authorized the purchase of 234 acres that include Kilauea Falls. Public access is part of the plan but not yet realized. People currently access the falls via a shared easement through private property; use your own judgment.

From the parking, walk the wide dirt road that drops through profuse flora, including a sprawling banana patch. After about 15 minutes, not long after you begin to get stream valley views, go right at an unsigned road that drops and traverses right (though you need to keep right an climb a little after the first descent). This juncture is the dump site of a huge Kilauea Coastal Preserve dredging project in 2011, which restored bird habtat at the river. The route drops into a tree tunnel in a bird-rich forest from where the stream is visible. Then take a concrete drive down steeply left and then go up another concrete ramp. The route then pierces a bamboo thicket, ferns and ape (elephant ear plants). About 35 minutes from the car, you'll reach a bedrock section of the stream and ascend another 5 minutes before coming to the fabulous, vista across the large pool to Kilauea Falls. *Be Aware:* Flash flood danger is extreme during rains on the last section of this trail. No safe route exists to the top of the falls. *More Stuff:* Continue walking on the main road to reach the 'back entrance' to **Kahili Beach** You'll reach Kilauea Bay at the stream mouth and near Quarry Beach. The panoramic hike to the bay is nearly 5 miles, round trip, with some 475 feet of elevation.

WHAT'S BEST: Put this beach with a stream on the A-list with Kaua'i's other out-of-the-way wonders. After wave play and beach time, seek a mini-adventure with a paddle up the verdant stream delta. Nearby is one of Hawaii's best botanical gardens.
PARKING: Take Hwy. 56 toward Kilauea. Turn makai .6-mi. after mm21 on Wailapa Rd. A yellow highway sign marks the intersection. *For Kilauea Bay:* Continue for .4-mi. and veer left down a steep but well-surfaced dirt road for .6-mi. to unimproved parking area at beach. Avoid this road during rains. *For Na Aina Kai Gardens:* Continue less than .5-mi. to the end of Wailapa Rd.

HIKE: Kilauea Bay to Quarry Beach (.75-mi.) or Keilua Point (up to 1 mi.); Na Aina Kai Botanical Gardens (guided tours)

For **Quarry Beach**, which is the point that forms the stream-side mouth of the bay, head down the beach to your left as you face the water. You need to cross the stream at a sand dam at the surf line. A path leads up to a road. It's a short walk to your right to the viewpoint at the old quarry, bordering the wildlife refuge. Continue seaward to cozy rock perches to watch the backside of waves rolling inland, and to look for whales during the winter.

Walking the other way on the bay's soft sand—called **Kahili Beach**—you quickly leave the beach and walk up flat rock ledges, gaining 50 feet, to a grassy perch just out of the salt spray. Continuing down from there is a small sweet beach—**Little Kilauea Bay**—which extends to the cliffs of Keilua Point.

Na Aina Kai Botanical Gardens & Sculpture Park is one of Hawaii's top attractions and will be a vacation within your vacation. The 240-acre grounds are decorated with more than 100 life-sized bronze statuary in garden settings, a hedge maze, and a huge pond with fountains—all the vision of owners Joyce and Ed Doty, who began the effort in 2000. The formal garden dioramas give way to ocean-view gazebos and a large hardwood plantation that extends to a wild beach. *Notes:* An admission is charged.

PADDLE: **Kilauea Stream** curves inland for more than a mile, wide and deep through an open valley with upland views, before losing itself in dense foliage and river rock. A killer flood of 2006, created when a reservoir failed in torrential rains, sent tons of debris and entire structures seaward. You'll have to carry the kayak several hundred feet. Go through two upright pipes on a narrow road to the riverbank.

SURF: Locals take advantage of an offshore break at the riverside mouth of the bay. This area is called **Quarry Beach** or **Rock Crusher**. Kilauea Bay, though not well known, has one of the island's better breaks. Spectators can cross the river to the quarry to view surfers looking down the barrel of the wave. *Be Aware:* Shore breaks can cause injuries and hazardous conditions during high surf.

Kong

"Kong" is the familiar name for the pointed peak on Kaua'i's northeast shore, looking much like the head of the mythical ape, forever watchful seaward. The peak's real name is Kalalea, which in Hawaiian means "prominent." But Kong's 15-minutes of Hollywood prominence came not from *King Kong*, but as the opening shot for *Raiders of the Lost Ark*.

The gap-toothed ridge in which Kong is centered, commonly called the Anahola Mountains, is the subject of Kauaian mythology that has been altered by recent geology: The ancient "Hole in the Mountain," an opening through the ridge behind Kong, was said to have been made when a rival king from the Big Island threw his spear across the entire island, piercing the ridge and earning the kingship for his effort. In the mid-1990s, a landslide closed the hole to a tiny crescent.

Kong's ridge is a branch of the Makaleha Mountains, the east-side range that intersects the sloping forest reserve and agricultural lands that sweep around the coast from Kilauea on the north to the Royal Coconut Coast on the east. This area is known for numerous hike-to coves, beachcombing beaches and coastal bike trails. With several trails and four-wheel drive roads leading into forest reserves, the Kong region also offers an excellent inland access toward Mount Waialeale and adjoining ridges.

Heading away from Kilauea toward Kapaʻa, begins a long coastline, perhaps the least-hiked of Kauaʻi's accessible shore. Waiakalua beaches are among the best-kept secrets, featuring three cocopalm coves. Down the coast from Waiakalua is Larsens Beach, better known and much larger—more than two miles of coral beach and ragged reef, fringed by low bluffs. Tide pools, reef currents and wave action make Larsens' shore ever-changing, and winter trade winds bring eclectic flotsam ashore.

Continuing toward Kong from Larsens, the coast becomes a series of coves and inlets large enough to be called bays—Papaʻa, Moloaʻa, Aliomanu and Anahola. Moloaʻa Bay, though the site of several homes, is a classic getaway cove for sunbathing, swimming, and short hikes along its bluffs. Off-highway paved roads around Moloaʻa, including the one to Larsens, make this a place to tour on a bike. Anahola Bay, just below Kong, and Aliomanu Bay, which lies beside Anahola, offer three snorkeling and surfing beaches, a navigable stream and a variety of beach hiking. Bordering Hawaiian Homelands, Anahola is the most-Hawaiian community on this side of the island.

Around the point, on the Kapaʻa side of Kong, are miles of coastline accessible by foot and mountain bike—some of it wild, and some of it through resort paths and beachside parks—extending all the way from Anahola along the Royal Coconut Coast to the Wailua River. Surfers and boogie boarders in this neck of the woods head for Donkey Beach, Kealia Beach or Wailua Bay, while snorkelers duck in at one of several lesser known spots behind funky Kapaʻa Town and the hotels of the Coconut Coast. Although waters are shallow here, the swimming can be good.

Sacred Forest, Hindu Monastery

This coral-reef coast is not without its paddling waters, with two streams to inland areas that practically no one paddles. Unlike other streams on the island that fit this description, Kong's are close to kayak outfitters. Outrigger canoes and kayaks also stroke the waters off the coast, although Kaua'i newcomers should check with locals before venturing beyond the breakers in a kayak.

Some of the best inland hiking is to be had on this east portion of the Kong trailheads. Above Kealia is the Spalding Monument, pointing the way toward the upper Makaleha Mountains and Waipahe'e Falls. Above Kapa'a on Olohena Road is more access toward these mountains, as well as three trailheads to Nounou Ridge, better known as the Sleeping Giant. The landmark Sleeping Giant is a forest reserve and excellent viewpoint to get a bearing on the east side.

Heading up the Wailua River—the place where the first ali'i, or kings, chose to call home—leads to the Keahua Arboretum. From the arboretum, bikers and

Anahola Bay, Coconut Marketplace

hikers can pick up the south end of the Powerline Trail that connects with Princeville on the north shore, or head up another ridge that twists through jungle to abut the Makaleha Mountains. Another trail from the arboretum leads to an up-close look at Mount Waialeale, below the rippling waters of its vertical face. Also from the arboretum are trails that poke out to views of Kilohana Crater above Lihue.

The rural roads around Kapa'a and the Coconut Coast are also a scenic tour for cyclists wishing to catch a glimpse of local-style living and maybe snag a papaya at an honor-system fruit stand. Behind the Sleeping Giant is a gardenlike expanse.

After a day spent recreating, Kapa'a Town is a good choice to grab a smoothie or a shave ice, and walk around the quaint streets and neighborhoods—a blend of the cultures that combine under the umbrella of aloha to make Kaua'i. Buddhist temples stand near Catholic churches, and brew pubs adjoin sushi bars and Hawaiian diners.

Anahola Stream, Coconut Coast in Kapa'a

MAP 2   TRAILHEADS 19-32

KONG

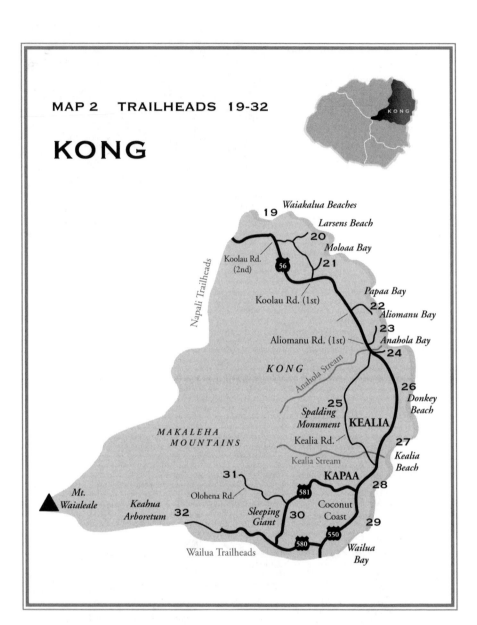

HIKE	HIKING
SNORKEL	SNORKELING AND SWIMMING
BIKE	MOUNTAIN OR ROAD BIKING
PADDLE	KAYAKING, CANOEING
SURF	SURFING, BOOGIE BOARDING

TH	TRAILHEAD	*Note: All hiking*
Makai	TOWARD OCEAN	*distances are roundtrip*
Mauka	TOWARD THE MOUNTAIN, INLAND	*unless otherwise noted.*
mm.	MILE MARKER, CORRESPONDS TO HIGHWAY SIGNS	

19. WAIAKALUA BEACHES   HIKE, SNORKEL, SURF

WHAT'S BEST: Adventurous hikes to idyllic, hidden tropical beaches. This is why many people come to Kaua'i.
PARKING: Head beyond Anahola on Hwy. 56, past second Ko'olau Rd. Turn makai on N. Waiakalua Rd., about .8-mi. past mm2. Go .7-mi. on N. Waiakalua to end of road at cul-de-sac, and turn left at telephone pole #17 on dirt road, which is lined with ironwood trees. Go .2-mi. to unimproved parking. Leave car free of valuables.

HIKE: Waiakalua Beaches (.5-mi t, 175 ft.); Pila'a Beaches (1.75 mi., 175 ft.)

Waiakalua Beaches are jewels tucked away on a remote section of coastline between Larsens Beachand Kilauea Bay. Start down the steep steps, improved by cut logs. Pause at a viewpoint not far from the trailhead and look right: You'll see the more secluded **Pila'a Beaches**—palm-fringed crescents of sand on a black rock coast, under cliffs rich with plant life. **For all beaches**, proceed down over roots and a slippery section, in shade all the way. One short rock section requires attention to foot placement, just above the soft sand beach. Go left to **Waiakalua**. Heliotropes, ironwoods, and palms grace the shore. From Waiakalua is a view of Crater Hill, and overhead are likely to be seabirds. But watch the ground, too, since big monk seals like to haul out here. At the end of the beach is a boulder-rock point. Scramble for a few minutes and you'll come to a second beach below Na Aina Kai Gardens, which is private property.

To reach the pretty **Pila'a Beaches**—a 'fantasy island' getaway—go to the right when you reach the bottom of the trail at the water. It's a .5-mile scramble on black boulders at the edge of coastal vegetation. After the balancing act, you'll cross a small stream and reach the first beach, which is backed by a parklike lawn. Normally, you can reach the second beach, which is home to several cottages, by walking sand between boulders around the cliff. Both beaches are beautifully situated among palms and other beach

Be Aware: A hiking pole and sturdy shoes will greatly aid the half-hour of boul-der hopping along the coast. Also, a short distance down from trailhead parking is a mountainside trail to the right that traverses steeply to Pila'a, but is difficult to follow; the coastal route, though not a cake walk, is easy to follow.

SNORKEL: **Waiakalua Beaches**, on pretty days, fill the bill for an ideal tropical beach, the perfect place to take a dip with the fishes. For a better swim, make the hike to **Pila'a Beaches**. Cross the stream and immerse yourself about midway along the first beach—superb! *Be Aware:* These beaches feature an exposed section of reef with strong and confusing currents. Get a good read before venturing in. A primary rip current travels directly outward from near the stream.

SURF: Surfers take a gander at **Waiakalua** from the viewpoint mentioned in the hiking section, and die-hards carry their boards down. This is a place for locals and advanced surfers to look for something exciting. Because of the reef break and remote-ness, Waiakalua is a risky surfing area. During periods of epic surf, big-daddy wave riders, partnered with buddies on jet skis, ride the rolling mountains: quite a show.

20. LARSENS BEACH   HIKE, SNORKEL

WHAT'S BEST: Larsens is definitely not on the tour-bus circuit. Roam an open beach-scape for miles, looking for wildlife and a well-chosen place to take a dip.
PARKING: Take Hwy. 56 past Anahola and turn makai at first Ko'olau Rd., which is about .75-mi. past mm16. Drive past Moloa'a Rd. and, at 2.25 mi. from hwy. turnoff, turn makai again, sharply right at a beach access pole. It's at telephone pole #7 and address 7200. Go .9-mi. down to a large parking area. Leave car free of valuables. *Note:* Ko'olau Rd. loops around to Hwy. 56. Coming from the north, turn left just after mm20 and proceed 1.1 mi. to the Larsen's road.

HIKE: Kephui Point (3.5 mi., 275 ft.)

Larsens Beach is visible from a grassy perch a short distance down from the parking—the beach is about 200 feet below and little more than .25-mile away. **Kepuhi Point** is beyond two beach seg-ments, lying to your left as you face the water. Take the trail down and go right at the first trail to the beach. Head to your left along the water. Along Larsens Beach,

Telephoto shot of monk seal at Larsens

Larsens Beach

which extends from Moloaʻa Bay to Kulikoa Point near Pilaʻa, you will discover drifts of yellow sand beside tilting sections of broken reef, foaming with aquamarine tidal action—and ideal home for seabirds and marine life. Larsens is an unusually complicated and interesting coast. The backshore slopes fairly gently, allowing for several red-dirt routes through ironwoods and occasional broadleaf beach trees. *Be Aware:* You may also discover a few flop campers and nudie sunbathers, although neither of these activities are lawful in Hawaii.

The first part of Larsens is also called Kaʻakaʻaniu Beach. After this first .5-mile beach, you leave the sand, taking a trail over a .25-mile stretch up and over a low point and dropping down to the next beach segment, a cutie called Waipake Beach. At the far end of Waipake you may see monk seals resting in the sand or on the reef (stay back). Rising at the end of the beach is a ruddy, hog-back bluff. Veer left on a gradual route before coming to the end of the beach, and follow a sketchy trail through ironwoods, staying close to water's edge. Laysan albatrosses nest on the hillsides. As you come down the other side—crossing a lush gully—you'll see Kepuhi Point. The point is a volcanic formation set low to the surf, with a frothing tidal pool and a blunt tip that thwarts the sea to create a sometimes thunderous display of white water. The entire length of Larsens is a beachcomber's delight, with the possibility of glass balls, buoys, message bottles, and shells. *Be Aware:* Inland is private property; use coastal paths.

SNORKEL: **Larsens Beach** is known for lethally dangerous swimming. Before dropping down to the beach, study the reef from the viewpoint mentioned in the hiking section. You'll be able to spot the main blue channel, at the far left of the beach; current usually runs right-to-left and out this channel. Throw a stick in the water to see which way it floats, and once you enter the water, be mindful of the direction your body starts moving on its own. Still, on certain days in the right spot, Larsens is a beautiful place to get in the water with mask and fins. The second beach over, **Waipake**, is the better choice for swimmers. Check out the protected sand beach just as you drop down, a prime spot for a day at the beach. *Be Aware:* Do not swim here without making sure it is safe. Conditions are often hazardous farther out.

21. MOLOA'A BAY   HIKE, SNORKEL

> **WHAT'S BEST:** A lush tropical bay, made for an afternoon of swimming, short walks and relaxing. Though homes encircle the parking area, privacy is a short hop away, with whales offshore and seabirds as your beach buddies.
> **PARKING:** Take Hwy. 56 past Anahola, pass mm16, and turn makai on first Ko'olau Rd. Go 1.25 mi. and turn makai again on Moloa'a Rd. Continue down .75-m and park on the left , where another road veers right.

HIKE: Seabird Point (1.5 mi., 125 ft.); Moloa'a Forest Reserve (.75-mi., 150 ft.; different parking area, see hiking description.)

From the parking to **Seabird (Kalaeamana) Point**, walk the road to the left and go left past the beach homes. Cross Moloa'a Stream and continue around the fine arc of this medium-sized bay to the far end. Under heliotrope and ironwood trees, is a sign for the shearwater preserve. Take the path to the right along the rocks near the cliff, leaving the bay behind on a short ascent. On the upslopes before reaching the point, Layson albatrosses have been known to rest or make their awkward, "gooney bird" take-offs. If you see these birds, or the smaller shearwaters, give them room. Stay on a contour at the edge of the bluff, skirting a grassy area, until reaching a sturdy fence that marks private property.

Hanalei taro, Nukolii net fisherman, Shipwreck Beach surfer, Waipoo Falls in Waimea Canyon

Kalalau Trail, Limahuli National Tropical Botanical Garden, Larsen's Beach, Anahola Beach Park

Kuilau Ridge Trail in Keahua Arboretum, Awaawapuhi, Wailua Falls

Wailua River paddlers, Alakai Swamp boardwalk, Salt Pond Beach Park, Kilauea Point National Wildlife Refuge

Moloaʻa Bay

The **Moloaʻa Forest Reserve** is not a spectacular hike, but it is a rare place to access the Anahola Mountains on this side; the trailhead is below a pointed peak named Amu. To get there, drive past the first Koʻolau Road for 1.5 miles. You'll be going up a grade, passing a series of guardrails; as the guardrails end—and about .1-mile after mm18—look mauka for a grassy turnout and a large silver mailbox. Park on grass shoulder on either side of road. *Be Aware:* The trailhead is hard to spot on this busy road. You might end up passing it and hanging a U-turn.

Beginning at mailbox, which reads "B-14, Hunter Checking Station-Moloaʻa," walk up the grassy embankment. Then go through the closed, not locked, metal gate to your left and follow the wide path as is curves upward toward Anahola. After a little more than .25-mile, notice a grass-cut trail veering left—the hunter's road continues toward Anahola. The left-veer takes you a few hundred feet to a blue-water viewpoint of Moloaʻa Bay. Also of interest on this little-used trail: Halfway to the viewpoint spur described above, you'll see a red-dirt embankment, from which a poor trail leads. This trail gives you an option to look at Amu, a feature of the Anahola Mountains. *Be Aware:* Hunter's area; weekdays are best for hiking.

SNORKEL: The perfect crescent of the **Moloaʻa Bay** is broken at various places by black-rock reef, making this an interesting place to snorkel around, with good visibility on calm days and enough fish to make it interesting. Moloaʻa is an excellent place to take a plunge and go back to the beach mat. *Be Aware:* Avoid the rocky areas during periods of high surf. The better choice for snorkelers are the **Moloaʻa Baths**: Walk from the parking and access the beach between the last two houses. Head right around the bay about 200 yards to some palm trees, where a finger reef protects the shoreline. You'll find several "baths," or channels in the coral, just right for a swim when the tidal conditions are right. The family will enjoy poking around the tide pools.

22.   ALIOMANU BAY-PAPA'A BAY

WHAT'S BEST: A one-two punch: Aliomanu contributes to Kaua'i's wealth of beach-comber's specials. A short trail deters many visitors from the white crescent of pretty Papa'a Bay. Easy to spend the day and then come back the next.
PARKING: Take Hwy. 56 past Anahola and Hokualele Rd. and turn makai on second Aliomanu Rd., only .1-mi. past mm15. Go .1-mi and turn left on Kalalea View Dr., toward Aliomanu Estates. Continue 4-mi. and then turn makai at beach pole (that may be missing). *For Papa'a Bay:* Go .25-mi. and park at a grassy turnout where the road turns right. *For Aliomanu Bay:* Make the right and park in the lot visible just down the road. *Note:* Papa'a Rd., the next road north of second Aliomanu Rd., is also a way to get to this beach if you're coming from the north shore. Turn makai and follow beach access signage for about .6-mi.

HIKE: Anahola Bay (2 mi.); Papa'a Bay (1.25 mi., 125 ft.)

Aliomanu Bay is a shallow depression in the coast between Papa'a and Anahola bays—you probably wouldn't think of it as a bay. From the parking, head down a red-dirt road, that makes easy curves to the beach, about .25-mile away. To **Anahola Bay**, head to your right as you face the water at Aliomanu Beach. You'll walk the coarse sand at first and then pick your way around Kuaehu Point, which is below a lone house with a bright blue roof. A trail through sand and over black rocks soon leads to a view of Anahola Bay and Kong. High tide may make for a wet trip around the point, but this beach is made for wading. Once around Kuaehu Point, you can continue down Anahola Beach, as described in TH23. *More Stuff:* You can access the south (Anahola) end of the bay taking Aliomanu Road .5-mile in from the highway (passing Kalalea View) and turning left on Kukana; a beach access is on your right after less than .1-mile.

To reach the dreamy beach at aquamarine **Papa'a Bay**, go directly seaward toward an access pole and through an opening to the left of a gate. After a short distance, hang a left on a trail that skirts along the bluff in front of newly built homes. Stay right at a 'fake' trail junction. At the far end of the bluff, a steep trail leads down through beach trees to sea level. From there, pick your way inland on a trail. For the last 75 yards, you'll have to walk over large black boulders, before reaching the fine strip of sand. At the far end of the beach are a small stream and coral shallows, a good spot to log beach time. The two large homes behind the beach were built by a Hollywood director.

SNORKEL: **Aliomanu Beach** has excellent scenic values, with kamani and ironwood trees interspersed along a grassy inland and a generous swath of yellow sand looking onto a two-mile long coral reef. Rocks and shallow waters make for interesting wave actions and tidal surges. All in all, this is a decent beach for snorkeling, although don't expect large, sparkling schools. *Be Aware:* Shallow waters, confused surf, and unpredictable northeast exposure can make for strong currents.

Papa'a Bay

Papa'a Bay can be a good snorkeling spot on calmer days, as the cove offers protection from the surf. A coral reef just offshore the stream is a fish hangout, while turtles like the deeper water near the black rocks on the route in. Swimming in the bay is normally clear and calm. *Be Aware:* During higher surf, a left-to-right rip current forms near the stream mouth, but it normally dissapates in the bay.

SURF: Locals head to **Papa'a Bay** to take advantage of a quick-breaking, offshore swell, called Flags. These fast-riding waves can be available at any time of the year. The usual entry point is in the rocky area where the trail first reaches sea level.

23. ANAHOLA BAY   HIKE, SNORKEL, PADDLE

WHAT'S BEST: Snorkel, beachcomb or paddle. Though not normally on the list of starred attractions, charming Anahola may just become your first choice for a getaway.
PARKING: Take Hwy. 56 past Kealia and turn makai on first Aliomanu Rd., which is past the Anahola Post Office and just past mm14. Go .5-mi. down the paved road to stream mouth at beach. Park there or at one of several access point to your left along the beach road, the last of which is about .75-mi. from the river. An excellent midway access is near a beach reserve sign near address 4746.

HIKE: Anahola Beach (up to 3 mi.)

Anahola Beach, where the Anahola Stream flows down from nearby Kong and enters the bay, is a narrow, long strip of yellow sand along a coral reef. Ironwoods, cocopalms and several kinds of broadleaf trees shade widely spaced beach cottages. The stream bank near the surf line is one of those perfect spots to sit awhile. Start the beach walk with the stream at your back, heading for Kuaehu Point and Aliomanu Bay (connecting up with TH22). About halfway on the walk, a few beach cottages sit close to the water and you may have to walk the top of a short seawall for a bit during high tide, or stay on the road for a short distance and to an unsigned access near address 4934. Just after the seawall, you come to a stream that gives you a romantic look at Kong, rising in the background, framed by cocopalms over still waters.

SNORKEL: All in all, **Anahola Bay** is an above-average snorkeling beach, with clear pools large enough to do lap swimming, a moderate number of fish, and a long coral reef. You'll find sandy access in selected spots, although rough coral borders much of the shore. The better snorkeling is farther down from the stream. *Be Aware:* Rip currents head out channels, particularly strong during high-surf conditions. Observe and test the waters. Also avoid the river mouth area when the river is high.

PADDLE: The **Anahola Stream** lazes inland almost a mile before entering tangles of flora near the highway overpass. The Anahola Valley is lush with tropical fruit trees. Birdsong dominates the airwaves. This is a non-commercial paddling area, but you'll usually see a canoe or kayak parked in the ironwoods at the stream bank, where Aliomanu Road comes down. *Be Aware:* Flash floods occur after heavy rains.

24. ANAHOLA BEACH PARK   HIKE, SNORKEL, SURF

> WHAT'S BEST: Stop in for a swim on the locals' side of the bay, taking in views of the Anahola Mountains in afternoon sun.
> PARKING: Take Hwy. 56 past Kealia. Turn makai on Anahola Rd., past mm13. You'll see a right-turn lane at a guardrail and a right-arrow sign. Drive .75-mi. to white-rock sign and palms noting the beach park. Veer left, and continue to the end of road.

HIKE: Anahola Beach Park to: Anahola Stream (1.25 mi.) or Pahakuloa Point (2.5-mi., 225 ft.)

Anahola Beach Park is the home beach for the Hawaiian community of Anahola. **To Anahola Stream**, go left on the beach, with its beautiful views of the Anahola Mountains, seen through a healthy grove of coco palms. You'll pass the camping area long before reaching the wide mouth of the stream, which is also accessible via TH23.

For Pahkuloa Point, take the dirt road just beyond beach parking, past picnic tables through ironwoods. On a gradual rise amid trees, the road rounds Kahala Point and then breaks open to grassy slopes. Avoid spur roads left and, about .5-mile from the trailhead, and you will reach rock-and-sand Lae Lipoa Beach, which you can walk instead of the road. At the end of this beach, follow the road as it ascends inland, passes another small rocky beach, and reaches the point. From here, you'll see across

Anahola Beach Park

a cliffy cove to where fishermen can drive in from Kealia. *Be Aware:* Though wild and remote, people can drive the coastal road from Anahola.

More Stuff: To see the botanic wonders of the Taro Patch take Kikoo Loop inland across the highway from the Anahola post office. Drive across the 1921 bridge and park. A streamside trail of about .25-mile ends at the lawn and tropical gardenscape, which is also the a site of 60's-style concerts. *Be Aware:* You need to ask to enter; if no one is around, call John at Taro Patch-Anahola Ancient Cultural Center. See page 242 in *Resource Links*.

SNORKEL: The waters off **Anahola Beach Park** are shallow and the water clarity is normally above average. But you'll have decent snorkeling in this relatively safe swimming area. The beach has sandy entry points and a good swimming lane that extends toward the river. *Be Aware:* Under high surf conditions, currents can be a problem.

SURF: The reefy right-break off Kahala Point toward the beach park is sometimes called **Unreals**. The real draw here, for body boarders mainly, is **Pillars**, about halfway between the beach park and the stream. To drive there coming from the highway, turn left on Poha Road and go .25-mile to the beach. You'll see the abandoned pillars of a pineapple pier offshore. *Be Aware:* Pillars can have a nastly break onto a shallow sand bar.

25.   SPALDING MONUMENT   HIKE, BIKE

WHAT'S BEST: Hikes and bikes of varying distances along the bird-rich, pastured upslopes of Kealia, with blue-water views and in-your-face exposure to Kong and the Anahola Mountains.
PARKING: Take Hwy. 56 from Kapa'a. Turn mauka at Kealia Rd., about mm10.5, across from the farthest Kealia Beach parking area. Head uphill on a paved road through bougainvillea. As you pass through fields, look for line of Norfolk pines up and to your left, which mark Spalding Monument. The decrepit monument is 2.25 mi. from Hwy. 56. *For Ahahola Mountains:* Go right .9-mi. from the monument and turn left on a dirt road left. Pass a mailbox for Kealia Hunting Station, Unit C. and continue .4-mi. to park under monkey pod trees where the road dips down.

HIKE: Spalding stroll (1.5 mi., 150 ft.); Anahola Mountains (2.5 mi., 300 ft.)

The **Spalding stroll** is is a birder's delight down a dirt drive fringed by tall Norfolk pines that lead away from the palm-encircled monument. Although the monument to honor a pineapple scion probably remains in disrepair, blue-water views from here sparkle. As you walk down the path—beginning to the left of Kaua'i Farms behind the monument—the embankment and flora sometimes obscure views, but you do get looks of the Kapa'a coast on your left and close-ups of a moist woodland valley on your right. In about a mile, where a road veers to the right toward a private home in the distance, the path starts to drop steeply. The stately pines will have given way to dwarfed ones, swallowed up by a profusion of other trees and shrubs. The road continues down to a valley inland from Kealia, but you'll probably want to turn around.

The **Anahola Mountains** hike is more about walking in the forest, and getting a good view of Kong, rather than reaching particular destination. *Be Aware:* This walk is best earlier on weekdays, when hunters are not present. Keep your car free of valuables, since break ins have occurred at this trailhead. Begin by keeping right where the road forks at a gate. Under a high leafy canopy, you'll dip right, and then climb left, with the mountains to your right across a broad stream valley. The road dips again and crosses a small stream on a bridge. Less than a half-hour into the hike—and before the main road reaches a pipe gate—go right on a track that drops through a sea of ferns toward the stream valley. You will get full-on views of Kong. Pick your own turnaround spot.

More Stuff: Adventure hikers (or bikers) can continue toward Kong, and loop around toward the Moloa'a access. Additionally, the main road continues from the pipe gate inland to Kaneha Reservoir, through scenery evoking the green hills of Africa, and ends near Waipahe'e Falls—a former tourist attraction that has been fenced off for years. At about 2 miles in, you'll get big views of the Makaleha Mountains to your left. An old airstrip and a number of other roads crisscross this agricultural upland, making for confusing going, so remember your junctions.

BIKE: The hunter's road to the **Anahola Mountains**, as described above, is a good choice for mountain bikers. You can either start at Hwy. 56 or start at the Spalding Monument as per hiking description. The **Spalding stroll** road continues down to Kealia on a snotty, rutted road, connecting with Haua'ala Road, which is part of an inland ride described in TH27, Kealia Beach. To make this fairly difficult loop, you hang a left at the bottom of Spalding Road and ride out to the highway along the stream. From the highway, go left to Kealia Road, and pedal back up to Spalding. All of this is about 6.5 miles. Plan on hosing down the bike after it's over.

26. DONKEY BEACH   HIKE, SNORKEL, SURF

WHAT'S BEST: A big beach offers room to roam on a wild-and-scenic coastline. With a high-end development planned on the upper slopes, Donkey Beach may not be the hideaway it once was, but it still delivers top-level scenic goods.
PARKING: Take Hwy. 56 past Kealia Beach. Pass mm11 and the Kealia Kai development. Look for signed trailhead parking, makai at the top of the hill, near mm11.5.

HIKE: Donkey Beach (.75 mi., 125 ft.); House Beach (2 mi., 225 ft.)

Rental cars mingle with surfmobiles at the trailhead parking. **For both hikes**, a shrub-lined concrete path leads down through a palm grove to **Donkey Beach**, which is rarely called by its real name, Kumukumu Beach. Donkey, a short distance to the right when you reach the coastal hike-bike path, is one of those better-known secret beaches, but its .5-mile wide crescent of sloping sand remains pristine. Walks to either side of the bay afford good views back toward the beach as well as of the rugged coast—Paliku Point, with a picnic pavilion, is to the right as you face the water, and Ahihi Point is

Donkey Beach

left. *Be Aware:* Some doff their duds at Donkey Beach, but nude sunbathing is unlawful on all Kaua'i beaches.

To **House Beach**, also known as Anapalau Beach, head away from Donkey Beach, going to your left as you face the water. The newer, wide path ends, but the coastal trail doesn't: Go right across a stream gully (with small falls and pools). You'll then pass a small cove of Ahihi Point, after which the trail contours through a hau thicket. (You could also take the more-direct trail down to the right as you reach the hau thicket, if you don't mind a steep slope through ironwoods to the beach.) You'll break out of the thicket to a treed road and 'around the bend,' see a rutted road to the right used by locals for weekend picnics that cuts down to House Beach alongside a stream. The cove no longer has a house. You'll find ample sand between nests of black rock, and shade is supplied by mostly heliotrope ironwoods. You may also find some refuge left by not-cool campers.

SNORKEL: With a shore break, **Donkey Beach** is seldom a good snorkeling spot, but at the edges of the bay you can, on calm days, enjoy swimming around with a mask on. *Be Aware:* Surf and rip currents can make this a dangerous Donkey. Snorkeling at **House Beach** is better—the best on the Coconut Coast during ideal conditions. On calm days, try walking out to the point (Anapalau) to the far left as you face the water, toward the lone ironwood, and swimming back in toward shore—through deep, clear water. Precautions observed, House Beach is a very good snorkeling experience. Families will love the **keiki beach**, with a protected, sandy entry, located to the right as you face the water (the first part of the cove you reach on the hike).

SURF: **Donkey Beach** is on the circuit for east-side surfers, but the break is better at Kealia. Avoid the chopped-up shore break by surfing inside the point to the right as you face the water, where waves peel off into the beach. Other boarders ride the tiers mid-bay. You can tell if the surf is up by looking for surfmobiles and pickups parked amid the shiny rental cars at the trailhead. *Be Aware:* A powerful shore break means impact injuries. Leave your car free of valuables.

27.   KEALIA BEACH   HIKE, SNORKEL, BIKE, PADDLE, SURF

WHAT'S BEST: Coastal biking and hiking, beachcombing, whale-watching, and a body-boarding extravaganza: spend the day at Kealia or drop in for a beach break on your way around the island.

PARKING: Take Hwy. 56 through Kapa'a toward Anahola. You'll see two improved parking areas: Look for a right-turn lane at mm10 or, .25-mi. beyond that, turn into larger lot near four picnic pavilions.

HIKE: Kealia Lookout (1.75 mi.); Donkey Beach (2.75 mi.)

To the **Kealia Lookout**—where you may spot a whale during winter migrations, and are promised a fine seaward view on all clear days—walk to your right as you face the water. Either stomp the sand or use the wide paved path that, along with series of small pavilions and footbridges, were part of recent park improvements. Near the far end of the beach, about .5-mile from the parking, you cross Kealia Stream. If the water is high, use the bike-pedestrian bridge near the highway. Regardless, at the end of the beach, get on the path and continue another .25-mile to a point visible from Kealia Beach. This is a spot below the scenic turnout on the highway between.

To **Donkey Beach**, go to your left as you face the water, walking on a former pineapple haul road that has been paved and is now used by hikers, cyclists, and surfers. This coastline, with its grassy hills dotted with ironwoods, is being converted to large-parcel real estate. Its flora was also given a crew cut by Hurricane Iniki. About .5-mile along on the road from Kealia, you'll round a gully and come to a pavillion just inshore of an old pineapple pier. The pier is an exciting side-trip for those steady on their feet. On the way to Donkey Beach, you'll pass by a pleasing pavilion, set off the path to the right, and cross a footbridge before dropping down to the large baylike beach.

SNORKEL: To your left as you face **Kealia Beach**, a black-rock breakwater creates a sandy area for snorkeling and wading. Swimming can be fairly good here, although fish are not abundant. Surfers usually don't frequent this part of the beach. *Be Aware:* Stay out of the water on big-surf days, and watch out for current sweeping the inside of the breakwater.

Kealia

BIKE: From **Kealia** is the island's best coastal riding, scenic and open—part of the Kapa'a coastal path opened in 2009. You have options: Ride toward **Donkey Beach**, as per hiking description, and continue almost to Anahola, which is 6 or 7 miles, roundtrip. The route beyond Donkey becomes a trail, not a path, and then then a dirt road after House Beach. The ride has its ups and downs, but is essentially flat,

Kealia store and post office

curving with the coast. You can also ride the other way from Kealia, toward the **Kealia Lookout**, and continue on the coastal path for about two miles to Kapaʻa. In Kapaʻa Town, TH28, you hook up with a coastal route taking you almost to Lihue without having to venture on to the highway.

Another option from Kealia, is the **Hauaʻala loop**, which takes you on a little-traveled, 5-mile swing through the Kealia Stream valley. Take off toward Kapaʻa on the path, crossing the Kealia Stream on the footbridge. Then cross the highway (heads up) and take a right, up Mailihuna Road. Pump uphill, past Kapaʻa High School, joining Kawaihau Road, .6-mile from the highway and in the ʻburbs. Now the fun starts. Hang an immediate right down Hauaʻala Road, which takes you down quickly to the valley, with views of the stream, shaded by banana plants and massive broadleaf trees.

After about 1.5 miles, Hauaʻala Road becomes dirt and crosses over Kealia Stream—water may be flowing over the road—surrounded by pools and under large monkeypod trees. Shortly after this serene juncture, and an uphill stretch, the road hairpins back toward the ocean, now on the other side of the stream. Just after the turn-back, you'll see the dirt road that comes down from Spalding Monument—be sure to go right here, on the lesser path at telephone pole #100. Hauaʻala Road continues its loop, down now, through puddles, surging roadside grasses and overhanging, vine-encrusted limbs. After this wild, rutted stretch, you pop out at small agricultural homesteads and reach exotic views of Kealia Stream. Then the tree tunnels transition to pasture and marshlands, about a mile inland. Continue to the tiny Kealia post office, in view of beach parking across the highway.

PADDLE: Kayakers should park at the footbridge, very near mm10. **Kealia Stream** gathers the waters from several streams and has a wide passage of navigable water for about 1.5 miles inland. You start out paddling in pasturelands—having to pick your way through grass patches at the beginning—and head increasingly into the subtropical flora as branches create sun-filtered shady pools. Birdsong is pronounced. This is a stream not used by commercial outfitters.

SURF: The shore break at **Kealia Beach** invites short-board surfers and body boarders, often several dozen at a time. Body boarding is often good off the breakwater to the left. Near the stream mouth at the other end, swells also attract surfers, although be aware of submerged rocks. Although Kealia can be good at any time of year, normally the onshore trade winds fight the break. *Be Aware:* Kealia is one of Kaua'i's most dangerous beaches, with rip currents, exposure to trade winds, and a shallow, onshore break. Head and neck injuries are possible.

28. KAPA'A TOWN   HIKE, SNORKEL, BIKE, SURF

WHAT'S BEST: Tool around a colorful Kauaian town, on foot or by bike, and enjoy one of its several coral beaches. Try Kapa'a on a sunny weekend to see the mix of cultures that blend to create island-style living. Then take a short hike inland to a hidden waterfall.

PARKING: The Kapa'a Town trailhead covers a 1.75-mi. portion of coast, beginning near mm7, just past the Kapa'a Shores condos, and extending to Kou Rd. on the other end of town, behind Otsuka's furniture store. *For parking:* Turn makai on Keaka Rd., at the Chevron, drive a short block, and park at Niulani Rd. along the water. *Note:* Additional access points are imbedded in activity descriptions below. *For Ho'opi Falls:* Head

Kealia Beach

toward Kealia on Hwy. 56 and turn mauka on Kawaihau Rd. (just past Otsuka's). Continue for almost 3 mi. and turn right on Kapahi Rd. Go .25-mi. and look for a gate on the left, about .1-mi. before the end of Kapahi.

HIKE: Kapaʻa Town stroll (up to 4 mi.); Hoʻopi Falls (.75-mi., 200 ft.)

Begin the **Kapaʻa Town** stroll at Keaka Road parking spot, and head toward the Waikaea Canal, about .75-mile to your left as you face the water. You start out in a quiet several-block grid of beach cottages, home to Fuji beach, which is a draw for kite boarders and moms with toddlers. A new arty footbridge leads across the canal to the large sandy beach behind the Pono Kai condos. The Pono Kai beach extends to Kapaʻa County Beach Park—with picnic pavilions and restrooms—which is behind a soccer field that borders the highway.

Pono Kai Beach

For most of this hike, you can choose between walking the beach or a wide concrete path. Palms and ironwoods shade the way. Keiki birthday parties, neighborhood events, and fishermen enjoying a daytime brewskie add to the atmosphere.

Passing the beach park—having walked .75-mile from the Waikaea Canal—you reach another newly rebuilt footbridge, at Kapaʻa Library. The pleasant path continues for another .25-mile, passing a community center and swimming pool, and coming to an end behind Otsuka's at Kou Road. Here, a groomed stand of cocopalms faces the shore leading to Kealia.

On the way back, you may wish to take a look at Kapaʻa Town: Walk the beach path back to the soccer field, and continue right on Niu Road. Then go left on the main street, checking out the shops and sights of Kapaʻa's triangular downtown. Continue down the main street to Inia Road, at the Pono Kai, and cut through the grounds of these condos to the beach and path back to your car.

Tucked away in a neighborhood, **Hoʻopi Falls** won't be a vacation highlight, but it is a pleasant-enough, woodsy getaway. Head down the dirt road at the gate and within ten minutes you'll reach the stream, under a canopy of large monkeypod trees. During low water, take a lower trail across bedrock downstream; in higher water, take a trail that veers right, about 40 feet above the stream. In either case, you'll reach the falls in about 5 minutes. Two, 20-foot cascades fall through a bedrock gorge, providing swimming holes and places for wannabe rock climbers to explore.

SNORKEL: **Baby Beach** is a sandy area for toddlers and moms. From Keaka Road, walk or drive two blocks to where Makaha Road comes in. The little beach section is between Makaha and Panihi roads. You'll see a long, shallow pool near the road.

Pono Kai Beach, the best swimming beach in Kapa'a, extends to your right as you face the water at Kapa'a County Beach Park—which is behind the large grass field at Niu Road. Pono Kai Beach has ample sand and trees providing a choice between sun and shade. The sandy shore makes for easy entry, and you'll find interesting rocks and a reef not far out, although schools of fish are uncommon. Current is generally onshore. Visibilty is often only fair. *Be Aware:* Don't drift too far out, especially if swells are large; outgoing current develops under these conditions.

Coral Reef Beach—which you can access most easily by parking at the Kapa'a Library and walking to your left across the footbridge—has shallow waters, but decent places of entry with the best fish along this part of the coast. Water clarity is good. For drying off, you can choose between a small strip of sand and a grassy area with shade among palm trees. *Be Aware:* Rip tides here can be dangerous, and sharp coral is also a factor.

BIKE: The **Kapa'a Town** coast is the most bike-friendly developed spot on the island. Read the hiking description for coastal walk, or just get on your bike and roll. *Note:* The town has a couple bike rental places, but Coconut Coasters is centrally located on the path and has a fleet of reasonably priced, spiffy beach cruisers; see *Resource Links,* page 239. Starting near the Kapa'a Shores condos on Niulani Road, make your way along path and footbridges, hugging the coast and heading toward Kealia. At the far end of town, near mm9 behind Otsuka's—across from Kawaihau Road—the route is wild-and-scenic to Kealia Beach—and beyond.

Going the other way on a bike, toward **Wailua**, is not quite as simple, but not difficult, either. To connect with the Coconut Coast, TH29, stay on Niulani Road until you are forced to loop out around the Kapa'a Shores condos. You can turn seaward toward the Kaua'i Coconut Beach Resort or even earlier at a beach access sign for little-known Waipouli Beach County Park. You have to pop out to the highway and cross the bridge near the Bull Shed restaurant. See Coconut Coast mountain biking descriptions to take it from there.

SURF: **Kapa'a Town** is not surf city. But local boarders sometimes try the reef break outside of Waikaea Canal. Head for the boat ramp on Kaloloku Road, and

Along the Kapa'a coastal bike path

look seaward to the right. Due to shallow break and tricky currents, don't try this area unless the local boys are out there. The real wave action in Kapa'a is among high-flying kite-boarders who put in at the end of **Baby Beach**, in a section called **Fuji Beach**.

29.   COCONUT COAST   HIKE, SNORKEL, BIKE

> **WHAT'S BEST:** Strolling or pedaling Kaua'i's lesser-known resort coast, with its classic coco palms and quiet coral beaches. Take a mellow walk to start or finish the day.
> **PARKING:** Take Hwy. 56 from Lihue and cross over the Wailua River. Pass mm6 and park makai at Coconut Marketplace.

HIKE: Coconut Coast stroll (up to 3 mi.)

The **Coconut Coast** is a 1.5-mile long coral beach sometimes called Papaloa, running from Alakukui Point at Wailua Bay to Waipouli, the area before Kapa'a. Behind a commercial district, this is Kaua'i's surprisingly beautiful, easy-walking coastal resort stroll. The modest resorts, spread apart, seem kitschy compared to the time-share be-homeths going up elsewhere in Hawaii. From the parking, walk through the courtyard of Coconut Marketplace (some decent stops for shopaholics) and continue behind the Islander on the Beach resort to a tree-lined water's edge. Go to your right on the paved path beside a narrow strip of yellow sand. Just past the Kaua'i Sands, walk out a trail to a patch of greenery, which is contemplative Alakukui Point, where you'll find remains of **Kukui Heiau**, a fishing temple. From the point, skirt sandy tidepools at the shore of two small coves, behind tasteful Lae Nani condos. If you hop black rocks at the end of these tidepool coves, you will reach the outer point of Wailua Bay.

Going the other way, to your left from the Islander, you have a choice between the paved path or the beach, which is a narrow strip of coarse sand and exposed reef running along a low bank fringed by palms and ironwoods. You'll pass a large grass field, which has survived various development plans for decades, and then come to the Kaua'i Courtyard by Mariott. Crossing a small ditch on the other side of the resort, you are again in an open area, with ironwoods and a coral beach—the scenic, usually quiet Waipouli Beach Park.

SNORKEL: On **Papaloa Beach**, just behind the Islander on the Beach as described in the parking instructions, you'll find sandy entrances in an otherwise sharp-coral beach with the reef running close to the shore. A fair number of fish swim here, and snorkeling can be good. *Be Aware:* The water is shallow and sometimes made turbulent by winds and wave action. *Cool tip:* Families and dawdlers will like the tidepool beaches at the **Lae Nani condos**, reachable via the short walk described above.

Waipouli Beach Park, just to the left as you face the water at the Coutyard Marriott, has the best sand in the area and several places that are shielded relatively from strong currents and wave action. Drive on Aleka Loop along a grass field to the path that is to the right of the resort as you face the water. *Be Aware:* Sha currents, and wave action combine to make this coast a place to take prec

BIKE: The **Coconut Coast** is ideal for exploring on a slow-moving mountain bike. Hug the water, being watchful for pedestrians and hotel paths, where walking the wheels is advised. Between the coastal paths and the highway, roads and parking lots provide safe passage. To connect with Kapa'a Town (and the coastal path to Kealia) you can ride the coast most of the way, though you need to pop out to the highway past the Kaua'i Beach Resort at Makaina, and cut back in again just past the Kapa'a Shores.

Going the other way, towards Lihue and Wailua Bay, you need to ride through the Coconut Marketplace parking lot and pick up Papaloa Road, which fronts the highway before joining it near the defunct Coco Palms Resort. You need to get on Highway 56 and cross the river via the marginal bike lane on the main bridge. After the river, cross the highway again and pedal toward Lydgate Park, TH34. A new concrete bike path makes for easy going from there.

30. SLEEPING GIANT   HIKE

WHAT'S BEST: A tree-lover's hike to an east-side landmark, 1,200-feet high, with coastal and inland views. This forest reserve ranks high on the list of excellent half-day hikes.

PARKING: Three different trails lead to the top of Sleeping Giant.

For the Sleeping Giant mountain-side trail (shortest): Take Hwy. 580, Kuamo'o Rd., mauka from Wailua Bay (at the Coco Palms). Continue on Hwy. 580 for 2.5 mi. and turn right on Hwy. 581, Kamalu Rd. Go about 2 miles on Hwy. 581, past Heamoi Place, and park at telephone pole number 11—public access is between two homes near address 1050.

For the Sleeping Giant Kuamo'o trail (not recommended for summit): Take Hwy. 580, as noted above, only at 2.3 mi., look for a sign and trailhead parking on your right across the highway from Melia Street.

Sleeping Giant

For the Sleeping Giant ocean-side trail (longest, ocean views): Head toward Kapaʻa on Hwy. 56 from the Wailua River and the junction of Hwys. 56 and 580. After .25-mi. at a traffic light, turn inland on Haleilio Rd. Drive about 1 mile and look for a trailhead as Haleilio makes a big sweep around to the left—near a water pump station.

HIKE: Sleeping Giant via mountain-side trail (3.25 mi., 775 ft.); Sleeping Giant via Kuamoʻo Rd. trail (to Vista Hale picnic shelter 1.5 mi., 325 ft., or to summit 5.5 mi., 925 ft.); Sleeping Giant via ocean-side trail (4 mi., 1,050 ft.)

All Sleeping Giant trails are part of Nounou Mountain Forest Reserve in the state's Na Ala Hele trail system. The Nounou Mountains, as you can observe from the coast, would be part of a ridge connecting with Kalepa Ridge, TH37, were it not long ago cleaved by the Wailua River. Inland of the Sleeping Giant was where the ancient Kauaian royalty, the aliʻi, chose to first settle.

For the **Sleeping Giant mountain-side trail**, which is the most direct way to the top, begin the hike by passing private homes on a gentle upslope for about .5-mile into forest. Here you reach the Kuamoʻo trailhead junction on your right. Continue up the trail alongside tall Norfolk pines. The trail then switchbacks steeply, traversing a variety of trees planted in the 1930s by the Civilian Conservation Corps. You meet the ocean-side trail, coming in from your left. Veer right to a picnic shelter near the top for views of the Coconut Coast, Wailua River and the Makaleha Mountains. To the summit, keep going to the right as you face seaward as the trail drops and then snakes up a ridgeline. One steep section before the top of the Giant requires your hands, but it is not dangerous. *Be Aware:* Thrill seekers will want to tiptoe to the left near the top to reach the chin of the Giant, but take your time since slips here lead to a free-fall.

The Sleeping Giant Kuamoʻo trailhead is best for the shorter walk to the Vista Hale picnic shelter or for a wooded, birder's car-shuttle hike to the mountain-side trailhead; it is a circuitous way to the summit. You begin in a pleasant grassy easement and then cross a footbridge over Opaekaʻa Stream, well above the falls. The trail switchbacks through hau and guava before busting out to a view of Kalepa Ridge at the picnic shelter. The route then undulates along the west side of Nounou Mountains through richly varied forest, meeting the mountain-side trail described above after about 2 miles.

The Sleeping Giant ocean-side trail requires the most elevation. It's main upside is the blue-water views on the way up. It is also sunnier and you'll see more flowering shrubs, compared to the more forested mountain side of the ridge. Fewer hikers use this access, which joins its sister route about .25-mile from the picnic area near the top.

31. OLOHENA HIGHLANDS   HIKE, BIKE

WHAT'S BEST: Hiking or biking an open ridge into the island's tropical interior, or riding around the rural countryside above Kapaʻa to get a take on local-style living.

PARKING: Take Hwy. 56 to the center of Kapaʻa Town and turn mauka on Hwy. 581. Hwy. 581 is Kukui Rd., which becomes Olohena Rd. Take Olohena up for about 6 mi., making sure to bear right where Hwy. 581 turns left and becomes part of Kamalu Rd. Continue up Olohena on narrower paved section until it ends at a Kondo Gate, a hunter's check-in.

HIKE: **Moalepe Trail** (3 mi. to 6 mi., 300 to 700 ft. depending on hike selection.)

The **Moalepe Trail**, one of the lesser-used segments of the Na Ala Hele state hiking system, begins on a gradual incline, a red-dirt road flanked by pasturelands. White egrets will often be seen winging their way up a narrowing valley. To your back are blue-water vistas and a good look at the Anahola Mountains. After a mile the ridge narrows, with ferns, eucalyptus, and monkeypod trees at arm's length. At about 1.5 miles, the Kamali Ridge across the valley is dramatically close, on its way to abut the Makaleha Mountains, which in turn are heading toward Waialeale.

After the 1.75-mile mark, the trail becomes decidedly steeper, gaining most of its 700-foot elevation on the way to join the Kuilau Ridge Trail, at 2.75 miles into the hike. Gravel is often added to this section, to aid equestrians, but count on big mud-holes winning out in the long run. You'll get close-ups of the Makaleha Ridge all the way. The trail junction—actually the trails just blend together, getting renamed in the middle—is at a hairpin left turn. The Kuilau Ridge Trail is described in TH32, Keahua Arboretum. *More Stuff:* The Moalepe Trail to the Kuilau Ridge Trailhead is a 4.5-mile car-shuttle, which works out well if you have a non-hiking driver in the

Kuilau Ridge Trail

group. Another easy-hiking spot nearby is the Wailua Game Management Area: When driving up Olohena, past the 581-Kamalu Road junction, turn left on Pu'uopae Road. After .5-mile, turn right on Kalama and continue 1 mile to the Rice Gate at road's end. This is a birder's walk that eventually connects with the Moalepe Trail.

BIKE: The **Moalepe Trail** is a gradual rise for nearly 2 miles, but after that, count on standing in the pedals. This trail is popular among equestrians, and horses turn the route into pudding—although gravel patches remedy this for a while. Although this trail does connect with TH32, Keahua Arboretum, it is not well-suited to mountain bikes on that end—it's muddy and wheels damage portions of the trail. Ride in on Moalepe for about 1.5 miles, and then try the countryside pedals described below.

32. KEAHUA ARBORETUM   HIKE, BIKE

WHAT'S BEST: Hike or bike into the tropical highlands—to the basin of Mount Waialeale, along a jungle ridge, or head out across the island to Hanalei Valley. Several of Hawaii's prime forested hikes are right here. So is a sacred forest.

PARKING: Take Hwy. 580, which is Kuamo'o Rd., mauka at the Wailua River (at the old Coco Palms). Arboretum parking is about 7 mi. from Hwy. 56. Park before spillway.

Note: The Keahua Arboretum area is best enjoyed under drier conditions. Four-wheel drive vehicles are recommended after the pavement ends. But when the water at the spillways is about six-inches deep or less, passenger cars can drive the Waikoko Forest Management Road across this first spillway, and even across a second, which is .5-mile farther in, and continue a mile or two beyond that. The roadway improves after the second spillway.

HIKE: Keahua Arboretum circle (1 mi., 150 ft.); Kuilau Ridge Trail (4.5 mi., 550 ft); Powerline Trail hikes: Kualapa Ridge (9.5 mi., 1,600 ft.), or trans-Kaua'i car-shuttle (13 mi., 1,700 ft.); Waialeale stream convergence (6 mi., 250 ft.); Waialeale basin (10 mi., 780 ft.) *Notes:* Hiking distances are from first-spillway parking. Different parking described below for Kaua'i's Hindu Monastery-Sacred Forest (.25-mi.)

For the tame stroll around the **Keahua Arboretum**, drive or wade across the spillway or cross the stream near the parking area. Walk up to your left, toward a picnic area, below which is a grassy basin, planted with both native and introduced tree species by the University of Hawaii. This young arboretum is intended as an outdoor classroom for students and tourists alike. Its maturation was stalled by Hurricane Iniki, but it's beginning to grow into its own. Begin to your left as you face the arboretum. A trail encircles the grounds, but the grasses can be thick on the homestretch and you may feel more comfortable going out partway and returning on the same path.

The **Kuilau Ridge Trail** is a hike to remember. The trailhead is about .1-mile up from the spillway parking area—on your right driving down. The beautiful forest walk

Kuilau Ridge Trail

begins up an often-wet dirt road, with tree-filtered views of Waialeale basin in the distance and two stream drainages in the foreground—bursting with shrubs, vines, and trees. You can also see the Powerline Trail making its way to the Kualapa Ridge. At about 1.25 miles, the trail levels, reaching a large grassy area with picnic shelter. From the picnic shelter are views seaward of Sleeping Giant and Hoary Head and, straight ahead, of anvil-shaped Makaleha Ridge.

Press on for the best stuff. The trail jogs right from the picnic area, and, for the next .5-mile, you're on a narrow, twisting ridge, amid lush tropical greenery with a Japanese-garden feel. A variety of birds will be seen and heard. This squiggly ridge is one of the most striking and scenic walks on Kaua'i. *Be Aware:* The profuse greenery at the edge of the trail hides steep drop-offs on either side. Stay on the trail.

Crossing the ridge, the trail makes a switchback, climbing to your right and then descending over a stream on a footbridge. *Note:* A sign at the footbridge says this is the end of the Kuilau Trail; disregard the sign and continue. For the next .5-mile you ascend a straight, wide path, through a tree tunnel formed primarily by peeling paperbark trees—from which paper is not made. At the top of the tree tunnel is a small grassy opening, where the trail hairpins to your right. This is where Kuilau Ridge joins Moalepe, the end-point for this hike. To get other views of the Makaleha Ridge, as well as the Kapa'a coastline, head down the Moalepe Trail for about .5-mile. Continuing all the way to the Moalepe trailhead, makes for a 4.5-mile car-shuttle hike.

The **Powerline Trail**, an an excellent trek, begins about .1-mile from the arboretum parking, on your right after the first uphill across the spillway. You'll see a hunter's checking station for Unit C, and a muddy scar of a road going up, an uninviting beginning to what is an excellent tropical forest view hike. The **Kualapa Ridge**, the high-point of the journey, is nearly 5 miles in on the Powerline Trail. You don't have to make it all the way to the top on this up-and-down ascent to get full value from this hike. The route's initial climb gives way after only five minutes to a grassy road under monkeypod trees. You'll swerve and undulate through a ferny forest, chugging upwards, with views toward the Kuilau Ridge and waterfalls, about 2.5 miles in. Birds are profuse, normally. The trail takes a 300 foot dive into a stream valley before the final ascent to the ridge, which is a good spot to turn around and shorten the adventure.

From the Kualapa Ridge you can see down the more-gradual north slopes of the trail to the Hanalei Valley, and, looking the other way, the upslopes of the Kilohana Crater area and the Sleeping Giant. These views are in addition to close-ups of the wrinkled ridges beside the Powerline Trail. The **trans-Kauai hike** is an all-day trek to be attempted by fit hikers on a sunny day. To acquaint yourself with Powerline Trail, you may wish to walk in from this trailhead as far as you want, and then pick another day to try the trail from the other side of the island, Powerline Trail North, TH12. *Be Aware:* Prepare for this hike with plenty of water, food, rain gear and a hiking pole.

To the **Waialeale stream convergence**—where three streams join—and to **Waialeale basin**—a point 4,000 feet directly below the fabled peak—stay on the Waikoko Forest Management Road. On the 4WD road, you circle up and behind the forest gardens, drop down and cross a second spillway and walk up a grade, under a canopy of subtropical trees. After the second spillway, you come to where power towers cross the road. From the power towers, the road undulates heading fairly straight for a mile, and then it makes a right, beginning a west-heading approach to the Waialeale basin. Continue for .5-mile. Then, for the **Waialeale stream convergence**, take a right-bearing fork. You'll see a sign announcing Hunting Unit C and telling people not to pick up lost dogs. This right fork follows a water ditch for a mile and ends under a tree canopy alongside the swift-flowing North Fork of the Wailua River, at a gauging station. If you carefully cross the river on rocks, you'll discover a point at which two major streams join the Wailua River, which is coming down from the Waialeale and headed for Wailua Bay. *Note:* Don't attempt to drive the road from the fork, even in four wheel drive.

For the **Waialeale basin**, take the left fork at the Unit C-dog sign. From this fork you are 2.5 miles from the basin. Continue up a grade through eucalyptus, avoiding spur roads and trails—this is a place where even hounds get lost. After .5-mile from the fork, you pass a spur road on the left to a picnic area, and enter an open forest of monkeypods and African tulip trees. A mile beyond the picnic road you come to a gate, with tall concrete poles that frame a view of Waialeale. Beyond the gate, the relief becomes pronounced, and the scenery real darned pretty. Be careful of getting too close to trailside viewpoints that may be nothing more than snarls of plantlife. *Note:* Even four-wheel drive vehicles should park at the gate.

The trail ends at a gauging station, a rough-poured concrete dam, creating a face-on spot to sit and enjoy the fast-flowing North Fork of the Wailua River. Across from the dam is a profusion of jungle greenery, leaves as big as elephant ears lost within great vine tangles. Upward is the concave face of Mount Waialeale, with a half-dozen gouges in its vertical face that become falls during rains. *More Stuff:* From the dam, a sketchy trail across the river leads through the jungle and along rocks to the Blue Hole at the bottom of Waialeale; this trail is difficult and should be attempted only by fit hikers traveling in pairs on nice days.

For rest and contemplation, try two stops at the 51-acre grounds of **Kaua'i's Hindu Monastery**: The intimate **Sacred Forest** is on

Waialeale Basin

Powerline South, road to arboretum

the main road, on your left as you head mauka near mm.5, at 7345 Kuamo'o Road. A modest shrine or two accent a thick, but walkable forest. This spot will calm everyone down, whether they like it or not. The **monastery** itself is down the road about .5-mile; turn on Kaholalele Road, near mm.4.5. The church, garden, and visitors center is at 107 Kaholalele. The groomed banyan on the path to the church is a world unto itself. *Note:* Visitors are welcomed but if you plan to go inside the monastery people ask that you use one of the sarongs supplied at the teahouse to cover up shorts.

BIKE: The **Powerline Trail** and **Kuilau Ridge Trail** are used by some advanced riders, who don't mind trails that are steep, muddy and rutted. You also can begin these cycles at the other access points: Powerline Trail North, TH12, near Princeville; and Moalepe Ridge Trail, TH32, above Kapaʻa. The best intermediate-level mountain biking option for Keahua Arboretum—one of the best rides anywhere—is the **Waialeale basin** trail, as described in the hiking section. Although mud may fly, the elevation is reasonable over the 5 miles, and the roads are very rideable, cobblestones notwithstanding. The toughest climbing for this ride is during the first mile as you negotiate steep hills on either side of the spillways. From the spillways, the ride is gradually up. On a bike, you can afford to explore the spur roads—although make sure to keep your bearings. *More Stuff:* Another adventurous option off this trail is to cut left where the power towers cross the road, as described in the beginning of the convergence and basin hikes. A network of roads lead to the Wailua River watershed, above the falls. Some of this area may be private property, however. You make the call.

Powerline mud, waterfalls on Mount Waialeale

Wailua

Wailua Falls

When the ancient Polynesians completed a 2,500-mile voyage from the South Pacific, thus making their mythical homelands a reality, their first steps were on the banks of the Wailua River. In the years to come, they built seven heiaus—temples—along the course of the river, the last near its source at Mount Waialeale. The heiaus line a sacred path from the bay to the birthplace of all waters.

To Hawaiians, Wailua was the Vatican, and for centuries the aliʻi, or kings, of all the Hawaiian Islands could trace their lineage to these hallowed grounds on Kauaʻi. Wailua in Hawaiian means, "waters of the spirits," a name reflecting the Hawaiians' reverence for their ancestors and kinship with nature.

Short walks from Wailua Bay and Lydgate Park lead to three heiaus, including one nearly intact. Intact heiaus are rare on Kauaʻi, since, when Christianity was embraced by the royals, the heiaus were sometimes used as livestock pens or their rocks removed and used for roadwork. Also at the mouth of the river are the remnants of a city of refuge, a place where vanquished warriors or criminals could escape to do penance.

Wailua Bay is the best surfing spot along the coast between the river and Nawiliwili. But most people get on the water here in canoes and kayaks, heading up the widest, deepest, longest river in Hawaii. A simulated Hawaiian village and the Fern Grotto, both tourist attractions, may be seen from the river. Naturalists can observe native subtropical vegetation, such as hala and hau trees, along with the rare pili grass, used to make grass houses, that still grows on the banks.

Beginning at Lydgate and extending toward Hanamaulu Bay are several miles of≠ secluded beaches. This coast runs behind the Wailua Golf Course as well as behind a resort hotel. At Nukoliʻi Beach, strollers will find interesting bits of coral and shells, and often will be able to see net fishermen casting from shore. Mountain bikers can find a trail most of the way—pushing the wheels as needed in one spot—completing a continuous run of coastal pedaling that goes from Hanamaulu Bay to Anahola Bay.

Hanamaulu is a locals' beach, where families gather on the weekends. Its sheltered cove makes for safe swimming as well as boogie boarding, and the bay's waters are safe for kayakers who can paddle out to Ahukini Landing at its mouth. An annual outrigger canoe race begins at Hanamaulu, heads into open water, and finishes by rounding Ninini Point and entering Nawiliwili Harbor.

Fern Grotto

Paddling by the Sleeping Giant on the Wailua River

The coast between Ahukini Landing and Ninini Point, despite being behind the airport, is a scenic ride or hike, and Ninini, with its lighthouse, is an eye-popping spot to watch cruise ships enter the harbor under Hoary Head Ridge.

Nawiliwili Harbor, Kauaʻi's largest port, displays both the muscle and romance of a tropical island. Walking around Nawiliwili, or riding a bike, can easily take up a day. Included in that day might be swimming or surfing at Kalapaki Bay, the beach below the Kauaʻi Marriott Resort that features Duke's Canoe Club. Walks along two breakwaters and a small harbor for cruising sailboats add charm to the lively harbor. Cruise ships offload tons of tourists.

Almost unnoticed in the harbor, but one of its more remarkable features, is Huleia Stream. The stream's calm waters lead into the Huleia National Wildlife Refuge and past the Menehune Fish Pond. Some of the movie *Jurassic Park* was filmed here, and, although private property restrictions prohibit exploring the shore, much can be seen from the water.

The most-visited spot in the Wailua area, however, is not the coast, but Wailua Falls, a few miles inland. A very steep trail takes hikers to the base of the falls. In ancient times, warriors dove from these falls to prove their courage to prospective wives. In recent times, the falls was depicted in the opening shots of television's *Fantasy Island.*

The entire Wailua area can be viewed from Kalepa Ridge, which runs just inland, parallel to the coast between Wailua Bay and Hanamaulu Bay—a vantage point of historical significance. From the sandalwood trees that grew on this ridge, Kauaian warriors kept watch for a dozen years, beginning in 1795, for the invasion of Kamehameha the Great—an attack that never came. Once, a fierce storm on the

Kaua'i Channel thwarted Kamehameha's ships, and a second invasion fizzled when warriors were stricken by disease after they again had set sail for Kaua'i.

The sandalwood trees on Kalepa Ridge were clear-cut in the early 1880s and the fragrant wood became Hawai'i's first export. A hundred years later, from a bunker on the ridge, American soldiers kept watch during World War II for another invasion that never came. The ridge affords a mid-distance view of the coast and a panorama inland of the Kilohana Crater and Waialeale ridge.

Kaua'i Marriott Resort on Kalapaki Bay

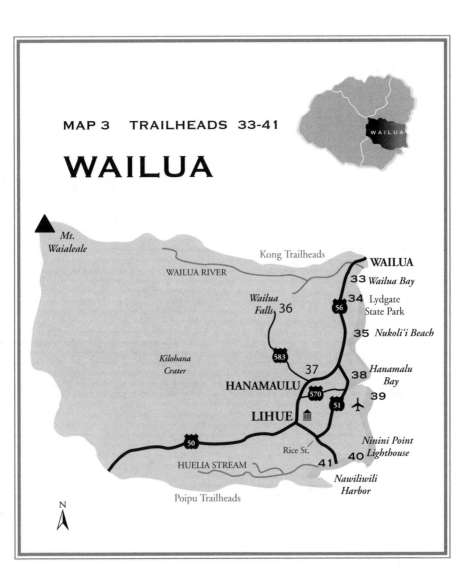

MAP 3   TRAILHEADS 33-41

WAILUA

WAILUA

*Mt.
Waialeale*

Kong Trailheads

WAILUA RIVER

WAILUA

33 *Wailua Bay*

34 Lydgate
State Park

*Wailua
Falls* 36

56

35 *Nukoli'i Beach*

*Kilohana
Crater*

583

37

HANAMAULU

570

38 *Hanamalu
Bay*

51

39

LIHUE 🏛

*Ninini Point
Lighthouse*

50

Rice St.

40

HUELIA STREAM

41

*Nawiliwili
Harbor*

Poipu Trailheads

N

T R A I L H E A D S
33-41

HIKE	HIKING
SNORKEL	SNORKELING AND SWIMMING
BIKE	MOUNTAIN OR ROAD BIKING
PADDLE	KAYAKING, CANOEING
SURF	SURFING, BOOGIE BOARDING

TH	TRAILHEAD	
Makai	TOWARD OCEAN	
Mauka	TOWARD THE MOUNTAIN, INLAND	
mm.	MILE MARKER, CORRESPONDS TO HIGHWAY SIGNS	

Note: All hiking distances are roundtrip unless otherwise noted.

33. WAILUA BAY   HIKE, PADDLE, SURF

WHAT'S BEST: A vacation variety pack: Walk the shore or paddle up the river of kings, the most sacred place in the Hawaiian Islands. Or take excellent family strolls to Kauaʻiʻs largest heiau and its most underrated botanical garden.

PARKING: The jct. of Hwys. 56 and 580 chops this trailhead up into four parts, although everything is located close together. Read hiking descriptions for places to park.

HIKE: Wailua Beach (1.25 mi.); Malae Heiau (up to .5-mi.); Wailua Marina and Smiths Tropical Paradise (up to 1.5 mi.); Birthstone Heiau and Royal Cocopalm Grove (.5-mi.)

Access to **Wailua Beach** is easiest if you're heading from Lihue toward Kapaʻa; cross the river in the right-hand lane and use the parking lot on your right immediately after crossing the river; if you miss this one, park at a second turnout on your right at the far end of the bay. In spite of its on-road location, Wailua Beach is a scenic stroll, especially when the river is running high after rains, colliding with choppy incoming surf. When the river is low, you can wade the sand bridge at the river mouth and connect with Lydgate Park. Photographers will want to curl right and walk under the bridge inland for a view up the wide river; this is where local canoe clubs put in. Or, heading left as you face the water, you can make your way around Alakukui Point and connect with the Coconut Coast.

To walk the **Wailua Marina and Smiths Tropical Paradise**, drive aross the bridge going toward Lihue and turn right immediately. This is a tourist-trot around the docks where boats depart for **Fern Grotto**. The grotto is a large dripping cavern creating acoustics for the old-timey serenade provided by your guides. The river boat tours, operated by the Smith family for generations, are a kitschy classic and well worth the price of tickets.

The marina docks, surrounded by several grassy acres, yield a splendid view across the wide Wailua toward the Sleeping Giant; quietly one of the most scenic views on the island. The cultural and botanical gardens inside **Smiths Tropical Paradise** are also well worth the modest admission price. Footbridges span lagoons amid flowering tropicals and forests of native and fruit trees. Kaua'i's Japanese, Polynesian, and Filipino heritages are represented. Shrieking peacocks waft down from towering banyans. You'll likely give the place two thumbs, especially if kids are along.

Though plant growth often hides **Malae Heiau**, it is the most intact of seven heiaus the ancients constructed, beginning at Wailua Bay and extending to Waialeale. Access is easiest when heading toward Lihue. Drive across the bridge, pass the entrance to Smith's, and look for a dirt turnout. You'll see a gate for a cane haul road. Head through that gate and look right for a 10-foot wide path that leads a short distance up to, and around, the 300- by 400-foot edifice. Its walls are about six feet high and more than twelve feet wide, vertical in the center and sloping down around the perimeter. *Notes:* The heiau is periodically cleared of brush, but it grows back quickly. Take care not to disturb the walls of this sacred place—officially a state historic site since 1928.

To the **Birthstone Heiau**, drive less than .5-mile up Hwy. 580 and park on the left at the Wailua River State Park Poliahu Area. A stairway with pipe railing leads up from behind this historic site to a small Japanese cemetery and a tree-filtered view of the Wailua River. Across the street from the Birthstone Heiau is small arboretum, a State Soil and Water Conservation Park. Next to the park is the **Royal Coconut Grove**. The royal grove lies behind the old **Coco Palms Resort**, closed due to Hurricane Iniki. Elvis stayed here when filming *Blue Hawaii*. (Plans to rebuild are slowly in the works.) The lagoon inside predates the hotel, built for enjoyment by Queen Emma. Entrance to the grove is prohibited, but you can get a good look at it by walking along the road.

PADDLE: Kayakers may access the **Wailua River** by turning on Hwy. 580, Kuamo'o Road, and making an immediate left, just past Smith's ticket area, into a Wailua State Park boat launching area. The Wailua Marina also has a boat launch area. This is Kaua'i's most popular river, and kayak rentals and tours are limited to prevent overcrowding. Even so, it can get cozy. Wailua River Kayak, located near the Safeway, is an excellent choice for independent travelers who want the enrichment provided by competent guides. They are family owned, run small daily tours—mornings are best—and can customize a trip for you; see *Resource Links*.

The Wailua is very wide, with several miles of slack waters. Two miles upriver is a confluence: The left fork is the South Fork of the Wailua River, which comes from Wailua Falls; the right fork is the North Fork of the Wailua River, which comes from Waialeale basin. The Wailua was the landing spot for the ancient Polynesian mariners, where the first Hawaiian settlements were established. **Fern Grotto**, part of Wailua River State Park, is a little more than 2 miles upriver, just up the left fork. The right

Lydgate Park, Fern Grotto tourboat, Malae Heiau

Uluwehi (Secret) Falls

fork leads past the privately owned Kamokila, a recreated Hawiian village where much of the movie *Outbreak* was filmed. Many tours go past the village and take out a little farther up, where the river narrows at rapids and shallow water. A trail leads from the left side of the river for about a mile to **Uluwehi (Secret) Falls**, a popular destination.

SURF: With its eastern exposure and river-mouth location, the surf at **Wailua Bay** varies more than most places. Surfers take advantage of an offshore break, from about the middle of the bay extending over to Alakukui Point. Body boarders try the shore break, though shallow water makes this hazardous to your health. The sails of kite-boarders will also be seen above the bay's waters. *Be Aware:* Swimming and snorkeling can be dangerous due to rip currents near the river and near the rocks at the other end of the bay.

34. LYDGATE PARK
HIKE, SNORKEL, BIKE, SURF

WHAT'S BEST: A short walk of historical significance or a longer beach walk. Kids will love a fantastical play area and the island's safest snorkeling. Lydgate is one of Hawaii's best family beach parks.
PARKING: *From Lihue:* Take Hwy. 56 toward Kapa'a and turn makai at mm5, on Leho Dr. Follow Leho, turn right on Nalu Rd., and continue to large improved parking lot. *From Kapa'a:* Take Hwy. 56 toward Lihue and turn makai after crossing the river, at left-turn lane for the Aloha Resort; this is also Leho Dr. as it loops back out to Hwy. 56. Then turn left on Nalu Rd. *For Lydgate Play Bridge:*

Drive to the south end of Leho Dr.(Lihue end) and take Nehe Rd. a short distance to a parking area.

HIKE: Hikinaʻakala Heiau (.25-mi.); Lydgate Beach (up to 3 mi.)

At the **Hikinaʻakala Heiau**—located at the river mouth just above the beach and below the hotel—are interpretive signs, describing heiaus in general, and this heiau in particular. Not much remains, but this was the first of seven heiaus leading inland from the bay toward Waileale. Adjacent to the heiau are the remains of the **Hauola City of Refuge**, a place for Kauaian miscreants to go during periods of banishment from proper society.

Lydgate Beach, a state park with showers and restrooms, is part of a beach that starts at the mouth of the Wailua River and extends about four miles, almost to Hanamaulu Bay. Large **Kamalani Playground** and picnic area is just inland of the park's man-made snorkeling pools. Heading away from the river on the beach, you pass a mid-way picnic area, then the **Play Bridge**. The developed area of the park is about .5-mile long, after which ironwoods encroach on a fairly narrow strip of yellow sand. A wide concrete bike path runs paralell to the coast, through an inviting camping area. The park's surprise on this end is a several-story, mazelike Play Bridge that could accommodate several classrooms of scurrying little people. Continuing on the beach walk, you'll pass the Wailua Golf Course, beyond which are the coral sands Nukoliʻi Beach, TH35—this is an appealing car-shuttle stroll if you have a willing driver.

SNORKEL: **Lydgate Park** features an oval, man-made swimming area, which breaks the surf near the river mouth. This large pool provides snorkeling free of concerns

Lydgate Park

about riptides. Fish at times may be outnumbered by snorkelers in the shallow water, which can sometimes be turbid due to wave action outside the enclosure. Lydgate is ideal for children. It's a sure thing for a swim and gets high overall marks.

BIKE: **Lydgate Park** is a pleasant segment of bikeable shoreline, connecting on one side with TH35, Nukoli'i Beach, and on the other with TH29, Coconut Coast. Heading toward Kapa'a and the Coconut Coast, you have to ride up to the highway and take the car bridge on a marginal bike lane. Biking the other direction, toward Lihue, you can roll along the concrete path until it ends past the play bridge. Eventually you spill out onto the sandy road along the beach. To avoid the beach trails, you can also push and ride along the out-of-bounds perimeter of the golf course, which is marked by upright pipes.

SURF: **Black Rock**, at the mouth of the Wailua River off the point of Lydgate Park, offers a fairly deep reef break. It's a long paddle out, to a right-break. Recommended for intermediate-level surfers.

35. NUKOLI'I (KAUA'I) BEACH HIKE, SNORKEL

WHAT'S BEST: Comb the east side's longest beach, looking for coral and shells, and watching Hawaiian net fishermen. You get far away in an instant.
PARKING: *First (easiest) Nukoli'i access:* From Lihue or the airport, head toward Kapa'a on Hwy. 56—from the jct. of Hwys. 56 and 51. Turn makai on Kauai Beach Dr., .25-mi. past mm3, toward the Kaua'i Beach Resort. Turn right just before resort lot, and follow the road .4-mi. around to developed lot, which is Nukoli'i Beach Park. *Second (prettiest) Nukoli'i access:* Continue .5-mi past Kauai Beach Dr., nearly to mm4, and turn makai on a dirt (Nukoli'i Beach)road along the edge of the golf course. Follow the road, which may have major potholes, around to parking area among ironwoods at beach.

HIKE: Nukoli'i Beach (up to 4.5 mi.)

Starting at the beach park (which is maintained by the resort) at the **first Nukoli'i access**, take off down the each to your left as you face the water. Nukoli'i is also called Kaua'i Beach and Kawailoa. This beach sees few visitors, especially beyond the immediate grounds of the resort. At any time of the day you may see net fishermen, plying their ancient trade. About .5-mile from the beach park, you pass the resort, where you cross a ditch. A sandy road, closed to vehicles, parallels the beach. Nukoli'i extends more than two miles, joining the beach behind the golf course—where the second access area described above brings you in—and continues seamlessly to Lydgate Park. Whales are a common sight offshore, during the winter and early spring.

SNORKEL: Wave action, shallow reef, and rip current team up to make Nukoli'i Beach an iffy choice for swimmers. One exception is **Kaua'i Keiki Beach**, a small reef-protected pool that is straight out and a little to the right of the beach park facilities; even so the tide has to be right to make this work. Another possiblity for adult dipping

Nukoli'i Beach

is the beach section that is up the beach, past the resort and just beyond the drainage ditch. Stay close to the shore during high surf.

36. WAILUA FALLS HIKE

WHAT'S BEST: Viewing the falls, from above or below, a scene many will remember from TV's *Fantasy Island.*
PARKING: Turn mauka on Hwy 583 which is off Hwy. 56, between Hanamaulu and Lihue. *For top of falls viewing:* Take Hwy. 583, also called Ma'alo Rd., 4 mi. to the end at the falls parking area. *For bottom of falls hike:* After passing under a cane-haul bridge near mm3.6, look for a paved turnout on the right with a guardrail; park at a dirt turnout at the beginning of the guardrail.

HIKE: Wailua Falls (1.75 mi., 275 ft.)

Be Aware: Drive to the falls viewing area before beginning this hike. If the river level is high at the top of the falls (normally it is comprised of twin cascades), or if it is raining, do not take this hike. Also *do not* take a lethal trail that is near the guardrail at the falls overlook. And finally, wear shoes you can get wet, since a river crossing is required.

For **Wailua Falls trail,** walk the paved road to near the middle of the guardrail, where the trail is clearly visible. Step over and begin a steep and often slippery descent. Roots and branches make for steps and handholds, and the trail is not dangerous. After reaching the bottom, head upriver a short distance through ferns and a shade canopy, courtesy of huge mango trees. The trail becomes sketchy, and reaches a ledge. Cross the river here (the ledge trails won't work, honest). On the other side, a hard-to-follow trail leads upriver to the vast pool beneath the falls. Follow your ears and watch your footing. *Be Aware:* Falling-rock is a danger under the falls.

37. KALEPA RIDGE   HIKE

> **WHAT'S BEST:** Walk the path of Kauaian warriors, a sweeping mid-elevation vista of the Wailua coast, Kilohana Crater and interior mountains.
> **PARKING:** Take Hwy. 56 toward Lihue from its jct. with Hwy. 51. At .4-mi. past the jct., turn mauka on narrow Hulei Rd., behind the red-roofed senior center Go .25-mi. and park before gate, where concrete ramp goes up straight in front of you. *Note:* A permit is no longer required for this hike; property owners are not liable. Use at your own risk.

HIKE: Kalepa Ridge (4 mi. to 8 mi., 525 ft. to 1,600 ft.,)

Kalepa Ridge is where Kauaian sentinels kept a watchful eye seaward for Kamehameha's invading ships from Oahu—which were thwarted by a storm, and then by disease. Walk around the chain-link gate and start up the concrete ramp. You'll gain 400 feet in elevation and pass a water tank. Continue to where the concrete ramp turns sharply left—that route continues to a telecommunications installation. Take either of two trails to the right at this point—they both go to the same place. The right-most trail crests the first Kalepa knob, a good choice for those wishing to bag the view of the coast and turn around. The left-side trail avoids the knob and continues along the ridge.

The Kalepa Trail, like life, has its ups and downs. Avoid side trails. After the viewpoint at the beginning, the next major knob on this ridge is Kokomo, nearly 1,000 feet up from the trailhead, and about 1.25-miles from where the dirt part of the trail begins. Those game for more may continue, dropping off Kokomo, and navigating a rough, eroded red-dirt zone, to Nailiakauea, another bump in the ridge. At this point, you are near, but high above, the Wailua River. Beyond Nailiakauea is another protuberance, called Mauna Kapu. Just below these features, as you face inland, is the Wailua River and Fern Grotto. Mauna Kapu is about 2 miles of rough walking from Kokomo. The ridge, comprising the Kalepa State Forest Reserve, is an ideal place to gain a perspective on the entire east side of Kauai. *Note:* Kilohana Crater is inland from the ridge. The expansive dome of green is not easily recognized as a former volcanic eruption—one that came millions of years after the first episodes formed the island.

38. HANAMAULU BAY   HIKE, PADDLE, SURF

> **WHAT'S BEST:** Picnic or swim at a locals' beach with a Hollywood history.
> **PARKING:** Turn makai off Hwy. 56 on Hanamaulu Rd., at a traffic light. Hanamaulu is .5-mi. toward Lihue from the jct. of Hwys. 56 and 51. From Hanamaulu Rd., veer right on Hehi Rd.and continue 1 mi. down to the beach park.

HIKE: Hanamaulu Beach Park (up to 1 mi.)

No hiking trails lead from **Hanamaulu Beach Park**, but short walks inland through boggy banana fields and around the park and beach of this cozy bay, will give you a look a the east-side's most Kauaian beach and community—on the weekends, expect a family party in one of the picnic pavilions.

Hanamaulu Bay is the only indent in a seven-mile coast running from Wailua Bay to Nawiliwili Harbor. Looking out to sea, on the right mouth of the bay, is Ahukini Landing, TH39. Hanamaulu Bay was the scene for several of the

Remnants of Hanamaulu sugar cane days

earlier movies shot in Kaua'i, including *Pagan Love Song*, in 1950, and John Wayne's 1963 classic, *Donovan's Reef.*

PADDLE: **Hanamaulu Bay** is the launching spot for canoe races that go around Ninini Point and into Nawiliwili Harbor. Although novice kayakers might want to avoid that voyage, except on the calmest of days, Hanamaulu is perhaps the best place to safely venture into the saltwater, with intimate views of the bay, shrouded with cocopalms and ironwoods. You can even get a few strokes inland on the stream, .25-mile or more, amid bananas and lush fields.

SURF: A gentle onshore break invites safe boogie boarding and body surfing, though the local boys don't often clamor to catch these combers.

39. AHUKINI LANDING   HIKE, SNORKEL, BIKE

> **WHAT'S BEST:** Say a scenic aloha before leaving Kaua'i, or on any day, with a walk around a historic pineapple pier. Or try the surprisingly good snorkeling waters.
> **PARKING:** Take Hwy. 570, which is Ahukini Rd., toward Lihue Airport and veer left, staying on Ahukini. Go 1.5 mi. to road's end.

HIKE: Ahukini stroll (.5-mi.)

Ninini Point Lighthouse

That **Ahukini Landing** can be so close to the airport is testament to Kaua'i's scenic beauty. Once a principal shipping dock for the flourishing pineapple trade, Ahukini today is a state-run fishing pier. The pier area is an interesting stroll, with a view of Hanamaulu Bay and a downward look at fish and the occasional manta ray or turtle in clear water. Ahukini's black rock breakwater is another walk option, as is the 'glass beach' to the right as you approach the parking area. The most common actvity here is the park 'n' stare, a tradition among Hawaiian drivers taking a break from the workaday world. *Be Aware:* Observe the surf before venturing onto the breakwater.

SNORKEL: With no beach and a dreary curbside appeal, **Ahukini Landing** will not impart love at first sight. But the water is deep and clear, sheltered by the breakwater, and fish are plentiful among scattered coral knobs. Scuba instructors give lessons here. Entry is easy, over rocks. All in all, Ahukini gets high marks. *Be Aware:* Stay behind breakwater to avoid current and wave action. Also, stay clear of the fishing pier.

BIKE: A fine dirt road fronts the shoreline from Ahukini Landing all the way to Ninini Point, TH40. The shoreline road is marked by a pipe gate, just before Ahukini Road makes its 90-degree turn on the way to the landing.

40. NININI POINT   HIKE, BIKE

What's Best: From the lighthouse is an exotic look at ships entering Nawiliwili Harbor. Sit a spell, and then take a long, level jog or bike ride along the coast and a resort lagoon.

Parking: Take Hwy. 51 from the Lihue Airport toward Nawwilwili. At .6-mi. past Hwy. 570 (the aiport road) turn left at beach access sign, which is Ninini Rd. You'll see an entrance station for the Kaua'i Marriott—not the main entry for the resort. Follow Ninini Rd., curving left and then right, around golf course. Stay left on a dirt road, rather than veering right toward the Mariott Lagoon condos. At 2 mi. from highway, look for a golf hole number 12 sign, shaped like an alligator; go left on dirt road for .4-mi. and park at Cyclone-fenced radio antenna installation.

HIKE: Ninini Point (less than .5-mi.)

Cruise ship leaving Nawilwili Harbor

Ninini Point is just down the dirt road from parking area. You'll see Ninini Lighthouse, which sits close to the sea at the mouth of Kalapaki Bay, also the entrance to Nawiliwili Harbor. Across the bay is Hoary Head Ridge, a backdrop for the white cruise ships that slide past the point: try to time your visit when a cruise ship is departing, often around 5 p.m. *More Stuff:* Tiny Ninini Beach is pocketed into the coast between the lighthouse and Running Waters Beach (described in next trailhead). From the parking at the fenced antenna installation, face the water and take a grassy road to the right, veering from the one you drove in on. In five minutes you'll pass a spur road on the left; stay right and then take a rough trail that drops left through thick flora and eroded slopes to the cove. This is a pesky hike, but a real getaway.

BIKE: To bike the **Ahukini coast**, take a grassy, two-track road to your left as you face the water, going behind the fenced installation. You'll roll along ironwoods and a low-set bank on a rugged coastline, with an open view inland (near the boundary for the airport). In about .5-mile you reach Kamilo Point. The road continues, veering inland slightly—past a "white balloon" communications tower—before dipping back out to the coast at other rocky beaches at 2 miles. Finally, at 2.5 miles, the road joins with Ahukini Road. *Note:* Improvements to the road and new development in 2011have altered this route. Another option for cyclists is to park at the entrance station and tour the area in a 10-mile loop. Start by riding out to Ninini Point and then down the coast to Ahukini Landing and back. Then pedal over to Running Waters and coast down to the Kaua'i Marriott. Loop back to the entrance station on the path that encirlces the resorts's huge man-made lagoon.

41. NAWILIWILI HARBOR   HIKE, SNORKEL, BIKE, PADDLE, SURF

> **WHAT'S BEST:** Get a look at the guts and the glitz of tropical Pacific seafaring life and enjoy the beach that lured Kaua'i's first major resort. Or paddle up a river into a wildlife refuge. It's easy to spend the day poking around Nawiliwili.

Nawiliwili Harbor

PARKING: Take Hwy. 50 to Lihue, turn makai on Rice St. and continue about 2 mi. down. Or take Hwy. 51 toward the harbor from airport, turn makai on Rice St. When almost down to the harbor, turn left toward the Kaua'i Marriott, on Ho'olaulea Way. Pass the resort's main entrance and turn right on Kalapaki Circle. Then turn right toward beach access and continue down to a 150-space parking lot. *Alternate or overflow access:* Pass the resort entrance, continue on Rice-Hwy. 51, and park at beach access on the left just before crossing small concrete bridge. *For Kukui Point:* After turning on Kalapaki Circle, pass the beach access noted above. Instead, keep left toward Shoreline Public Access and parking for Chapel by the Sea. *For Running Waters Beach:* Pass Kalapaki Circle, cross a bridge, and stay left (passing the road to Kalanipu'u Resort).

HIKE: Kalapaki Beach walk and Nawiliwili Jetty (up to 2.25 mi.); Kuki'i Point (.5-mi, 100 ft.); Running Waters Beach (.5 mi., 125 ft.); Nawiliwili Small Boat Harbor (1 mi.)

For Kalapaki Beach walk and Nawiliwili Jetty, skip out to the beach from the parking area and go right, either on sand or the paved path through the the resort's poolside gardenscape. Before straying too far, you'll probalby want to duck into the grounds of the Kaua'i Marriott, which feature an elevated promenade with balconies above a glamorous pool. In the lobby is the *Princess*, the huge koa canoe, circa 1860, that belonged to the great Prince Jonah Kuhio. Near the front of the resort is a realxing lagoon with koi ponds, waterfalls, artwork, and colorful birds. Built in 1962 as the Kaua'i Surf, this resort has weathered two hurricanes, and prompted a zoning law requiring that island buildings be "no higher than a coco palm."

Continuing around the .25-curve of sand of Kalapaki Beach, you will pass Duke's Canoe Club, named for Olympic champion Duke Kahanamoku, and then walk over a footbridge (or wade the stream) to Nawiliwili Beach Park, a canoeists' enclave and locals' hangout, which is next to the Anchor Cove shopping center. **Nawiliwili Jetty** extends seaward from the beach park, about .5-mile into the harbor. You can drive out the entire distance, but a path closer to the water gives you a close-up look at surfers and boaters. Across from the bay is Hoary Head Ridge. To your right from the end of the jetty is Huleia Stream and the small boat harbor.

Kuki'i Point is the mini-lighthouse across from Nawiliwili jetty light at the entrance to the harbor. The short walk delivers a large scenic payoff. From the parking by Chapel by the Sea, walk to the end of the road. Go right on a golf course path, which curves down, around a green. Then follow a rocky trail to Kuki'i Point. *More Stuff:* From the parking lot, a path the skirts the resorts to **Running Waters Beach**. The last part of the walk is over smooth-lava shelf favored by fishermen. Though a longer route, this is a more scenic walk than the other trailhead, which is described below.

Running Waters Beach was a scenic getaway, before the institution-like Kalanipu'u Resort was built in 2010. From the lot, a trail leads between the old restaurant (which, like Ahukini Landing, is awaiting redevelopment). Running Waters is a sloping curve of sand, pocked with black rocks. It lies outside the breakwaters of Kalapaki Bay.

To **Nawiliwili Small Boat Harbor**, you need to make a mile drive from the entrance road to the Marriott. Pass Anchor Cove Center going around the harbor away from Kalapaki. Turn left on Wilcox Road and pass Matson shipping and the anchorage for the massive cruise ships. Continue and then turn makai on Halemalu Road toward

Running Waters Beach

the boat harbor, and Niumalu Beach Park. Several kayak outfitters, as well as sailing and fishing guides, are based in this low-key area. Boats in the harbor will strike a romantic chord for anyone who has fantasized sailing the South Seas. For the full effect, try walking the jetty that shields the vessels from both the harbor and the fresh waters of Huleia Stream—an underrated jaunt.

SNORKEL: **Kalapaki Bay** is known for surfing rather than fish-peeping, but relatively sheltered waters do provide a scenic and reliable place to don the mask and fins. Waters are fairly murky. People lap swim just offshore of the beach. Kalapaki is a roomy bay, but if you drift too far off shore you might run into trouble with surfers and boating lanes.

Running Waters is better for sight-seeing and relaxing than anything else. Large waves from varying directions wash the rocky shore, making this a turbulent area for swimming on most days. But, during calm periods, Running Waters is known as a good area for experienced snorkelers who don't mind the new imposing resort development.

Duke Kahanamoku

PADDLE: Kayakers will enjoy stroking into well-protected **Kalapaki Bay**, but keep an eye out for surfers and boat traffic. For access to the **Huleia Stream**, go to the Nawiliwili Small Boat Harbor, as described above. Outfitters there rent kayaks and offer guided tours up the wide stream, which goes into the Huleia Wildlife Refuge. The refuge was a setting for the movies *Jurassic Park* and *Raiders of the Lost Ark*. It is not readily accessible on foot, due to private property restrictions and wildlife refuge regulations. As wide as any river except for the Wailua, the stream curves inland for about 2 miles. About 1 mile in, you pass the Menehune Fish Pond, a streamside reservoir constructed by Kaua'i's legendary settlers around 200 to 400 AD. A mile past the fish pond, waters ripple over a cascade, the end of navigable waters. No hiking is permitted inland, except with a licensed outfitter. *Be Aware:* Brace yourself for a headwind on the homeward paddle.

SURF: **Kalapaki Beach** is site of Duke's Canoe Club, named for surfing legend Duke Kahanamoku. His hardwood longboard is

displayed inside. Duke's beach has several good surfing spots, although often too tame for the local boys. The onshore break is suitable for bodyboards. Farther out, near Kuki'i Point, is an area called **Lighthouse**, a left-slide next to a rock wall suitable for good surfers only. Near the breakwater across from lighthouse is an area sometimes called **Hang Ten**, near the right side of the bay; Hang Ten also has rock hazards. Both these Kalapaki spots often suffer from low surf. On the other hand, good breaks for beginning and intermediate surfers may be found on any given day. **Kalapaki Bay** is also an excellent choice for stand-up paddlers.

Kalapaki Bay, stand-up paddler, Marriott weather station

Poipu

Along the Mahaulepu Heritage Trail

The last volcanic eruptions on Kaua'i took place 40,000 years ago from craters that are now obscured by cacti and brush, a long tee shot from the golf links and resort hotels of Poipu Beach. Kaua'i's first eruptions were 10 million years ago, under the sea.

More recently, but long ago in the 1300s, the Poipu shores at Mahaulepu were the scene of a great battle, when a powerful king from the Big Island, having conquered all the other islands, landed here with a flotilla of war canoes. The Kauaian king, Kukona, outfoxed the powerful enemy, coaxing the invading forces inland, where they were defeated. Rather than kill the captured king, Kukona is said to have taken him on a tour of the island. The next unified invasion of Kaua'i was not attempted for almost 500 years, by Kamehameha the Great, and his forces did not succeed either.

Beginning in Mahaulepu, which is on the ocean side of Hoary Head Ridge, and extending to Lawai Bay, the south coast is a varied coastline of reef-protected coves, wave-bashed bluffs, and sandy beaches. These features make Poipu ideal for hiking, cycling, and all water sports. Horseback riding is also popular here.

On the arid bluffs between Shipwreck Beach and Mahaulepu is the Heritage Trail, known for shorebirds, whale viewing, and historic sites—one of the best coastal walks in the islands. The Grand Hyatt Poipu at Shipwreck Beach is rated among the world's top tropical resorts.

The whole coast from Spouting Horn to Mahaulepu is well-suited for exploring on a mountain bike some of it by zigzagging through resort areas and other parts by riding on four-wheel tracts and disused cane roads. One dirt road, just up from the Poipu-Spouting Horn junction, leads inland to parts of the island not reachable by any other means.

Windsurfers are drawn to the waters with the surfers off Shipwreck Beach. Ocean kayaking and canoeing are popular within the protected waters of Poipu Beach, but paddlers should get the advice of a local before stroking out to sea.

Poipu Beach is flanked by resorts and condominiums, basking in the south shore's desertlike climate. In the winter, Poipu will have sun when the rest of the island may not. The beach is a two-mile run of small sandy coves separated by short peninsulas, creating pools suited for snorkeling and swimming. Surfers come here year around to Brennecke's Beach, but the real surfing action along this coast is during the summer when Kona winds bring larger swells.

Koloa Landing, at Whalers Cove, today is often bypassed by tourists heading for Spouting Horn or Poipu. But in the 1800s Koloa Landing was the third busiest anchorage in Hawaii among whaling and trading ships, surpassed only by Honolulu and Lahaina on Maui. Although the shore is rocky, snorkeling is good at Whalers Cove, but not quite as good as a little farther up the coast at Prince Kuhio Park. Named in honor of Prince Jonah Kuhio Kalanianaole, delegate to the U.S. Congress in the early 1900s, today the place is just "PK's." An audience gathers at PK's to watch the surfers during the summer, and in the winter the little beach is packed with snorkelers.

The road ends at Lawai Bay, not far from Prince Kuhio Park. Two of Kaua'i's three National Tropical Botanical Gardens are located up the Lawai Valley—Allerton and McBryde gardens. The gardens, part of a botanical research center working to preserve and study tropical plants, were once the retreat of a Hawaiian queen. Many movie companies, including those shooting *Honeymoon in Vegas*, *Jurassic Park*, and *Donovan's Reef*, have selected the gardens for locations. Visitors wishing to see the gardens must take a tour, starting from the visitor's center across from Spouting Horn.

Spouting Horn is where pressurized sea water erupts like a geyser through a lava tube, created from sea swells trapped below. Reputedly, a second, larger geyser was located nearby, but it was dynamited in 1910 by plantation owners who wanted to keep salt spray from killing cane crops just inland.

Agricultural lands and rural neighborhoods comprise the lands sloping up from Poipu toward Kahili Peak. The hikes to Kahili Ridge provide exhilarating views of the

Grand Hyatt lagoon, Poipu Beach

south shore, as well as a close-up of the ridge's complex flora and topography. Kahili rises above Koloa Gap—the passageway between Lihue and Poipu. The view from this jungled spine was once utilized by outlaws who could swoop down on horseback and surprise their victims.

An easier walk, and perhaps the best place on Kaua'i to view the south and west shores, is Kukuiolono Park on a hillock above Kalaheo. The park will interest history buffs and botanists, as well as provide a 260-degree blue-water vista.

Shipwreck Beach, Spouting Horn, Poipu Beach

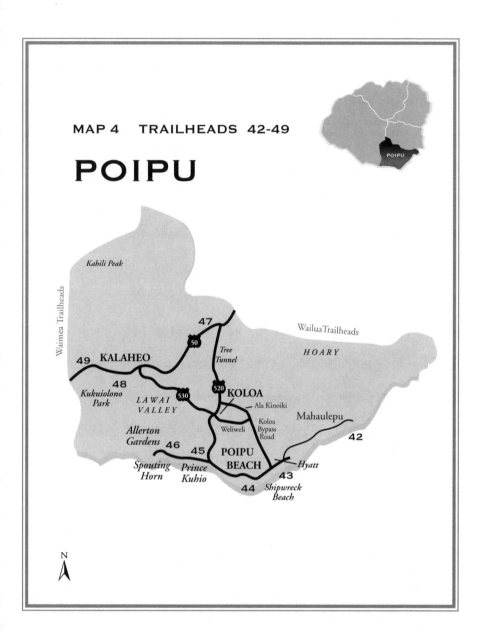

MAP 4   TRAILHEADS 42-49

POIPU

POIPU

Kahili Peak

Waimea Trailheads

47

50

WailuaTrailheads

Tree
Tunnel

HOARY

49 KALAHEO

48
Kukuiolono
Park

LAWAI
VALLEY

530

520 KOLOA

Ala Kinoiki

Mahaulepu

Allerton
Gardens 46

Weliweli

Koloa
Bypass
Road

42

45

POIPU
BEACH

Spouting
Horn

Prince
Kuhio

Hyatt

43

44 Shipwreck
Beach

N

TRAILHEADS
42-49

HIKE	HIKING
SNORKEL	SNORKELING AND SWIMMING
BIKE	MOUNTAIN OR ROAD BIKING
PADDLE	KAYAKING, CANOEING
SURF	SURFING, BOOGIE BOARDING

TH	TRAILHEAD
Makai	TOWARD OCEAN
Mauka	TOWARD THE MOUNTAIN, INLAND
mm.	MILE MARKER, CORRESPONDS TO HIGHWAY SIGNS

*Note: All hiking
distances are roundtrip
unless otherwise noted.*

42. MAHAULEPU   HIKE, SNORKEL, BIKE, PADDLE

WHAT'S BEST: You wouldn't expect this wild coast to be so close to the resorts of Poipu Beach. Take a swim, nap where the monk seals sun themselves, or walk along the south shore's wild coast.

PARKING: Take Hwy. 50 from Lihue and turn makai on Hwy. 520, which is Manuhia Rd., the Poipu tree tunnel. Go 3 mi. and turn left, before Koloa, on Ala Kinoiki. Continue about 3 mi. to a stop sign at Poipu Rd. Turn left. Pass an open gate, just beyond the Grand Hyatt Poipu, and continue past a road to stables. Turn right, about 1.5 mi. from Hyatt. Enter gate for Kawailoa Bay—open normally from 7 to 6. Continue .5-mi to first beach parking, turn left, continue .5-mi and park in unimproved area at Kawailoa Bay. *Note:* Beyond the Hyatt, the road is unpaved and usually seriously potholed.

HIKE: Haula Beach (1.5 mi., 150 ft.); Mahaulepu Beach (1 mi.)

The bright seascape from Kawailoa Bay to **Haula Beach** may inspire you to paint with watercolors. Start to your left as you face the bay—a road goes in that direction but most hikers will prefer to take coastline trails, curling through the ironwoods along low tawny bluffs. Waves often pound the point at Kawailoa Bay, and when conditions are right you may hear a resultant moaning of air coming up just inland through old lava tubes. Open sand dunes and sculpted cliffs highlight the middle of the walk. Then you drop into a cove, with a rugged little beach. Continue along the shoreline.

After this first cove, you'll encounter a fence. You may pass unobstructed at the shoreline—a dicey little move around a post over a 20-foot drop. (Inland near the corner of the fence you'll also find and unsigned gate.) From the fence, stroll up the slope and curve around to the left, reaching a view of the beach from an ironwood forest. Head inland and pick your way down to the beach. Haula Beach is the only access to Haupu State Forest Reserve, which rises above it. It is a generous curve of sand, in

the shadow of steep-rising Kawelikoa Point. *More Stuff:* Lands around this point are private, including mysterious, photogenic Kipu Kai Beach. A hunter's trail leads from the upslope of the beach and switchbacks up the ridgeline to an awesome view spot.

Going the other way from Kawailoa Bay, toward **Mahaulepu Beach**, walkers will find easy going around a sandy point and then a long straighaway, bordered by the

Haula Beach, Kawailoa Bay

ubiquitous ironwoods. Monk seals commonly beach themselves at this beach—stay back from this endangered species that is the only mamal native to Hawaii. The far end of Mahaulepu Beach is known Gillan's Beach, the name of the guest cottage at the backshore. Scamper up the bluff and you'll be on the Mahaulepu Heritage Trail headed for Shipwreck Beach and the Hyatt.

SNORKEL: Small **Kawailoa Bay** is enticing for snorkelers and swimming can be good. But at times you'll find a choppy surface. Watch for sleeper waves along the shoreline. For the most sea life, swim out and left toward the low reef. Above this reef—walk to the left at the bayshore—is an excellent **keiki beach** and a shaded spot to plant your beach stuff. Local kids jump from the nearby bluff.

Mahaulepu Beach, is also fairly good, best accessed from the first beach parking area. Look for cars; a short trail to the beach is hidden in a hedge of ironwoods. The best swimming is to your left, a couple hundred yards down the beach. A rock barrier, about 30 yards out and running along the shore, creates a huge oval pool for beginners and younger children. Safer spots are nearest the sandy point. For some tide pool soaking action, or nonaction, head to the beach's headland, at **Gillan's Beach**. *Be Aware:* High surf at Mahaulepu indicates dangerous current conditions.

Mahaulepu Coast

BIKE: Sandy beach roads, horse trails, and cane roads in disuse all make **Mahaulepu** mountain biker friendly. Some of the best riding is inland. You can take Mahaulepu Road (go left where the beach road turns right before the gate) back toward Koloa, and get a look at the Koloa Sugar Mill, which was the first on Kaua'i. Closed in the late 1990s, the behemoth, red-stained structure is being swallowed by tropical foliage.

Cyclists also can make a 10-mile **Koloa loop**. Start by parking in Koloa. Take Weliweli Road from Koloa, but turn left on the cane toward Mahaulepu, rather than the paved Koloa-Poipu Bypass Road. Once at Mahaulepu, skirt the coast along Shipwreck Beach, TH43, and **Poipu Beach**, TH44. At the far end of Poipu, just past the Sheraton, head to the right, and come back up the pavement on Poipu Road to Koloa. *Be Aware:* Heed private property signs on cane roads, and watch out for cars on Poipu Road.

PADDLE: Experienced paddlers put in at Kawailoa Bay and head to the left around the point to **Kipu Kai Beach**, which is not accessible by land to the public. This is a spectacular place and one of the best ocean kayaks in Hawaii. Check weather reports and seek advice from local outfitters before embarking on this challenging trip.

43. SHIPWRECK BEACH-GRAND HYATT Hike, Surf

What's Best: The Grand Hyatt Poipu is a fitting start for a majestic nature-history walk along bluffs above the deep blue Pacific. Then take a short, quirky walk to the site of Kaua'i's last eruption.

Parking: Take Hwy. 50 from Lihue and turn makai on Hwy. 520, the tree tunnel road. Before Koloa, turn left on Ala Kinoiki, a bypass road. Continue several miles. At stop sign, turn left on Poipu Rd., and, just past the Grand Hyatt Kaua'i, turn makai on Ainako St., a beach access road running between the Hyatt and Poipu golf course.

Hike: Grand-Hyatt and Mahaulepu Heritage Trail (4.25 mi., 275 ft); Pu'u Wanawana Crater (.5-mi., 150 ft.)

Whether before or after the nature walk, you should take a stroll through the **Grand Hyatt Kaua'i**, one of the world's top beach resorts. Go right at the parking lot and weave your way around the saltwater lagoon-pool and through the resort's gardens. Inside, Asian-inspired architecture manages to be both grand and intimate. Decor includes museum quality artwork, and cultural events often take place on weekends. *More Stuff:* A paved path extends from the Hyatt through the greenbelt of Poipu Kai condos, reaching Poipu Beach Park at Pane Road, which is off Ho'one. It extends from the side of the resort opposite beach access parking.

For the superlative **Mahaulepu Heritage Trail**, start toward your left as you face Shipwreck Beach in front of the Hyatt and walk down the beach toward Makawehi Bluff.

Shipwreck Beach

The landmark bluff greets the pounding surf at that end of Keoneloa Bay—which is the proper name for the Shipwreck. (The most recent wreck of 1970 was taken away by Hurricane Iniki.) Several footpaths lead to the top, where intrepid divers sometimes wow beachgoers. Shorebirds nest in rock pockets. Make your way down the coast, at first through a network of sandy paths and hardened dunes, woven amid dwarf ironwoods. The trail drops to sea level, jogs inland, and ascends along a tall wall that borders a golf course. At the top, you'll find the large, lava-rock platform and other remains of Ho'ouluia Heiau, a large fishing shrine.

The path continues along the ledge of the golf course—watch for drop-offs, but also keep a seaward eye peeled for whales and spinner dolphin. Just before dropping into Mahaulepu Beach, the route snakes across Kamala Point. Near the water you will find Makauwahi Sinkhole, a finger off Hawaii's largest limestone cave. The trail then drops to the sand at Gillan's Beach, which is around the point from Kawailoa Bay.

Pu'u Wanawana Crater is a short drive from Shipwreck. Hiding in plain sight, the crater is the site of Kaua'i's most-recent eruption—recent in geologic terms. Head mauka on Ala Kinoiki Road, up just .1-mile from the stop sign at Poipu Road. Park at a dirt turnout, walk around a yellow gate, and stay left on a two-track road that rises up to a road that goes around the crater. Go to your right about 75 feet and look for a trail leading into a thicket of upright shrubs with cacti tentacles carpeting the ground. The path leads through the foliage, twisting a hundred yards or more, and reaches a vantage point at the Stonehenge-like volcanic teeth that mark the perimeter of the crater. *Be Aware:* Use your own judgment when using this route. Access may be through private propery.

More Stuff: For an easy, 1.5 mile excercise walk, try the paved path to Makahuena Point. Head to your right as you face the water at the Hyatt's beachside path. The path skirts the green margins of sedate condos (and newer giganitc timeshare resort) that carpet this bluff between the Hyatt and Poipu Beach.

SURF: **Shipwreck Beach** is a popular spot for bodysurfing and body boards, as well as short board surfers. Its popularity and location in front of a major resort hide the dangers of the waters here. Shipwreck is known for a shore break with rock hazards, swells in the winter and high surf in the summer. Make observations before entering the water, and avoid on rougher days. The coast off Shipwreck Beach is also popular among windsurfers, but only experts should venture into these seas.

44. POIPU BEACH   HIKE, SNORKEL, PADDLE, SURF

WHAT'S BEST: Surfers, strollers, snorkelers, and people-watchers all can end their quest somewhere along sunny Poipu Beach. The arid surround and condos are a disappointment to some, but not to those seeking blue sky when it's raining elsewhere on the island.

PARKING: Take Hwy. 50 from Lihue and turn makai on Hwy. 520, which is Manuhia Rd., the tree tunnel road. At Koloa, turn right at stop sign and then turn left at the gas station on Poipu Rd. Continue to the roundabout and go left on Poipu Rd.
First (Sheraton) parking: Turn makai on Kapili Rd toward the Sheraton, about .5-mi. after veering left. Kapili Rd. ends at Ho'onani Rd., where you turn left and park immediately on right at public access lot. This is the quieter end, farthest from the beach park.
Second (midway) parking: Continue on Ho'onani Rd. for about .25-mi. and park near the Kiahuna Plantation Resort. Puts you in the middle of the Poipu Beaches.
Third (Poipu Beach Park) parking: Continue on Poipu Rd. past Kapili Rd., about .75-mi. and turn makai on Ho'owili Rd. to Poipu County Beach Park.

HIKE: Poipu Beach stroll (2.5 mi.); Moir Gardens (.25-mi.)

Poipu Beach is more than a mile long, consisting of four small sandy coves separated by natural black-rock breakwaters extending not far seaward. This is not a nature walk, as beach chairs, boogie boarders, and sunbathers abound. Starting at the first parking, take a groomed path through a pleasant palm grove, around the back of the Sheraton, coming upon its sloping sandy beach. Continue, either along the beach on a path that runs parallel to where the luau show takes place around five o'clock, usually Monday, Wednesday, and Friday. A major overhaul of the grounds was done in 2011. Leaving the Sheraton, with its double-scoop beach, you'll walk the expansive greenspace of Kilohana Plantaion Resort—not swank, but a premier location for Poipu lovers.

After passing the rocky area (a former heiau site), you come to the newly refurbished, low-key-luxury of the Ko'a Kea Hotel & Resort at Waiohai Beach. This beach soon blends into Poipu Beach Park. The park has a sandy peninsula, with a rocky tip, that

Brennecke's Beach

Poipu Beach

creates a beach area to either side of the spit. Monk seals like it. The park extends inland from the beach to Poipu Road. Continuing along the park, the next, rougher beach you come to is Brennecke's, across from the restaurant of the same name. *More Stuff:* A paved path leads from Pane Street at the end of the park through resort homes to the Grand Hyatt, about 1.5 miles distant.

To **Moir Gardens**, a.k.a Pau a Laka, go to the Outrigger Kiahuna Plantation, which is across Ho'onani Road from the second beach access parking. Look for a Plantation Gardens sign. Begun in the 1930s, the gardens include native plants, succulents, and a display of cacti rated among the ten-best in the world. The gardens surround a lagoon and the plantation restaurant, near which is also a fabulous orchid garden.

SNORKEL: Poipu Beach commonly offers some of the safest and sunniest swimming on Kaua'i, especially during the winter. At **Sheraton Beach** and **Waiohai Beach**, a reef offshore breaks up the swell and waves, creating a large and fairly deep swimming area. A little shore-breakers might test your balance. Fish are not copious.

At **Poipu Beach Park,** towels may carpet the sand on weekends, but the place is spacious. There are pavilions on the lawn at the backshore, but don't overlook the shaded tables to the far left as you face the water. The park inland across the street is the site of art fairs and events. Families and waders like the baby beaches to either side of the sand spit, but snorkelers can power out farther, beginning from the right side of the spit. *Be Aware:* Farther out, surfers, sailors, and reef action pose hazards.

Another snorkeling spot, often overlooked because it's in the seam between the roads that fork to Poipu and to Spouting Horn, is **Whalers Cove**. Take Hoʻonani Road away from the Sheraton about .5-mile. Look for a turnout on the left. Whalers Cove has good snorkeling with clear water and plenty of fish, but getting past boulders at water's edge requires some balance. The cove looks better from the water than the shore.

PADDLE: **Whalers Cove**, going away from the Sheraton on Hoʻonani Road, has a canoe landing. Go past the turnout described in the snorkeling section and look for a sharp left as the road heads away from the cove up Waikomo Stream. This is access for ocean exploration, recommended for calmer days.

SURF: With occasional trade swells in the winter and Kona wind in the summer, Poipu is year-around surf city. During the summer, beginners surf **Poipu Beach Park**, off the spit in front of the pavilion. The beach features both right and left breaks. In the cove next door, rougher **Brennecke's** also breaks both ways. During the summer, try the reef off **Waiohai Beach**, to the right of the sand peninsula. This is for average surfers, but a shallow reef covered with sea urchins creates a hazard. **Horseshoe** is in front of the Sheraton. This is mostly a summer beach, with a long paddle from shore. Horseshoe (a.k.a. Cow's Head and First Break) is recommended for top surfers.

45.   PRINCE KUHIO PARK   HIKE, SNORKEL, PADDLE, SURF

WHAT'S BEST: This coast may lack curbside appeal, but it has some of the island's best snorkeling and summer surfing. You'll also find beaches tucked away.
PARKING: Take Hwy. 50 from Lihue and turn makai on Hwy. 520 toward Poipu. At Koloa, turn right at stop sign, then left immediately on Poipu Rd. At bottom of grade, veer right from the roundabout toward Spouting Horn, on Lawai Rd. Go 1 mi. on Lawai Rd. and park off road at Prince Kuhio Park—near Beach House Restaurant.

HIKE: Koloa Landing (1.25 mi.)

The coast along **Prince Kuhio Park** is generally rocky, developed, near a road carrying tourists to Spouting Horn, and close to well-known Poipu Beach. For these reasons, this good snorkeling and surfing area may be overlooked. For the neighborhood stroll to **Koloa Landing**, walk to your left as you face the water, through small Prince Kuhio Park. This historic park features a monument to Kauaʻi's longtime congressional representative. You'll find grassy terraces, picnic areas, and a pond. From the park, cross Lawai Road and veer off to the water side on Hoʻona Road. Look for a beach access pole near 5152 Hoʻona Road. Head out onto the beach—known as **Waterhouse Beach**—and make your way along the sand and then around black-rock tide pools, accented by dry areas filled with bits of white coral. Around the point from Waterhouse Beach is Whalers Cove Resort. Continue along the shore toward the Waikomo Stream inlet. You will see a wooden stairway, which is the public access to Koloa Landing. Go up the stairs, through the resort parking lot, and back out to Hoʻona Road.

More Stuff: **Kukuiula Bay**, a sportfishing harbor, is another good spot for a scenic break. Drive away from Poipu on Lawai Road for a mile and veer left on Amio Road. The breakwater can be walked for a whale's eye view of the bay. Also nearby is the new (2009) **Kukuiula Village**, some 45 restaurants and specialty shops designed to look like a old-timey sugar town. From the roundabout, take Ala Kalanikaumaka Road and bring your gold card. Mature tropical trees and flowering gardens with water features make the Kukuiula "main street" a pleasant stroll. Merriman's Restaurant, Bubba's Burgers, Living Foods, surf shops, and galleries are among the many inviting shops in this in two-level plantation-style complex.

SNORKEL: **Longhouse Beach** is on the other side of the Beach House Restaurant from Prince Kuhio Park. Despite its unappealing roadside setting, Longhouse—also called Beach House, Keiki Cove, or PK's—offers excellent snorkeling, with enough sand, easy entrance and a nice population of fish swimming close to shore in deep, clear water. You might see a turtle swimming through coral heads. *Be Aware:* During high surf, strong current runs from left to right.

Waterhouse Beach, described in hiking section, has an excellent baby beach, a protected, shallow spot for dunking and wading—the best beach on this coast to log some relaxing beach-towel time. Snorkelers will have better luck at **Whalers Cove** at Koloa landing, which is also noted in the snorkeling section of TH44, Poipu Beach. It looks a lot better from the water than the shore.

Kukuiula Bay

SURF: The offshore break at **Longhouse Beach** draws good surfers, mostly during the summer. Longhouse breaks in four places, which locals call—starting from left to right as you face the water— **PK's** (for Prince Kuhio), **Centers**, **Acid Drop**, and **Heroins**. Sometimes PK's is just called Longhouse. Just don't call it late for surfin'. From April through October, people line the shore at the Beach House Restaurant to watch the show. PK's and Centers draw good surfers—none of these beaches are for beginners. The kahunas test their skills at Acid Drop and Heroins. All Longhouse breaks are well offshore, two-way breaks—and vary greatly due to wind conditions.

PADDLE: Outrigger races from Nawiliwili Harbor end at **Kukuiula Bay**, located a mile a way from Kuhio Park. Another popular paddle from Kukuiula Bay is toward Spouting Horn and Lawai Bay, which is not accessible to the public via land, except for garden tours. The bay is sheltered, although you need to be mindful of boat traffic.

46.   ALLERTON GARDEN-SPOUTING HORN   HIKE

> **WHAT'S BEST:** Two of the nation's five National Tropical Botanical Gardens are right here. Across the street is Kaua'i's sea geyser.
> **PARKING:** Take Hwy. 50 from Lihue and turn makai on Hwy. 520 toward Poipu. Turn right at stop sign in Koloa, and then left on Poipu Rd. At bottom of grade, veer right on the roundabout toward Spouting Horn on Lawai Rd. Go about 2 mi. on Lawai Rd., turn makai and park at Allerton Garden visitors lot.

HIKE: Garden Visitors Center and Spouting Horn (1 mi.); Allerton Garden (1 mi.); McBryde Garden (1.5 mi.)

A path leads from the **Bill and Jean Lane Visitor Center** to **Spouting Horn**, which is directly across Lawai Road. Spouting Horn is Kaua'i's saltwater version of Old Faithful. Here, flumes of sea-foam erupt through an opening in a reef, powered by pressure of waves trapped below. You watch from a safe distance behind a fence, just off a parking lot that is fringed by low-priced trinket booths. Many a camera lens and shutter finger have poised at this sight of Spouting Horn. Stay well back from the blowhole.

The garden's visitor center, built using a grant from Bill and Jean Lane, former publishers of Sunset Magazine, is a restored 1920s sugar plantation home, set here on the coast after Hurricane Iniki destroyed the other center farther inland. A path leads through the grounds, featuring a number of native plants, tropical fruits, and interpretive areas—a beautiful, free, and informative introduction to the island's greenery.

Both garden walks are ticketed tours, leaving from buses at the center. The tours are popular and advance reservations are recommended for Allerton; an admission is charged. The National Tropical Botanical Garden is a nonprofit, privately funded organization, under Congressional charter to do scientific research and plant conservation. Three of the five NTBG sites are on Kaua'i.

The **Allerton Garden** was once a retreat for Queen Emma and is known for its landscape design and flowering tropical plants. The gardens were the brainchild of Robert Allerton, who in 1937 at age 64 bought the property and labored for many years with his lifetime companion, John Gregg Allerton. With a private beach and lush stream valley, Allerton Garden has been the set for a number of movies, including *Honeymoon in Vegas, Thorn Birds, Jurassic Park,* and TV's *Fantasy Island.* Separate botanical 'rooms' are decorated with fountains and statuary. *Be Aware:* The Allerton tour (probably) will no longer include the beach and estate. To see these attractions, ask about the **Sunset Tour**, usually held on Saturdays. This more-expensive-but-worth-it tour also includes libation.

Allerton Garden

You're left to wander and gander at your own pace in **McBryde Garden**, which is aimed more at scientific research. A dreamland of native plants and trees, as well as spices exotics, are spread along a falling stream, crossed by a bamboo bridge and punctuated by cascades, pools, and a gazebo. Sit a spell here and there. Independent travelers and plant peepers will appreciate the McBryde. *Be Aware:* Many of the plants are rare and endangered; don't touch and stay on the path.

More Stuff: The **Hoiki Tour**, normally Tuesdays and Wednesdays, is for more adventurous visitors and includes the upper McBryde Garden watershed, the nursery seedbank where research is conducted, and an exploration of lava tubes on the west side of the main stream. The garden staff also plan to develop hiking trails in the upper reaches of the garden, including a small temple built by Greg and Robert.

Kaiwa Point, outside the gardens, is one of the island's best whale watching spots. Take Lawai Road to its end. Make a U-turn at the Allerton gate and park at a dirt turnout at the end of a chain-link fence. You'll see a rough, unmarked trail that takes you down to the rocky coastline. At the water, walk to your right, making your way through grass patches and boulders to Kaiwa Point, which forms the south mouth of Lawai Bay. Access here was altered in a good way in 2011 by a native-plants garden put in by 1,000-acre Kukuiula residential property bordering Allerton. Largely open space, the high-end neighborhood may include hiking trails and bike paths.

47.   KAHILI RIDGE   HIKE

WHAT'S BEST: A thrilling walk up a tropical ridge with blue-water views.
PARKING: Take Hwy. 50 from Lihue. Turn mauka .5-mi past Hwy. 520, which is the turnoff to Poipu. Look for Kahili Mountain Park sign, .25-mi. past mm7. Go .75-mi. up the road and turn left toward Kahili Mountain Park. Then circle around to left, between office and Adventist School, with cabins to your right across a grass field. Continue past cabin number 30, and park off road when you see a water tank on your right. You should see signs for "Hiking Trails" and "Ridge Trail."

Note: Kahili Mountain Park and Adventist School are private property. They have been generous in granting permission to use these trails, but keep in mind that landowners are not liable for any injuries that may occur to hikers. The cabins (Kaua'i's best rustic) may be rented under special conditions. See their website, kahilipark.org, or, better yet, stop by.

HIKE: Kahili Pine Grove (.75-mi., 200 ft.); Kahili Ridge (2.75 mi., 1,700 ft.)

For the easy **Kahili Pine Grove**, walk .1-mile down the road from parking, making sure to look inland to view your destination, a stand of several hundred Norfolk and Cook pines. Once you get there, you can't see the forest for the trees. Across from a Dead End sign, is the trailhead, which is signed. About 50 feet in on the walk, keep right, just after the trail makes its first small step up. (There is more than one route.) The trail loops around to the right, through fern hedges and then through a stand of

Kahili Ridge

ironwoods before leading into the grove. These are mostly Norfolk pines; their cousin, the Cook pine, has bushy branches, whereas the Norfolk is distinguished by its long, frondlike limbs. Outside the grove in all directions is an impenetrable growth.

The **Kahili Ridge Trail** is a challenging climb up a narrow feeder ridge that abuts Kahili Ridge. Begin at a road behind the water tower. After only .1-mile, you veer left off the road, following a homemade sign into a tunnel of a trail through pink-flowering shrubbery. Branches from this bush will provide helping hands to navigate up and down this often muddy trail. Less than .5-mile in, and 200 feet up, you pop out to views of the 197-acre park, with Hoary Head Ridge and the Poipu shores as a backdrop.

The ridge trail gets steeper, never making switchbacks, before reaching another plateau, about 1 mile from the trailhead. You get a seaward view here, but now the mauka view draws attention, with four or five waterfalls often streaking down Kahili Ridge. By this juncture the trail has narrowed to a foot or two wide, falling very steeply on both sides. But any acrophobia is assuaged in most places by the thick foliage, through which you couldn't roll a bowling ball. Still, exercise caution, for what appears as an embankment to the trail may be just tufts of flora.

The trail continues flat along this ridge for just a short distance, before launching skyward again, through trees whose roots provide steps to go with branch handholds. This rise gives way to another plateau, now that much closer to the face of Kahili. You make another significant upping, your final, before reaching the windswept heights. The trail ends at a radio antenna, down the ridge from Kahili Peak, which is not readily accessed. *Be Aware:* Narrow sections of the trail skirt drop-offs that are dangerous, escpecially with wind to throw off your balance and after rains create a slick surface. A hiking pole will help greatly, escpecially on the descent in place where handholds are scarce. Remember: It's easier going up than coming down.

48.   KUKUIOLONO PARK   HIKE, BIKE

WHAT'S BEST: A short walk with long views, a scent of flowers and a sense of history. This park is a peaceful retreat for road-weary visitors.
PARKING: Take Hwy. 50 to Kalaheo, which is about 5 mi. past Hwy. 520, the turnoff to Poipu. In Kalaheo, at at mm11.2, turn makai at the traffic signal, on Papalina Rd. Continue, passing first Pu'u Rd., for 1 mi. Turn right on the second Pu'u Rd., and right again immediately, at the stone archway that is entrance to the park.

HIKE: Kukuiolono Park and Pavilion (.75-mi, 100 ft.)

Kukuiolono Park is a golf course and wild-chicken habitat with grounds that feature an exotic Japanese garden and a Hawaiiana exhibit of rocks with archeological significance. From these attractions—which are located in trees just up the hill from the parking area—a paved golf path leads seaward to a picnic pavilion, resting high above the gentle slopes of the Lawai Valley. Coco palms, ironwoods, plumeria, and Norfolk pines line the path to the pavilion, where you'll find a 270-degree view of the south coast. Walter McBryde, 19th century sugar magnate, is buried in the park. New gardens and pathways added in 2011 have buffed this jewel.

BIKE: Pu'u Road is a one-lane country road that encircles the park. It has enough curves and dips to provide exercise, but overall is fairly level pedaling. Bananas and shade trees line the road, along with tall grasses. Pastoral and blue-water views open up here and there. For this 5-mile ride, park outside the entrance to Kukuiolono Park. With the park gate at your back, head to your right. You'll be on Pu'u Road most of the way, until reaching a neighborhood area closer to Kalaheo, where you turn right on Papalina Street and follow it back down to the park.

For another paved, rural-residential ride, go down **Papalina Road**, just outside the park gate. After coasting down a mile through a modest neighborhood rich with trees, you come to the administrative offices of the National Tropical Botanical Gardens. You can view the upper reaches of McBryde garden from the back patio.

49.   ALEXANDER RESERVOIR   HIKE, BIKE

WHAT'S BEST: A little-known back way to jagged Kahili Ridge, for cyclists and hikers, affords long views from the island's high country.
PARKING: Take Hwy. 50 past Poipu turnoff, through Kalaheo, and past the jct. of Hwys. 50 and 540. Turn mauka on unmarked red-dirt road, .2-mi. beyond of the Hwy.

540 turnoff. Proceed .3-mi. up the cinder road. Park off road, where a gated red-dirt road reduces to narrower road, in view of a large stone home. *Note:* If the gate is closed at the highway, walk in and add .6-mi. to roundtrip distance.

HIKE: Alexander Reservoir (5 mi., 775 ft.); Kahili Ridge (9 mi., 1,625 ft)

The **Alexander Reservoir** trail—a red-dirt, four-wheel track—begins on a gradual, pastoral incline, up the Wahiawa Valley, situated between Kahili Ridge and the Hanapepe River Valley. Over the first mile you have views of unusual rock escarpments and of Hanapepe Bay. You then enter a tree canopy, walking under the boughs of huge monkeypods, eucalyptus, and a number of flowering trees. Alexander Reservoir feeds two falls, Kaukiuki and Waiolue, which you may be able to hear on windless days, to your left beginning .75-mile from the reservoir—but which you cannot access by trail.

Nearing the reservoir the road wyes—either fork gets you there, but the left one should be less muddy. Both options take you to the right along the south shoreline of Alexander Reservoir, which looks like a fairly large woodland lake. Due to seepage, the road below the reservoir often turns to a mud swath that would bog a Humvee. Birds like this zone, with egrets most noticeable among a number of species.

From Alexander Reservoir, the route to **Kahili Ridge** becomes less of a road and more of a wide trail—steeper, curving and rutted, but very walkable. You'll be climbing another 800 feet before reaching road's end near the ridge below a radio antenna. Above the reservoir, you'll pass a large stand of Norfolk pines and pop out of the tree canopy with views of the upper Lawai Valley. You continue ramping up on the lip of this drainage, as foliage becomes dwarf and fern hedges dominate. The sky opens up and the route levels as you reach another fork; go right at telephone pole #2901.

After the fork, for the last mile, the trail is on top of the world, with saw-toothed Kahili Ridge beckoning straight ahead. Up the valley to your left looms Kawaikini, the tallest peak on Kaua'i at 5,243 feet. Also on the left are the ridges of upper Hanapepe Valley. The open flat below on the left with dwarf trees is Kanaele Swamp. To your right—as the trail wiggles and climbs—is the vertical relief of two rippling green ridges coming together. The route ends tantalizingly close to the ridge, at a knob; but only a goat, and not a smart one at that, would continue on the overgrown and sketchy trail from here. *Be Aware:* The margins of the trail are only mats of flora in places; don't venture off trail.

BIKE: **Alexander Reservoir** is well-suited for a hike 'n' bike. Park at the trailhead and pedal up to the reservoir, and hike the rest of the way to the ridge. You will have a pleasant coast down from the reservoir. Fit and experienced cyclists can make the entire ride. The tough parts—aside from the savage mud bogs—are steep ruts just beyond the reservoir, and some rutted hard-pack on the final approach to the ridge.

Waimea

Kilohana Overlook

In 1778, Hawai'i became the last major landmass to take its place on the modern globe. In that year British Captain James Cook and his ships, the *Discovery* and the *Resolution* dropped anchor in Waimea Bay, thus ending the Hawaiians' fifteen centuries without contact from the rest of the world's cultures.

Cook and his men, having sailed the South Pacific for a dozen years, recognized at once that these new people were of Polynesian descent, but prior to making landfall not even this great navigator knew that Hawai'i existed. Four hundred years had elapsed since the last Tahitian migrations, and islanders in those southern waters, like Cook, had known nothing of their descendants far to the north.

Cook's Kauaian visit lasted only three weeks, long enough to trade coveted iron nails with locals for equally coveted fruits and livestock, and for Cook and his officers to share a few peppery awa cocktails with the Kauaian aliʻi. Cook's most-significant legacy, however, was not a welcome gift: Although he had prohibited fraternization with the local women, his men managed to infect them with venereal disease.

Upon surveying Kauaʻi, these first Europeans chose the gently sloping coast of the drier west side for safe anchorage. But they barely caught a glimpse of what awaits today's visitors. Not many hikers in the tropics expect to find cacti growing on cliffs of red-walled river canyons. Waimea Canyon is appropriately called the "Grand Canyon of the Pacific."

About ten miles long and almost 4,000 feet deep, Waimea Canyon takes its place alongside canyons of America's Southwest as a scenic wonder. Trails lead into the canyon, as well as along its cliffs and throughout the diverse forests that border its upper rim at Kokeʻe State Park—a wonderland for birds and countless varieties of trees. Forests include both native varieties and others planted by the Conservation Corps in the 1930s. Within Kokeʻe are a museum and interpretive nature path, as well as miles of trails through forests chock-full with a fantastical array of flora. Some trails—including the Cliff and Waipo Falls trails—pop out to big views of Waimea Canyon.

The west side of Kokeʻe State Park forests gives way to Napali—The Cliffs. All along the northwest quadrant of the island, ridges and valleys fan out like spokes on a wheel, starting at road's end on the north shore and continuing around to road's end on the west shore at Polihale State Park and Barking Sands Beach. Each ridge ends at a cliff along a coast with no roads. This is a wild forest reserve area that hikers and cyclists can spend weeks exploring.

At least eight of the Napali ridges can be hiked or ridden by mountain bike. The hikes begin through tropical greenery and end at bluffs, some 1,500 feet above the surf, with canyon walls of neighboring ridges to the left and right. Viewpoints at trail's end look down at remote valleys, once inhabited, and all steeped in Hawaiian mythology.

Heading up from Kokeʻe park headquarters, the road ends at a lookout of the Kalalau Valley. Road's end is the beginning of the Pihea Trail. From Puʻuokila Lookout, the Pihea Trail starts along the precipitous rim of the Kalalau Valley and then turns inland, going across the Alakai Swamp on a boardwalk. Alakai Swamp is a 60-square mile bog of dwarf vegetation that was once the caldera of Hawaiʻi's first volcano. The boardwalk ends abruptly at a platform looking 4,000-feet down into the rippling green Wainiha River Valley and, beyond the valley, to Hanalei Bay on the north shore. Even the most-avid among red-dirt adventurers may take several trips to Kauaʻi before comprehending its geographic jigsaw puzzle.

Down from Waimea Canyon is a shoreline than includes the longest strip of sand in Hawaiʻi—some 17 miles—beginning where the road ends at Barking Sands Beach in Polihale State Park. Beach hiking and surfing are superlative at Barking Sands, as well as at Majors Bay and Kekaha, two other beaches that continue around the west side from Polihale (though a military base poses some restrictions).

This trailhead section also includes two of Kaua'i's quaintest places to walk around, each distinctly Hawaiian—Waimea and Hanapepe. Waimea Town, once the island's capital, is where the Royal Hawaiians make their monthly trips by ferry from Ni'ihau. Waimea, meaning "red waters," has a river for kayakers and a bay for surfers. An ancient trail also leads up Waimea Canyon from Waimea Town, along the ancient remnants of Menehune Ditch, a water-conveyance system.

Between Waimea Town and Hanapepe is Pakala Beach, one of the best surfing beaches. Pakala is also dubbed Infinities, because the rides can go on forever. Right near Hanapepe is Salt Pond Beach Park, the best swimming spot on the west side, as well as the site of the ancient—and still functioning—salt ponds. In the 1800s, sailing vessels coveted the salt, not only for its taste, but also as a vital preservative for meats and fish.

Hanapepe is another uniquely Hawaiian town, funky around the edges with Kauaiana shops along its small main street. Browsers will enjoy the town's suspension footbridge over a river, and trails into a canyon that would be a main event were it not for nearby Waimea Canyon. Private property limits access as far as Hanapepe Falls—of *Jurassic Park* fame—but three rural roads and

Napali Coast, Hanapepe Falls

trails give hikers and cyclists a taste of the canyon floor. Paddlers can get the farthest into the green-and-red gorge.

Port Allen, Kaua'i's working harbor, with a power plant and commercial dock, is a taking-off point for snorkeling adventures and the "Forbidden Island" of Ni'ihau. Kayakers can try the bay before heading up Hanapepe River. From Port Allen, hikers can also walk a coast trail to Wahiawa Bay, a destination for snorkeling tours not easily reached directly, since the bay borders the private property of a coffee plantation.

The Waimea area doesn't have hotels—with one notable exception in Waimea Town, and other ventures on the drawing board—so many visitors zip through on the way to Waimea Canyon or Barking Sands. But the west side could be an island unto itself and still be a world-class destination for muscle-powered sports nuts.

Waimea Rodeo, Kokee hula performers, Alakai Swamp

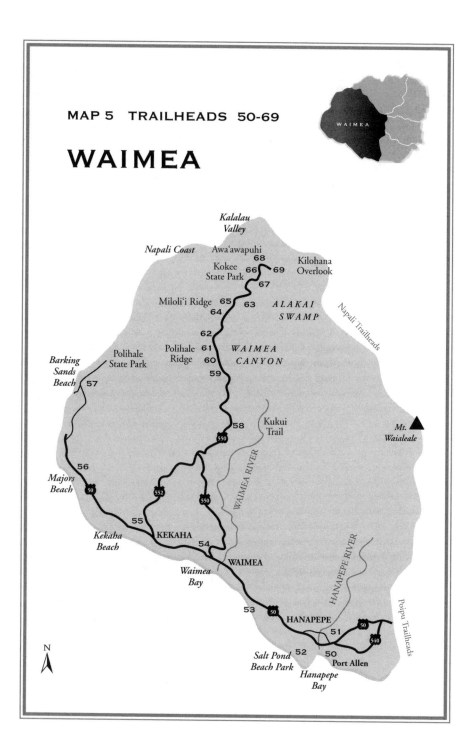

MAP 5 TRAILHEADS 50-69

WAIMEA

WAIMEA

Kalalau
Valley

Napali Coast   Awa'awapuhi

68

Kokee   Kilohana
State Park 66   69 Overlook

67

Miloli'i Ridge 65   63   *ALAKAI*
64   *SWAMP*

62

Polihale   61   *WAIMEA*
Barking   Polihale   Ridge 60   *CANYON*
Sands   State Park   59
Beach   57

Napali Trailheads

58   Kukui
Trail   Mt.
550   Waialeale

56
Majors   *WAIMEA RIVER*
Beach   50   552   550

55   *HANAPEPE RIVER*
Kekaha   KEKAHA
Beach   54
WAIMEA   *Poipu Trailheads*
Waimea
Bay

53   50
HANAPEPE   51
50   540
Salt Pond   52   50
Beach Park   Port Allen
Hanapepe
Bay

N

T R A I L H E A D S
50-69

HIKE	HIKING
SNORKEL	SNORKELING AND SWIMMING
BIKE	MOUNTAIN OR ROAD BIKING
PADDLE	KAYAKING, CANOEING
SURF	SURFING, BOOGIE BOARDING

TH	TRAILHEAD	*Note: All hiking*
Makai	TOWARD OCEAN	*distances are roundtrip*
Mauka	TOWARD THE MOUNTAIN, INLAND	*unless otherwise noted.*
mm.	MILE MARKER, CORRESPONDS TO HIGHWAY SIGNS	

50.   PORT ALLEN-NI'IHAU   HIKE, SNORKEL, SURF

WHAT'S BEST: Take a look at Kaua'i's sightseeing and whale-watching port, or hike to an out-of-the-way snorkeling bay. Or, spend the day cruising to the island of Ni'ihau, where you can place your face in some excellent snorkeling waters.
PARKING: Take Hwy. 50 past Kalaheo, and turn makai on Hwy.541, Waialo Rd., at mm. 16. Go .75-mi. on Waialo and park at large lot near dock and outlet shops. Additional parking areas described below.

HIKE: Glass Beach (less than .25 mi.); Wahiawa Bay (2.5 mi., 150 ft.)

Port Allen is not a place most people would want to spend their entire Polynesian vacation; fuel tanks, utility pipes, and power poles are not postcard fodder. Yet a tour around the port gives you a look at what makes Kaua'i tick and offers shopping opportunites at dockside outlet stores. Bargain price T-shirts are on hand, as are most of the sightseeing ships' offices. The dock at Port Allen is popular for sportfishing, whale-watching, snorkeling, and Napali Coast touring. You might find a last-minute deal.

To **Wahiawa Bay** and **Glass Beach**, turn left on Akaula Road, which is uphill from the dock area. The road runs between dreary metal warehouses and fuel storage tanks and is unpaved and bumpy. The beach is where the road drops to the water. Colorful smooth glass pieces used to outnumber the sand particles at this tiny cove, but collectors have taken out bucket loads. The road continues a short distance and ends at a Japanese and Hawaiian cemetery. A rough fishermen's path leads down the coast from here to the bay, winding its way alongside the edge of the shore and tide pools set in flat lava reefs. The mouth of the bay is about a mile from the cemetery. Wahiawa Bay is a deep, narrow inlet, bordered inland by the Kauai Coffee Company plantation, which is private property.

SNORKEL: The ultimate Kaua'i snorkeling trip awaits 20 miles offshore at the 'Forbidden Island' of **Ni'ihau** and the tiny island of **Lehua** that lies next door—a bird sanctuary. Several tours depart Port Allen, but the most experienced and popular are HoloHolo Charters and Captain Andy's. They'll both zip you there in a diesel catamaran, and swing by the Napali coast on the way. Ni'ihau is privately owned, off-limits to all but native Hawaiians. Lehua is a cinder cone off its eastern shore. Snorkeling locations will depend on weather and sea conditions, but count on crystal clear water.

Offshore Ni'ihau and Lehua

Wahiawa Bay boasts a comfy sandy beach, ideal for sun bathers, but with shade as well. The base of its cliffs is lined with submerged rocks, and the bay is well-protected, especially during the winter when the trades blow from the northeast. Inland is private property owned by Kauai Coffee. Tour boats used to anchor in the bay, and the snorkeling can be very good—provided high surf is not present.

SURF: **Hanapepe River mouth** (between the small boat harbor at Port Allen and the river) is a spot for beginners and boogie boarders. Small waves and rock-free waters make for safe conditions.

51. HANAPEPE

HIKE, BIKE, PADDLE

WHAT'S BEST: Exploring old-style Hanapepe Town and its river canyon—on foot, by bike, or paddling a kayak. Nose around and you'll be rewarded.
PARKING: Take Hwy. 50 through Kalaheo. Veer mauka toward Hanapepe on Hanapepe Rd., which is about .25-mi. past mm. 16. Continue short distance beyond left turn and park near Pa Lane at parking for Swinging Bridge.

HIKE: Hanapepe Town stroll (up to 1.5 mi.); Bougainvillea view (.25-mi., 150 ft.); Swinging Bridge-Hanapepe River (up to 3.5 mi.)

On the **Hanapepe Town stroll**, you'll see that dilapidation and gentrification have balanced out, resulting in a quiet, old-style hamlet sprinkled with interesting shops. A town walking map ($2) is available at many businesses. It suggests you continue down Hanapepe Road past the 1911 Bridge and loop left on the highway, and then left again, following Hanapepe Road back to town—the same way you drove in. As an option, many visitors will want to do an up-and-back, staying on Hanapepe Road. Either way, you'll find historical markers affixed to some two-dozen buildings that illustrate the stroll. *Note:* To see the place pop, catch an art night, normally held every Friday, beginning at 6.

For the **bougainvillea view**, walk back the way you drove in, past Ko Road, and take a paved path with a pipe railing leading up to the left. Flowering plants blanket the cliff. This short walk, which is the kids' route to Ele'ele School, gives you a perspective on the town, bay, and river.

For the **Hanapepe River**, walk across the **Swinging Bridge** that spans the wide river—the bridge is a destination itself. A levee trail on the other side goes both to the left and right. To the left, or downriver, you walk about .5-mile, to the 1911

Hanapepe Town

Hanapepe River

Bridge, about .5-mile up from where the river enters Hanapepe Bay. Going to the right across the Swinging Bridge takes you, after about 1.25 miles upriver, to a broad, agricultural area, with a variety of fruit trees, including bananas, as well as fields of seed corn. On the first part of the walk, you'll have river views, looking through large broadleaf trees at the red walls of the gorge, while, on your left, as a contrast, you'll pass a tropical junkyard, replete with rusting vehicles and chicken coops. Roosters and barking poi dogs are a likely audio. The path loops away from the river, ending at a farmhouse—this is where Awawa Road comes in, as per mountain bike description.

BIKE: Two decent rides await mountain bikers in Hanapepe, both up the valley on different routes. **Ko Road**, which is your first right on the way into town, snakes in 1.5 miles before coming to a locked gate. Beyond the gate is a hunter's road. Ko Road is bordered in places by the 200-foot high canyon, with views of the river and a patchwork of agricultural lands. Mountain bikers can ride the other side of the river by pedaling down Hanapepe Road from the Swinging Bridge parking area, crossing the river on the 1911 Bridge, and turning right on **Awawa Road**. Awawa Road takes you through a tree tunnel and past country homesteads. After 1.5 miles the roadends at a large cornfield.

PADDLE: The **Hanapepe River** makes lazy, very scenic curves inland from the bay for 1.5 miles. You see cacti as well as bananas. Kayakers can put in at the river mouth, off Puolo Road: Backtrack from the Swinging Bridge to the highway and turn right. Cross the river and turn left immediately on Puolo Road. Continue, passing a ball field on the right, and park after .25-mile, where the road makes a sharp right. This puts you at the mouth of the Hanapepe River across from the swimming beach at Port Allen. The put-in involves a short carry. You'll also have the the option of stroking around Hanapepe Bay. You need to be mindful of boat traffic in the bay.

52.   SALT POND BEACH PARK   HIKE, SNORKEL, SURF

WHAT'S BEST: Salt Pond is best place to take a snorkeling beach break while touring the west side. Follow your swim with a picnic or seacoast hike along ancient salt ponds.
PARKING: Take Hwy. 50 to .75-mi past Hanapepe River and turn makai on Hwy. 543, Lolokai Rd. toward Salt Pond Beach Park. Keep right at Lele Rd. The beach park is 1 mile from Hwy. 50. *Best access to see the salt ponds:* Keep left at Lele Rd. and then go right along the airstrip on Kuiloko Rd. This takes you to a less-used, unpaved lot.

HIKE: Salt Ponds and Pa'akahi Point (3 mi.)

Salt Pond Beach Park is an unflattering name for this more than pleasant park. From the parking, walk across the lawn of the picnic and camping area and then arc left around the beach. Almost unnoticed inland as you first leave the beach (at the alternate parking spot) are the **salt ponds** from which the ancients—and present-day Hawaiians—have extracted life-giving salt from seawater. You need to veer inland toward black plastic: It doesn't look appealing, but make the effort. (Kaua'i's sea salt is coveted for its mix of some 82 minerals and reddish color, derived from island clay.)

Salt Point Beach Park

Ancient salt ponds

Then backtrack from the ponds and hug the coast on a red-dirt road. The hike takes you around the chunky peninsula that forms the west side of Hanapepe Bay, across from Port Allen. As you walk you encircle Port Allen Airport, an asphalt strip that is the occasional launching pad for ultra-lights and tour helicopters. Locals are fighting a plan to increase helicopter facilities here, which would disrupt the pond's historic uses. In the middle of the peninsula, Puolo Point is the location of Hanapepe Light which identifies the bay for sailors. From Puolo to **Pa'akahi Point**, the last .5-mile of the outward segment, black rocks supply the resistance for some explosive wave action. Near Puolo Point, dolphins and whales often swim close to shore.

SNORKEL: Nature has made a saltwater swimming hole at **Salt Pond Beach Park**, complete with a crescent of sand and swaying palms. A reef protects the shoreline, but don't drift beyond the reef, as currents get tricky not far out. Due to silt and wave action, visibility is most often just fair, and fishes are not profuse. To the right and left of the big beach are a **keiki ponds**, made for splashing. Though not huge in area, these keiki ponds have clear water and

Camping at Salt Pond

the best snorkeling, when the tide is high enough.

SURF: Windsurfers and boarders alike take advantage of an offshore break outside the reef at **Salt Pond Park**. It's a long paddle out, and known only as a summer spot for surfers. Some locals also try the harbor break, at the mouth of the harbor just off the airport runway— **Pa'akahi**

Point. Access is difficult, down a rocky embankment, and the right-breaking swells are recommended for good surfers only.

53.   PAKALA BEACHES

WHAT'S BEST: Surfers rave about Pakala's long-breaking waves, but hikers will find a long, palmy beach walk, or a shorter one to view a quiet sugar-shack community right out of the 19th century.

PARKING: Take Hwy. from Hanapepe. Pass the makai turnoff to Makaweli and cross a highway bridge, at mm21, near an emergency phone. Park on highway shoulder, just on other side of the bridge.

HIKE: **Pakala Beaches (up to 2 mi.); Makaweli (1.5 mi.)**

Access to **Pakala Beaches** starts just below the highway bridge. From the turnout, cross the highway and walk inside a guardrail to the bridge. A path runs beside A'akukui Stream for about .25-mile under the boughs of large monkeypod trees to the beach. Turning right at Pakala Beach—which is also called A'akukui Beach or Infinities, because that's how long the waves roll—leads you about 1 mile to rocky Po'o Point. The point forms the mouth of Hoahuana Bay, along which the beach lies.

Going to your left at the beach, you cross the stream (if it's not too high or turbid) and follow the coco palm-lined shores that border **Makaweli.** Makaweli is collection of several dozen weather-worn, red-dust-stained sugar shacks, festooned with nets, glass balls, and hanging laundry, choked by tropical greenery and set in a grid of narrow, potholed dirt streets that make perfectly good sleeping spots for the occasional poi dog. Palm trees overhang a narrow strip of sand. This is not a tourist town. *Be Aware:* Although the people here are friendly, out of respect visitors might want to tread lightly at this quiet community.

Pakala Beach

Beach at Makaweli

SNORKEL: The water is shallow and the stream mouth used to have a reputation of being unhealthy due to upstream agricultural use. Although you would not come to **Pakala Beach** just to snorkel, you can find places to wade or take a float. Cross the stream toward Makaweli and try the first beach you come to. *Be Aware:* Surf can make shores turbulent all year around, with rip currents in shallow waters.

SURF: **Pakala Beaches**, or **Infinities**, draw surfers all year, but during the summer the swells are particularly inspiring. If the surf is good, cars will be parked at the highway. To the east side of the beach, or left as you face the water, is Pakala Point, where left-hand slides take boards up the coast to infinity. To access this break, you need to walk to your right up the beach about .25-mile and paddle out through deeper

Plantation house, Makaweli

water for about 100 yards. Curls often begin at several sections, accommodating a fair number of surfers. Locals ride these fast tubes for two or three hundred yards. In the winter, the offshore break toward Makaweli can be better. *Be Aware:* Infinities has a dangerous, shallow reef. Even the big boys and girls prefer high tide.

54.   WAIMEA TOWN

HIKE, PADDLE, SURF

WHAT'S BEST: This most-Hawaiian of towns offers a mix: a long walk on a swimming beach, a navigable river, and exotic hiking into the "heart of darkness." Waimea is the West, cowboys and all.

PARKING: Take Hwy. 50 past mm22. Cross bridge over the Waimea River. *For the beach and town walk:* Turn makai (left) at the first opportunity, on Alawai Rd. Go a short distance and park at river mouth at Lucy Wright Beach Park. *For Menhune Ditch and canyon trail:* Turn mauka (right) on Alawai Rd. After .5-mi., Alawai merges with Menhune Rd. Directions continue in the hike description below.

HIKE: Waimea Beach and Town walk (up to 2.5 mi.); Menhune Ditch or Waimea Canyon Trail (.25-mi. to 16 mi.)

You won't find many tiki torches in **Waimea Town**, but you will find some of Old Hawai'i. Outrigger canoes rest along the beach, fishermen hang out on the pier, families picnic and talk story. Waimea has the most native Hawaiians among its population, including Royal Hawaiians who take the ferry from Ni'ihau.

For the **beach and town walk**, start at Lucy Wright Beach Park, which was the landing for the first Europeans to set foot on Hawaii, in 1778, arriving in vessels led by Captain James Cook. About .25-mile down the beach is Waimea State Recreational Pier, where you can walk over the water. Cut in from the beach at the pier and go left on an alley. You'll pass the authentic plantation cottages of the Kikialoa Land Company, which are set back all along the beach in gardenscapes. (The defunct sugar mill facilities are just inland.) At the end of the alley are the spacious grounds of **Waimea Plantation Cottages,** a low-key, upscale vacation spot. Turn back after the resort, though you could continue across the rodeo grounds to Kikiaola State Boat Harbor, almost a mile from the pier and at the end of Waimea Beach. Walking back, you may wish to jog inland through sleepy Waimea Town. Quiet roads parallel the beach along the highway. Or, across the highway, other roads zigzag through Waimea's mom-and-pop commercial district. Be sure to check out the West Kaua'i Technology & Visitors Center (across from the old sugar mill); bland name for a place with fun cultural exhibits and friendly staff. They offer historical tours of the town.

For both the mellow **Menehune Ditch** stroll and the more challenging trek up the **Waimea Canyon**, continue on Menehune Road. About 1.3 miles from the highway, you'll see a suspension footbridge; park at a grassy turnout on the left before the bridge, or at another cliffside turnout .1-mile after the bridge. Embedded in the rock is a plaque commemorating the archeological site of the Menehunes' water-conveyance ditch, including the short tunnel section that remains. You'll also want to walk the bridge, but the roads on the other bank of the river are signed 'no tresspassing.'

For the **Waimea Canyon Trail** along the river, continue driving on the narrowing road until its end, about 2.5 miles from the highway. (You may pass an unkempt homestead with unfriendly signs along the way.) The road ends in a jungle setting at a small farm for bananas and other tropical fruits, with a home and signs reading 'Mid Pacific Research Station.' Park on the left before the home, in a grassy area. *Note:* The family here is friendly and generous about granting permission to access the trail. Ask permission, or leave a note on your dash if no one is around.

Proceed straight on the dirt road, past the bananas and papayas, continuing left of a gate and along a fence. Then go through a gate, entering the Pu'u Ka Pele State Forest Reserve. The trail goes up to the left, through switchbacks, climbing about 150 feet, until you hit a ditch. You follow the ditch up the canyon, with birdsong and the rushing river for a soundtrack. You may need to push plants away in a spot or two, and step over a few rocks. In about .5-mile, you'll see an Indiana Jones-type suspension bridge crossing 20 feet above the river. Cross this plank-and-cable bridge—the safety of which cannot be assured—and meet up with the four-wheel drive trail coming upriver from the first trailhead. Stay on this road, as it swerves up the canyon, crossing the river.

About 2 miles in from the trailhead, the trail climbs again, about 500 feet, and follows a ditch above the river for about 1.75 miles before dropping down again to the river. By this time you may feel like you've stepped into a Joseph Conrad novel. Signs of civilization are to be found in the form of a water conveyance system, built in the early

Around Waimea Town

1900s built by plantation owners to feed the cane fields of the west slope. From where the trail drops to the river to where it meets the Kukui Trail, TH58, is another 3.5 miles. To see this area, you're better off taking the Kukui Trail down from the canyon. *Be Aware:* Don't attempt this hike when river is high or when thick clouds indicate mountain rains inland. Prepare for a full-fledged trek. Although Kauaian hunters are a friendly lot, this trail is best for weekdays when hunters are not out.

More Stuff: To see the humble remains of Fort Elizabeth, turn makai at mm22.3, before crossing the bridge into Waimea. In the early 1800s, the Russians established the edifice, but abandoned their efforts with the emergence of British and Americans.

PADDLE: **Waimea River** is navigable for maybe 2 miles inland, although after about a mile in you want to watch for rocks and debris. Not many people paddle upriver here. Waimea also invites a bay-and-river combination, as waters along the beach are normally fairly calm. You're more apt to be joined by an outrigger canoe than a kayak.

SURF: The river mouth at **Lucy Wright Beach** is usually a place for novice surfers and boogie boarders. But Wright's is not always okay for keikis: Summer swells break far offshore, and build in four tiers to a shore break that can be dangerous. Currents can be strong under these conditions.

55.   KEKAHA
HIKE, SURF

WHAT'S BEST: Pull off the road and catch a sunset view of Ni'ihau on miles-long sand beach hike. When rains darken the rest of the island, sun seekers head for Kekaha.
PARKING: Take Hwy. 50 past Waimea. Pass Kikiaola Small Boat Harbor. Kekaha Beach Park access (restrooms) is at mm25. *Primary parking:* At lifeguard and picnic pavilions mm27. *Targets Beach parking (locals, shortens hike by .75-mi.):* Turn on a dirt road, mm27.3-mile at a small bridge(past the lifeguard station, across from 'Pioneer."). Drive in .1-mi. and park near ironwood trees.

HIKE: Kekaha Beach (up to 3.75 mi.)

Kekaha, not long ago a thriving sugar town, is now known for its long, long beach and as a gateway to Waimea Canyon. And when clouds hang over other parts of Kaua'i, sun often shines on Kekaha. Open sand and normally big surf stretch for miles, part of the longest sand beach in Hawaii. Offshore is a view of Ni'ihau. Dunes shift around near shore and create long sandy-walled pools. When the surf's up, you're safer on the higher flat sand. Just past the lifeguard station is **MacArthur Park**, melting in the sun, with several covered picnic tables. *Be Aware:* With strong legs and a sense of purpose you could hoof it 10-plus miles along Majors Bay and the Pacific Missile Range Facility to Polihale State Park. Alas, since 9-11 the government boys have closed the beach about 2 miles from the lifeguard station.

Kekaha

SURF: **Kekaha** gets pounded with south swells in the summer, and has predicable winter surf. But this beach is too far away from Kaua'i's other surfing beaches to be well-known or become crowded. Good-to-average surfers try their luck at a half-dozen spots. Among the most popular is the reef near mm25 at **O'omano Point**, sometimes called **Davidsons**. The reef, which provides the break, also presents a hazard. There are four other breaks along **Kekaha Beach**, from the community park to the lifeguard station. A locals' favorite is **Targets**: Use secondary parking and walk right at the beach to inland the landfill. *Be Aware:* Watch high surf before paddling out. Drownings and impact injuries do happen; don't bodysurf.

56. MAJORS   HIKE, SNORKEL, SURF

WHAT'S BEST: A beach-lover's beach, with sand two-hundred yards deep and many miles long, made for surfing and bagging some R&R. The catch these days is you need to apply for permit or enlist in the military to enter the base.
PARKING: Access is at the Pacific Missile Range Facility, which is past Kekaha on Hwy. 50, at mm30. *Note:* Due to heightened military security, permits are required to visit the beach. Call 808-335-7936. A two-page application and background check takes two weeks to process and costs $20 per person. They may e-mail an applicaton, which you can snail mail it back to them at MWR, Box 128, Kekaha, HI 96752. But normal procedures call for personal pick-up and delivery. The permit to visit all open beaches is good for a year.

HIKE: Majors Bay (3 or 4 mi.)

Majors Bay, another name for Waiokapua Bay, is the middle segment of the long beach—the longest in Hawai'i—that runs from the foot of the Napali coast at Polihale State Park around to Kekaha. Majors is next to what's left of Mana, the settlement of old-Kaua'i. Your permit allows access to several recreational areas, depending on what operations may be taking place on the base. One area is in the middle of the bay, and another is toward the north end, where monk seals have been known to loll about. If you need shade with your beach, however, bring it with you, since Majors is nothing but sand, air and water.

Starting at either area on Majors Bay, walk toward your left as you face the water. You'll be heading toward Kokole Point, visible from Kekaha. Majors Bay is the kind of place to get lost right out in the open, a deep expanse of soft sand that gives way to a mesmerizing view of Ni'ihau. The Kawaiele Bird Sanctuary, located just inland between the two entrance gates, invites feathered friends to fly into the view. Albatrosses, also known as gooney birds, are often soaring in numbers.

Going to your right from the parking areas at Majors you can get to the coral reef that signals the beginning of Mana Point. At certain times, you can access **Barking Sands Beach** from the base, by taking a road to the right as you enter the main gate; called Recreation Area One. The road leads to the reef at the far end of Barking Sands, and then becomes a four-wheel drive sand road. The sand road continues for about .75-mile, ending near Queens Pond at Barking Sands, as described in TH57.

SNORKEL: On occasion, swimming is possible at **Majors Bay**, but more often, all year, the surf is unsafe for snorkeling. A rip current from right to left, or north to south, is also a hazard. The best snorkeling area—the reef near the airstrip—is sometimes off-limits. Receding tide sometimes creates keiki ponds.

Majors Beach

Polihale State Park

SURF: **Majors** draws surfers, featuring some of the west side's biggest breakers during the winter. During the summer, swells can be outrageous. This is not a beginner's beach at any time of the year—some locals have proposed surfing championships be held here. Some surfers head toward the north end of the base, toward Barking Sands, but this access through the base is often limited.

57. POLIHALE STATE PARK   HIKE, SNORKEL, SURF

WHAT'S BEST: Walking from the Napali coast over the sands of time—where longest beach in the Hawaiian Islands ends and the Napali coast begins. Big mana.
PARKING: Take Hwy. 50 through Kekaha to end of highway beyond m32. At mm33, turn left where a sign says "Polihale State Beach." *Be Aware:* Floodwaters (and lack of-funding for repair) sometimes cause this road to close or be limited to 4WD. If puddles close out the entire road near the beginning, turn around. If not, continue for 3.25 mi. on an unpaved road, dodging its ruts and mud-holes. *For main Polihale parking:* Turn right after 3.25 mi. at a T-intersection with a telephone pole and large monkeypod tree. At .9-mi. from this junction is access to the dune camping road. At 1.5 is additonal parking. For main parking continue across a spillway, and park near a pavilion—1.75 mi. from the tree intersecton. *For Queens Pond:* Turn left at the monkeypod T-intersection. Drive .25-mi. and park before the road turns sharply right uphill and becomes deep sand.

HIKE: Polihale and Barking Sands beaches (up to 4.5 mi.)

Polihale State Park, which includes portions of **Barking Sands Beach**, is at road's end on this side of island. Here, a massive sand dune butts into Napali—The Cliffs.

Inland from the tree-and-shrub-covered dune, is a wedge of agricultural lands, Mana. The entire beach runs for about 17 miles, but you can't walk the whole way due to restrictions at the military facility. Polihale park has restrooms, showers, picnic shelters and car-camping sites scattered atop the dune, providing the most remote camping on the island. *Be Aware:* For all hikes bring water, sun protection, and footwear to guard against hot sand. Note also that, unless a minor miracle has taken place, facilites will be poorly maintained.

From the parking walk onto the sloping, fine sands. Going to your right, the beach gives way to black rocks in less than .5-mile, at the base of the Polihale Ridge. This may be the prize spot in the park, set below towering cliffs at a beach that goes on forever. You can walk the rocks another .25-mile to Polihale Springs, or Sacred Springs, which flows from Polihale Heiau, where the spirits of the dead are said to have departed the island. This walk requires extensive rock-hopping, but it is not difficult.

The hike to your left along the coast will walk the legs out from under even the most ambitious beach walkers. About a mile from the last picnic grounds at Polihale Beach, as you begin to see coral reef offshore, the beach inland is Barking Sands. The beach gets its name from a "woofing" sound these 60-foot high dunes make when settling, or when someone walks down them. Kauaian mythology says the "woofing" is the otherworldly echo of an ancient fisherman's dogs—the first man to love dogs as companions rather than as a culinary delicacy. As you proceed, the reef and shoals become more pronounced—a vast, eternal seascape. *Note:* Due to military security, the beach may be closed to walkers, about 1.75-mile south the beach pavilion parking, which is about .75-mile beyond Queens Pond. You definitely don't want to put on a ski mask and skulk inland. *Be Aware:* Don't turn your back when walking the surf line and watch out for rogue waves.

Polihale State Park

More Stuff: The Kapaula Heiau is up a drainage across from the camping area. Look for a short, steep inland valley from the dune at the campsite—the only place you would even consider walking inland. It's located a short distance on a road that leads to a water tank, which is above the heiau. But the site is overgrown and hard to locate.

SNORKEL: Queens Pond is often a safe swimming

area on an otherwise dangerous swimming beach. Head up the sandy road and through the dunes to the beach. Queens Pond is a few hundred feet to the right as you face the water. It is formed by a crescent-shaped reef that touches the shore at either end, making a large oval swimming area. When conditions are right, surf is spilling over the outside of the reef. Under extended calm conditions, Queens Pond can dry out and be a sand box. *Be Aware:* During storm surf it may be too turbulent for swimming. Rip current can be extreme.

Queens Pond

SURF: **Polihale State Park** is known for a multi-tiered shore break with lots of wave action and fairly short rides. The waves normally pound all year, with winter surf and currents posing a significant hazard. You want to consult the locals before trying Polihale; this is a big beach, and its quirks are not commonly known, since hazards shift with the sand. No lifeguards are on duty.

Another spot, but one for experienced surfers only, is **Queens Pond**. Follow directions in the snorkeling description above. The break here, especially in the summer, may not be pondlike. Get advice from locals; if it's a good day to surf, they will be here. *Be Aware:* Barking Sands and Polihale State Beach are among the island's most dangerous. Swimmers should stay clear of the water in all but calm conditions.

58. KUKUI TRAILS   HIKE

> **WHAT'S BEST:** A hike to the bottom of a rainbow-hued canyon that rivals those in Arizona or Utah. This trail is one of Kaua'i's scenic superstars.
> **PARKING:** Take Hwy. 50 to Waimea and turn mauka on Hwy. 550 just past mm23, which is Waimea Canyon Dr. (*Note:* Hwy. 550 is several miles shorter and also more scenic than taking Hwy. 552, the route suggested by highway signs.) Continue on Hwy. 550 past its junctin with Kokee Rd., Hwy. 552. Go .75-mi. past mm8 and look for trailhead signs on right and park off road, or drive ahead a short distance, make a U-turn at a turnout, and drive back to paved turnout parking on the opposite side of the highway.

HIKE: **Kukui Trails: Iliau Nature Loop** (.25-mi.); **Wiliwili Camp, to bottom of canyon** (5 mi., 2,075 ft.)

Kukui Trail

The **Iliau Loop** is a promenade around a flat area below the parking area, on which the native scrub vegetation of the canyon rim is identified. The loop takes in a railed viewing area, to your left, and its inspiring vistas of the variegated red-and-green canyon walls, often streaked with a waterfall or two. You can see up Waimea Canyon and also Waialae Canyon, which wyes off to the right. *Note:* Prime picnic tables await a couple hundred yards to the right on this loop trail.

Wiliwili Camp is at the bottom of the canyon and alongside the Waimea River. **Kukui Trail** is the only way for bi-peds to walk the bottom of the canyon from the Koke'e area. Once down, you can go upriver another 3.5 miles to Lonomea Camp, or downriver, connecting up with the Waimea Canyon Trail, TH54; but most day hikers will have done enough after making it back up. The Wiliwili Camp trail begins to the right off of the nature loop trail. You start out switchbacking, and then walk out onto an eroded promontory that makes a destination for those not wishing to go all the way down. From the promontory, having descended the majority of the way, you hike left, traversing an eroded hillside, and then right, switchbacking down to the bottom through a leafy forest. The canyon floor, still about 600 feet above sea level, will give you a faraway feel (Burma?), with towering century plants and cacti. Go left on the trail and you get to it's first hairy portion, where it is cut into a cliffside, a high-dive above the river as courses through contorted geology.

Be Aware: Be mindful of flash floods, since river crossings, required farther uspsteam, can be treacherous. Prepare for a full-on day hike, with rain gear, food, and water.

59.   PU'U KA PELE   HIKE, BIKE

WHAT'S BEST: A short hike to an astounding viewpoint of mythological significance. Mountain bikers can take a different flight.
PARKING: Take Hwy. 50 through Waimea. Turn mauka on Hwy. 550, At mm10.3, take a break to check out spiffed-up Waimea Canyon Lookout. Then drive to just past mm11, and park on the left, off road on shoulder at the access sign for Papa'alai Rd.

HIKE: Waimea Canyon Lookout (.25-mi.); Pu'u Ka Pele (.75-mi, 150 ft.); Lapa Picnic Area (4.5 mi., 575 ft.)

The **Waimea Canyon Lookout** gets hammered with tour buses, particularly mid-morning when the cruise ships are in Nawiliwili, but don't let that dissuade you. Railed viewing terraces on several levels provide plenty of room to behold the panorama.

Pu'u Ka Pele, or Pele's Hill, is an extinct sulfur vent located to the right of the highway, on the edge of Waimea Canyon across the highway from Papa'alai Road. The hill is said to be where Pele, the volcano goddess, left Kaua'i to create more fiery mischief farther south in the archipelago. At a pit at the top is Pele's footprint, made when she leapt from the island. From the road, walk across the highway and go up a concrete driveway

to a phone company building, visible from the highway. Concrete stairs lead to a series of log-and-dirt steps with a cable handrail aid a steep and rutted route. A fenced phone installation at the top takes up space but doesn't detract from the view. *Be Aware:* Don't venture out onto unsafe rocks. Also, although this is a historic trail within a state park and used frequently by hunters and hikers, it is along an improved easement utilized by the phone company. Use your own judgement, enter at your own risk, and stay away from buildings and lines.

Lapa Picnic Area is a bird-watcher's hike along Contour Road, which runs along the forested contour on the left side of the highway. This hike, though generally a contour, takes you through some undulation. Start down Papa'alai Road. After about .5-mile the trail makes an "S" turn and crosses Koke'e

Waipo'o Falls, Canyon bottom

Ditch. You then head seaward for another .5-mile, passing a road on your left that is the continuation of Papaʻalai Road toward the two ridge roads. Pass this road and bear right, now on Contour Road. It loops inland through subtropical forest, turns toward the ocean for .5-mile, and finally hairpins right, back to the Lapa Picnic Area.

BIKE: A good way to get to know these Napali ridge roads is to tour **Contour Road**. Six different four-wheel drive roads head seaward from Contour Road, all going out its own ridge, each with valleys steeply falling to either side. To ride Contour Road, follow the hiking description for the picnic area, but continue past the Haeleʻele Ridge Road. After another twisting-and-turning mile you reach Polihale Ridge Road and, 1.5-miles later, come to Kaʻaweiki Ridge Road—hang a right here and pedal about one curving mile back up to the highway. *Be Aware:* On Contour Road, expect mud, puddles and fallen branches. It's best to use these roads on weekdays, when hunters are not present (and when the gate is usually locked).

60.   HAELEʻELE RIDGE   HIKE, BIKE

> **WHAT'S BEST:** A tree-lover's ridge hike or bike for a bird's eye view of Barking Sands and a blue-water look at Niʻihau.
> **PARKING:** Take Hwy. 50 through Waimea and turn mauka on Hwy. 550 toward Waimea Canyon. At mm12, park on left, off-highway on the shoulder near a sign for Haeleʻele Ridge.

HIKE: Haeleʻele Ridge (13 mi., 1.900 ft.); Kepapa Spring (11.5 mi., 1,575 ft.)

Haeleʻele Ridge drops to a bluff that is due east, as the albatross flies, and 1,400 feet above road's end at Polihale State Park. The red-dirt surface gets snotty with rain, so watch your footing. Haeleʻele trail is a broad swath through a forest of eucalyptus, Norfolk Pines, and other trees. Beginning in Waimea Canyon State Park, the trail takes you into the Puʻu Ka Pele Forest Reserve. From the trailhead you hook left around the Lua Reservoir, and then cross Contour Road, about 1.5 miles in. From here you gradually come out of forest along a 3-mile descent. After about 2 miles on this descent—and that distance from Contour Road—is a side road to **Kepapa Springs**, which feeds Sacred Spring at Polihale Beach. Kepapa Springs road to the south, or left, becoming a trail after .75-mile. *More Stuff:* A rougher trail crosses the springs' drainage and traverses up a spur ridge, lenghtening this hike considerably. *Be Aware:* Stay well back from cliff edges.

Continuing on Haeleʻele Ridge road, you drop down the remaining 500 feet over the last 2 miles to trail's end. During the last .5-mile, through a rocky section, the trail stops being a sort-of road and becomes a true trail. *Be Aware:* Hunter's use this area on weekends.

BIKE: **Haeleʻele Ridge** is ideal for fit, experienced cyclists. If caution is used—that is, staying aware of slick surfaces, ruts, branches and roots—the route is not difficult to navigate. The difficulty comes in having the wind and strength to ride back up. Coasting down, after leaving the junction with Contour Road, saves a lot of steps.

61. POLIHALE RIDGE

HIKE, BIKE

WHAT'S BEST: Exploring where the Napali begins on this side of Kauaʻi, and where the spirits of the dead left the island from a sacred heiau below.
PARKING: Take Hwy. 50 through Waimea and turn mauka toward Waimea Canyon on Hwy. 550. Pass mm12, continue .8-mi., and park at picnic area on your left. Look for trailhead sign for Polihale Ridge Road. *Note:* From the guardrail at the highway is a knock-out view across the canyon to Waipoʻo Falls.

HIKE: **Polihale Ridge (10.5 mi., 1,875 ft.)**

Polihale Ridge descends steadily through a forest of pine, eucalyptus and other trees, as well as flowering shrubbery. Conditioned hikers can step out on this four-wheel drive surface. You begin at the A-plus picnic grounds, with a newer pavilion and several covered tables. Head down and take the first left, paralleling the road for a short distance, and passing a house with a large garden. Go through the yellow gate just beyond the house. From here to the end, the route is due west. For the first mile or more, you drop through moist forest, reaching Contour Road. The trail from Contour Road falls steadily, through large koa trees, mixed with ironwoods and Norfolk pines. About a mile from Contour Road, and 1,000 feet farther down from the trailhead, Polihale Ridge narrows, not to a spine, but you'll see pronounced relief of the valleys on either side. *Be Aware:* Hunters drive this road on weekends and holidays.

Polihale Ridge

Puu Hinahina view

The road forks near the end, just past a small water tank, each fork a short spur leading to an exciting view from a 1,400-foot escarpment. The left fork ends at a turnaround among ironwood trees. Walk through the trees to an eroded, red-dirt area for a big of road's end at Polihale State Park. On calm days, you will be able to hear surf pounding, and using a hang glider, you could be there in a few minutes.

To the left is canyonlike Haele'ele Valley, and three ridges are visible: Haele'ele, Kolo, and Mana. The right fork ends after .25-mile at an eroded area, looking down 1,000-feet into the Hikimoe Valley. The next ridge over, Ka'aweiki Ridge, is close enough for those with keen eyes to spot a wild goat or two. You can see surf at a wild cove. Polihale Ridge, according to Hawaiian religion, was where the spirits of the deceased left the island for the other world. Aloha.

BIKE: **Polihale Ridge** is made for mountain bikes. It's a tough down-and-up pedal, but the down part isn't so tough. Ruts, cones, and roots, along with a slick surface, present the usual hazards, but this ride takes more endurance that skill. Save enough engergy and daylight to get back up.

62. PU'U HINAHINA   HIKE, BIKE

WHAT'S BEST: Combine a short walk to a dramatic canyon lookout. Or go for an long adventure hike or bike down your choice of two west Napali ridges.
PARKING: Take Hwy. 50 through Waimea and turn mauka on Hwy. 550 toward Waimea Canyon.

For Ka'aweiki and Kauhao ridges: Go only .1-mi. past mm13 and turn left. Drive in, avoiding spur roads to the left and right, and continue straight for almost .4-mi. Park where the road forks. The right fork is Kauhao Ridge; the left fork is Ka'aweiki Ridge. *Note:* Under most conditions, you can drive another .5-mile either way at this fork, and park where each ridge road intersects Contour Road. Access is made somewhat confusing by a series of community and church camps situated between the highway and Contour Road.

For Pu'u Hinahina: Continue to mm13.6 and go right into an improved parking lot.

HIKE: Pu'u Hinahina (up to .5-mi.); Kauhao Ridge (8.5 mi., 2,150 ft.); Ka'aweiki Ridge (10.5 mi., 1,950 ft.)

Pu'u Hinahina Lookout is sometimes overlooked, since other viewpoints precede it, but it affords a spectacular view down Waimea Canyon. Glancing left from the lookout, you can review the terrain of the Halemanu Valley Hikes, TH63. To the right, as you face the lookout stairs, is a short path to a **lookout of Ni'ihau** and Lehua islands.

For Kauhao Ridge trail, take the right fork from the parking on a forested stroll to Contour Road. For the first 1.5 mile after Contour Road, the trail twists and drops through rumpled topography, before coming upon the wide ridge. Open eucalyptus and koa forest allow occasional blue-water vistas, with glimpses of Ni'ihau and its lesser known satellite island, Lehua. About 3 miles in, stay left at a road fork (though the right fork loops back to join the left). A short trail leads from road's end on Kauhao Ridge to a lookout of the Napali. At this lookout you are about two miles up the coast from Polihale State Park. *Be Aware:* Don't get close to eroded cliffs.

For Ka'aweiki Ridge trail, walk left from the parking and cross Contour Road, about .5-mile later. This ridge lies between Kauhao and Polihale ridges. Ka'aweiki is narrower than its neighbors, with deeply cut Hikimoe Valley on its south side and Ka'aweiki Valley to the north. The trail is not inherently dangerous for the sure-footed, but watch your step during the last 1.5 miles. You reach a 1,300-foot cliff with a straight drop to the Pacific *Be Aware:* Hunters may be out on weekends, so pick a weekday.

BIKE: Just as with their sister ridges in Pu'u Ka Pele Forest Reserve, **Ka'aweiki** and **Kauhao ridges** are a mountain biker's wonderland. If these and nearby roads were on the mainland, Kaua'i would rival Moab as mountain bike city. *Be Aware:* Slick, packed dirt, road debris and ruts make these ridge roads a place where accidents do happen. Also make sure as you're breezing down that you have enough oomph to get back up. Both rides are for hearty cyclists.

63. HALEMANU VALLEY TRAILS
HIKE, BIKE

WHAT'S BEST: A tree-lover's hike-world with waterfall and canyon vistas, perfect for a day when fog is higher up the mountain.

PARKING: Heading up Waimea Canyon on Hwy. 550, continue to mm14 and park off road at marked trailhead, at sign near Kokee State Park Boundary—as you leave Waimea Canyon State Park.

HIKE: Halemanu Trails: Cliff Lookout (2 mi., 525 ft.); Canyon Trail to Waipo'o Falls (4 mi., 1,150 ft.); Kumuwela Lookout (7.25 mi., 1,450 ft.); Black Pipe Trail loop (3.5 mi., 825 ft.)

Notes: Distances are for on-highway parking. A steep road from the highway leads .75-mi. to trailhead; if you choose to drive this road, subtract 1.5 mi. from hiking distances. If you plan to do a lot of hiking in the woodlands of Koke'e, stop by the park museum and purchase an inexpensive map. Within the park area is a fishnet of trails and access roads which can be interconnected in a number options.

The **Halemanu Valley** trails skirt the edge of the forested birdlands where Koke'e Park gives way to the eroded red escarpments of Waimea and Po'omau canyons. **For all trails**, go down the steep, wide Halemanu Road from the highway, which takes a big bend at the bottom and comes to another trailhead sign after .75-mile. Go right a short distance to where the road ends, usually in a big mud-hole, and the trails begin.

After a short distance the trail forks: The **Canyon Trail (and other options)** are the left fork and the **Cliff Lookout Trail** is the right. The Cliff Lookout is a scamper up to an overlook with a pipe railing and picnic table. You'll get a big sense of place. From Cliff Lookout, you can see down the canyon to your left, including the eroded promontory that is part of the Canyon Trail.

Continuing left on the Canyon Trail to the falls and other destinations takes you down another 600 feet. You drop through dense forest and cross over part of the extensive irrigation ditch system. After the ditch, the

Halemanu Trail toward Waipo'o Falls

Canyon Trail then climbs to where you get a view down the canyon, and where the **Black Pipe Trail** joins from the left. The Black Pipe Trail—perhaps best done to make a semi-loop on the way back from the falls—loops through a plethora of trees back to the road you walked down. After about .5-mile on the Black Pipe Trail, make sure to switchbak left up a hillside of koa trees, rather than continuing to down to the stream. About.25-mile after this little climb, you go left again when you come to a road. Keep circling to your left on the Black Pipe Trail. You'll come to the trailhead sign that is just down the road from the highway.

For **Waipo'o Falls** and **Kumuwela Lookout**, you continue on Canyon Trail past the Black Pipe junction, dropping a few hundred feet onto a dramatic barren ridge with canyon views. Continue down the eroded ridge—watch your footing on log steps—and drop to Koke'e Stream. A very short spur trail goes left to a cascade and pool. The trail continues a few hundred feet to the top ledge of Waipo'o Falls, falling 800 feet into the canyon. *Be Aware:* You don't get a good look at the falls. Check it out from across the canyon at Polihale Picnic Area, TH61.

To Kumuwela Lookout, the trail crosses Koke'e Stream at the falls and then goes up gradually along a grassy slope. You contour to your left across the head of the canyon, dipping in and out. About 1.75 miles from the falls, you reach Kumuwela Lookout. You can see all the way down Waimea Canyon to the ocean, almost an entire cross section of the island. To your left is Po'omau Canyon, which wyes off Waimea Canyon to the northwest and abuts Alakai Swamp. *Be Aware:* Don't try to cross the top of the falls if the water is at all running swiftly. *More Stuff:* From Kumuwela Lookout you can continue about 2.5 miles back to the road near Koke'e Museum, a shorter route if you have someone to do the car shuttle.

BIKE: Mountain bikers can park at the trailhead and take off down **Halemanu Road**. By veering left at the first trailhead sign .75-mile in, and then veering left again after less than .5-mile, you can connect with **Faye Road**. Faye Road leads to Koke'e Park headquarters. Doing this involves escorting the wheels over a short trail that connects the Halemanu Road with Faye Road. You can also ride a spur off Halemanu Road by veering right after the trailhead sign. This spur takes you to the junction with the Black Pipe Trail, which can be ridden in most sections, but be sure to dismount for hikers. To explore this area, you may wish to buy a map at the park headquarters, if you care to know where you are. On the other hand, as long as you stay on rideable roads and avoid trails, the region is small enough so that you will be able to ride yourself out of being lost or disoriented.

64. MAKAHA RIDGE ROAD   HIKE, BIKE

WHAT'S BEST: See a spectacular Napali ridge the easy way—by driving and taking short walks.

Miloli'i vista

PARKING: Head up Waimea Canyon on Hwy. 550. Pass Pu'u Hinahina Lookout, and turn makai on paved Makaha Rd., almost to mm. 14/550. *For Makaha Arboretum:* Go about 3 mi. on Makaha Rd. and look for an unpaved road on left (which loops out to the main road about .5-mi. later). *For Miloli'i vista:* Go 4 mi. to the guard station and make a U-turn. Bactrack about .25-mi. to the top of the rise, with a red-dirt embankment and pine trees on the left—near where a utility line crosses over the road.

HIKE: Makaha Arboretum (3 mi., 350 ft.); Miloli'i vista (.25-mi.)

To **Makaha Arboretum**, which has sugi pine trees mixed among a number of native and introduced species, look for (unsigned) Pine Forest Drive on your left as you are making a long, straight descent to the Makaha Ridge. The trail to the arboretum spurs off this road about midway along its loop.

The pine forest here, not tropical at all in its appearance, underscores that climates exist for virtually every growing thing on the Garden Isle. After walking down for about .5-mile on Pine Forest Drive—and before crossing a drainage—take the road that drops away from the ridge and then contours seaward along the rim of Kauhao Valley. A mile after leaving Pine Forest Road, you come to a picnic area. Makaha Ridge isn't always a great lunch spot—during Hurricane Iniki in 1992, winds reached 227 mph, the most powerful ever recorded in Hawai'i.

The **Miloli'i vista** packs much of the scenic punch that you have to walk 10 miles and climb 2,000 feet to see on other ridge hikes. Make like a goat and wander down the crumbly red-dirt slopes that lead to near-vertical escarpments of the valley, about 1,500 high. There are many routes for curious and cautious hikers. *Be Aware:* Cliff

Nualolo Trail

edges are dangerous. Though not at this exact spot, fatalities have ocurred in Miloli'i Valley, even among experienced hikers—including in 2007 to the island's beloved teacher and photographer, David Boynton.

Bike: Beginning at the highway, the 4-mile **Makaha Ridge Road** is an easy roll in for cyclists, although you're looking at a 1,500-foot pump on the return leg. Cheaters can have someone drive down and pick them up. The paved road, which does have some flat dips along the way down, ends at a military guard gate. A side pedal to **Makaha Arboretum**, as per the hiking description above, is also a worthy excursion for mountain bikers.

65.   MILOLI'I RIDGE   Hike, Bike

What's Best: A long ride or hike to land's end on a little traveled Napali ridge.
Parking: Take Hwy. 50 to Waimea and turn mauka toward Waimea Canyon on Hwy. 550. Go almost to mm14 and turn makai on paved Makaha Ridge Rd. Go .3-mi. on Makaha Ridge Rd. and park off road on right at Miloli'i Rd.

Hike: Miloli'i Ridge (11 mi., 1,800 ft.)

Miloli'i Ridge road contours parallel to the highway for the first 1.25 miles, twisting through moist forest. It then drops and hooks seaward, beginning the first of its long descent over a 5.5-mile run. After 2.5 miles—amid a mature koa forest in the Napali-Kona Forest Reserve—you come to a picnic shelter. The shelter is set on a grassy flat with tree-filtered views of Makaha Ridge and Nualolo.

From the picnic area, the road becomes a wide trail. Most of the descent is over the last 3 miles. You descend an eroded cut-bank, and then the trail goes up and over two knobs that lie along the ridge. During the last 1.5 miles you descend more gradually, through a fresh-scented pine forest. Avoid spur trails and keep right as the trail keeps dropping. Finally, the road ends at a grass patch amid pine trees looking 1,600-plus feet down to Miloli'i Beach, where remnants of a heiau tell of the people who once lived there. Across the way is Nualolo Ridge. From the grass patch, you can walk up the eroded rise to your left, which leads out onto the ridge, with ultra views everywhere. Look for goats scampering about. *Be Aware:* Stay away from crumbling slopes.

BIKE: **Miloli'i Ridge** should be attempted by fit, experienced cyclists. Although not inherently dangerous—beyond the usual ruts, roots, slick mud and road debris— the road is a workout, with several steep segments. Less experienced mountain bikers might consider a hike 'n' bike: Ride to the picnic area, about 2.5 miles in, and walk the rest of the distance.

66.   NUALOLO TRAIL   HIKE

WHAT'S BEST: Hike through the forests of Koke'e and break out to a narrow bench high above the Napali coast—one of the most exhilarating vistas in the world.
PARKING: Take Hwy. 50 to Waimea and turn mauka toward Waimea Canyon on Hwy. 550. Go .3-mi. past mm15 and look for trailhead sign on left, just before entering Koke'e State Park headquarters.

HIKE: Nualolo Trail to: Kuia Natural Area (.4-mi., 225 ft.); Napali Kona Forest Reserve (5.5 mi., 850 ft.); Lolo Vista Point (7.75 mi., 1,600 ft.)

The **Nualolo Trail** descends through moist forest and then dry shrublands to a precipitous terminus at **Lolo Vista Point**. Prepare for a fairly challenging day hike. From the trailhead road, you jump up to the left and then climb steeply for the first .25-mile, entering the **Kuia Natural Area Reserve**. From the area reserve you drop steadily through forest with the occasional clearing. Birds love it here. The descent continues, as forests give way to open areas, home to koa trees, ginger, and ferns. The trail swerves, making a left bend and then back to the right again as you descend a broad ridge top. About 2 miles in, you'll get the first blue-water views. At almost 3 miles from the trailhead, you enter the **Napali-Kona Forest Reserve**, as the trail drops steeply down a knob to drier, eroded relief.

Your route continues straight out the bench, descending steeply, and coming to the Nualolo Cliff Trail junction, which is the connector to the Awa'awapuhi Trail. The last .5-mile of the Nualolo Trail is the big thrill. The trail drops down an eroded slope and onto the curving lip Nualolo Valley—a 2,000-foot free-fall to your right into a big bowl. Fortunately, the fall to the left into Kawaiula Valley is not as sharp, and you can lean that way. The bench at Lolo Vista Point broadens out, with only dwarf flora in the vicinity, and it has a sturdy railing. Several Napali ridges provide views north and south. The rugged beach below where Nualolo Valley meets the Pacific is Napali Coast State Park. *Be Aware:* The earth is crumbly on the valley rim. There are places where people venture beyond the railing, but stay well back of edges.

More Stuff: The Nualolo Cliff Trail crosses around the rim of Nualolo Valley for 2 miles and connects with the Awaʻawapuhi Trail, TH67. The Nualolo Cliff Trail can be in poor condition due to erosion—not recommended for those who fear heights. A car-shuttle hike between Nualolo and Awaʻawapuhi trails is about 8.5 miles. If you plan this, inquire at the Kokeʻe Museum for current trail conditions.

67. KOKEʻE STATE PARK   HIKE, BIKE

> **WHAT'S BEST:** Discover the least-known face of Kauaʻi, hidden in a birdland forest of countless varieties of trees, vines and flowering shrubs. Repeat hikers and cyclists flock to these forests.
> **PARKING:** Head toward Waimea Canyon on Hwy. 550. Go past mm15 and keep right at sign to Kokeʻe Museum and park headquarters. Continue on Hwy. 550 .1-mi. and turn right on Kumuwela Rd., which is marked with a sign to Camp Sloggett. Drive .4-mi. to first turnoff to the right and a sign for the camp and park. *Note:* The road beyond this junction is not always suitable for passenger cars.

Notes: If you plan on hiking this area extensively, stop by the museum and pick up an inexpensive park map. Plan on spending some time at the Kokeʻe Museum which serves as an interpretive center, gift shop, gallery and bookstore. Then wade through the roosters to the Kokeʻe Lodge next door for a bowl of their hearty homemade chili. The grand meadow in front is ideal for a picnic, and is also the site for the Queen Emma Polynesian Festival in October.

HIKE: Halemanu-Kokeʻe Trail (2.5 mi., 375 ft.); Kumuwela-Waininiua loop (2.5 mi., 750 ft.); Ditch Trail loop (4.5 mi., 700 ft.); Berry Flat loop (2.75 mi., 250 ft.)

The **Halemanu-Kokeʻe Trail** is a good choice for birdwatchers and would-be botanists, wishing a self-guided forest tour with easy hiking. Koa and ohia lehua trees dominate the forest, a drier forest that is still making a comeback from Hurricane Iniki in 1992. If you have a field guide, some plants to look for are mokihan, maile, pukiawe, hala-pepe, and ikiuki. Flitting among the branches, and providing the music, you may see iʻiwi, apapane, elepio, and amakihi. In ancient times, exotic bird feathers were plucked here—the birds were captured and released.

To begin, walk toward Camp Sloggett—on the first road to the right off Halemanu Road—for .1-mile and look for the trailhead on your right. After 1.2 miles, the trail comes to Halemanu Road. You can turn around here; or make a longer loop hike by turning right on Halemanu Road. For a loop, follow Halemanu, keeping left, for about

.2-mile to road's end, where you take an unnamed trail to the left. Stay on this trail for .2-mile to where you connect with Faye Road. Turn right on Faye, which joins Hwy. 550 in .5-mile, and from there it's another mile back to Koke'e and your car.

For the **Kumuwela-Waininiua loop**, walk to the next right-turn from Kumuwela Rd, which is just past the Camp Sloggett road. Go down the road, crossing Koke'e Stream near several homes. About .25-mile after the stream crossing look for Waininiua trailhead on your left. The Waininiua Trail ascends gently but steadily for almost .5-mile, through koa trees and vines, before reaching a segment Kumuwela Road. Turn right on Kumuwela. After a short distance a spur road leads to your left; this left turn goes to the Ditch Trail and you need to keep right. Continue on Kumuwela Road for 1.25 miles to where Kumuwela Trail comes in from the right, which is the route back to the car. You may wish to take a side-trip here: By continuing down Kumuwela Road for .5-mile to its end, you reach Kumuwela Lookout.

Turning right on Kumuwela Trail, you walk through dense woodlands, with a unfathomable number of trees and shrubs. This woodland area, at the beginning of the 1900s was trampled and eroded by feral pigs and goats, with cows thrown in for good measure. In the 1930s, the animals were curtailed and a number of plants introduced. The trail continues for nearly 1 mile, before reaching Kumuwela Road, at its end. Walk Kumuwela Road, past the Waininiua trailhead and back to your car.

Alakai Swamp

For the fairly strenuous **Ditch Trail loop** start out by following the above description for the Kumuwela-Waininiua loop. The Ditch Trail is perhaps the most scenic among the interior Koke'e Trails. Inquire at the park museum or headquarters before taking this trail, however, as it sometimes deteriorates with bad weather. As you complete the Waininiua Trail section, and then turn right on Kumuwela Road, look for another road within .1-mile cutting back to your left. This is Waininiua Road, a .5-mile section that contours around and joins the Ditch Trail. Once at the Ditch Trail, turn left— the right-heading section is often not well-maintained. Turning left takes you both through woodlands and spots affording views of Po'omau Canyon. In about 1.5 miles of tough-walking terrain, the Ditch Trail joins with Mohihi Road. Go left on Mohihi Road, which becomes Kumuwela Road, and continue 1.75 miles back to your car.

The trailhead for **Berry Flat loop** is just under 1 mile in from Hwy. 550, at the first road that forks to your left. You can park at the Camp Sloggett Road, and walk to this trailhead, which adds .75-mile to the Berry Flat hike, making it about 3.5 miles roundtrip. Berry Flat, or Pu'u Kaohelo, is a forested nature trail, featuring koa, ohia, lehua, sugi pine and even a variety of redwood. Start up the road fork, which goes for .2-mile, and locate the trailhead on your left between two residences. The trail wiggles through a thicket of vines and ferns, under a shade canopy. At least two spur trails lead to nowhere; keep right as your contour in a circle for 2 miles, reaching Mohihi Road. Turn right on Mohihi and follow it back about .5-mile to your car.

More Stuff: For a loop of the Alakai Swamp-Pihea trail, you need to drive in 3.2 miles from Hwy. 550. Kumuwela Road become Mohihi Road. Although the road in can be driven much of the way by passenger vehicles, it should be avoided in rainy conditions and is recommended for four-wheel drive. These trails are other access to the swamp, which is described in TH68, Pu'uokila. *And More Stuff:* Mohihi Road continues for several more miles to Camp 10, with access to Po'omau Canyon Lookout Trail, Kohua Ridge Trail and Mohihi-Waialae Trail. Access to these trails should be in four-wheel drive vehicles. *Be Aware:* For all Koke'e trails bring rain gear and water. Keep your bearings and backtrack if you are unsure of your location.

BIKE: As you may gather from the hiking descriptions, the **Koke'e trails** lend themselves to mountain biking. **Kumuwela** and **Mohihi Camp roads**, about 17 miles if you rode them all, and many visitors will consider this area more interesting riding than hiking. A mountain bike solves the dilemma of whether to take a rental car off-highway, which is a violation of most rental agreements. One hike-and-bike recommended for mountain bikers is to ride in about 4.5 miles on Mohihi Camp Road and take the walk to **Po'omau Canyon Lookout**, which is just after the road across Waiakoali Stream. The .5-mile walk takes you over a footbridge, passing Norfolk and sugi pines, to a viewpoint at the head of Po'omau Canyon. You look down to where this canyon joins Waimea Canyon. **Camp 10** is about 6 miles in on Mohihi Road, a slippery ride with stream crossings and a few roots to contend with.

68. AWA'AWAPUHI

WHAT'S BEST: This is one of Kaua'i's beauties. Hike through natural tropical gardens to an adrenaline-rush ridge, the jewel of the Napali. Or take a lesser-know adventure to the 'Valley of the Lost People.' Or, take a paved stroll from the car to a grand view.
PARKING: Head up Waimea Canyon on Hwy. 550. Pass Koke'e Museum. *For Awa'awapuhi,* park at mm17 on left at signed trailhead. *For Valley of the Lost People,* continue to mm17.4 and park on the left at a dirt turnout, where the road makes a right-uphill bend with a concrete water ditch and berm on the right. *The Kalalau Valley Overlook* will be on the left clearly signed near mm18.

HIKE: Awa'awapuhi (6.5 mi., 1,675'); Valley of the Lost People (2.25 mi., 275ft.); Kalalau Lookout (.25-mi.)

The **Awa'awapuhi Trail** is to tropical ridges what the Golden Gate is to bridges and the Eiffel is to towers: powerfully beautiful and unique. For this reason it gets more hikers than many other trails, but not so many as to feel crowded. The trail decends for most of its distance through abundant forest and then teeters across grassy spines to overlooks some 2,500 feet above the Napali Coast State Park. *Be Aware:* Prepare for rain and wind, and gear-up for a full-fledged day hike. Don't go beyond the railings at the overlooks.

You begin walking through a good example of native dry forest—although dry for Kaua'i is different from dry in, for example, Nevada. The trail is in the Napali-Kona Forest Reserve, although the Awa'awapuhi Trail is managed as wilderness due to the rich number of native dryland plant species you see along the way.

Awa'awapuhi

Just under 3 miles into the hike, the Nualolo Cliff Trail joins this trail from your left, which takes you 2 miles across the percipitous head of Nualolo Valley and joins the Nualolo Trail, TH66. You can use this route for an 8.5 mile loop back to your car at Awa'awapuhi, including 2 miles up the road.

Be Aware: The Nualolo Cliff Trail is not always in the best shape. Inquire locally as to its condition before making this loop. The **Awa'awapuhi overlooks** are less than .5-mile from the Nualolo junction, a breathtaking scamper to two different vantage points. You overlook the Nualolo and Awa'awapuhi valleys, down vertical green escarpments. These valley floors, accessible only by boat and then a scramble up from the shore, are part of the Napali Coast State Park.

The **Valley of the Lost People** (formally called Honopu Valley) is where a band of the island's last Menehunes lived. The unoffical trail was closed due to deterioration, even before Hurricane Iniki in 1982, but local hikers manage to keep it passable—unless Mother Nature does a number. At the top of the bend in the highway, the trail starts as a level path through a thicket of vines and saplings. Stay left at a first junciton after five minutes, and then go right at a second junction a few minutes later (plastic ribbons normally mark the spots). After nearly 20 minutes you'll reach another junction in a clearing—go *left* at this third junction, dropping through a fern hedge with overhanging trees. (Look down the valley to a knob on the ridge; the trail contours left around this knob.) After the descent, the trail traverses in the open, amid ferns and ohia. Honopu Valley is down to your left, and you may hear its stream. Footing is tricky, but not dangerous. You will contour around the front of the knob you viewed from above, and find yourself in a healthy grove of koa trees, as well as red-flowering ohias. Pick your own turnaround spot. Intrepid hikers can continure farther into the valley, but be prepared and make sure to memorize your return route and keep track of time to allow enough daylight for the return.

New paths, tables, and a restroom make the **Kalalau Lookout** a sure thing for a family comfort stop. The view's not bad either, though be sure to also continue to the Pu'uokila Overlook a mile ahead at the end of the road.

More Stuff: The Kaluapuhi Trail begins about .25-mile up Hwy. 550 from the Awaawapuhi trailhead; look for a red-dirt path heading up on a curve in the road. This forested, one-mile excercise trail rejoins the road to Pu'uokila Lookout.

69. PU'UOKILA HIKE

WHAT'S BEST: A tropicbird's view of Kalalau Valley, or a walk into a primordial swamp to the edge of the world. (!!!) The lookout view graces book and magazine covers throughout the world—including *Kaua'i Trailblazer.*

Kalalau Valley from Pihea Trail

PARKING: Head up Waimea Canyon on Hwy. 550. Go past Koke'e State Park and the Kalalau Lookout at mm18. Continue 1 mi. to road's end at Pu'uokila Lookout.

HIKE: Pihea Overlook (2 mi., 350 ft.); Alakai Swamp Trail-Kilohana Overlook (7.5 mi., 850 ft.)

After taking in the view at the **Pu'uokila Lookout**, start down the trail along the rim of the valley—a rutted, often slick slope that is indicative of the trail's worst parts for the first mile. A hiking pole will help. In some places, you'll need all four limbs to negotiate the trail over sections of steps cut into hard-packed, greasy dirt—though the trail is not hazardous for the cautious hiker. The Pihea Overlook is on a hands-on spur trail beyond the junction with the Swamp Trail. At 4,280 feet, the **Pihea Overlook** is the highest point along the rim. You'll have to double back for the swamp trail.

To **Kilohana Overlook and Alakai Swamp**, look for a signed junction a mile in from trailhead parking—just after completing a difficult hands-and-feet staircase. You drop down away from the rim, on a trail which at first is muddy and steep. But after a short distance you hit the boardwalk and series of stairs, rails, and ramps that make the rest of the walk a relative breeze. The rain forest is superlative. *Note:* This trail approximates **Queen Emma's route** of personal healing, which she took many tmes after the death of her husband King Kamehameha IV—and after the couple had lost thier son, Albert, when he was a child. The queen's soirees were with hula dancers, who performed different rituals out of respect for each life-giving plant.

After about .75-mile on the boardwalk, you reach the junction with trails coming up from Mohihi Road (see TH67). To the Kilohana Overlook from the junction, go left toward Alakai Swamp. You stairstep down, cross the stream and then lose the boardwalk for a stretch as you climb up from the drainage through dwarf fauna on the other side. At the top you pick up the boardwalk again and march right through the 60-square-mile swamp—an open bog of ferns, grasses, shrubbery and dwarf trees spreading out at 4,000 feet above sea level. The caldera from Hawai'i's first eruption has evolved over millions of years to become the highest elevation swamp in the world. From edges of the swamp, including the ridge of Mount Waialeale, are the origins of all rivers and streams on the island.

Vegetation dwarfs and becomes more sparse over the last mile or so. Then the boardwalk ends at Kilohana, a small platform on the edge of the Wainiha Pali, 3,800-foot-high jungle cliffs rising above a river valley. If clouds are in your face, wait awhile since they are fickle and may well give you an opening, if you've been good. Wainiha Valley is a fissured green gorge similar in size to Waimea Canyon, but is rarely seen because it is privately held. See TH4. Hanalei Bay is in the center of a north shore view.

Be Aware: Do not venture into the swamp. You'll be knee deep in mud and have a good chance of getting lost. When rain and fog come in, getting off the boardwalk can be a fatal mistake.

Alaka'i Swamp boardwalk

A BRIEF HISTORY OF KAUA'I

Captain James Cook, an Englishman, made landfall in January of 1778 at Waimea Bay, thus "discovering" the "Sandwich Islands." But the Polynesians discovered Kaua'i about 16 centuries before the English, perhaps as early as 100 AD. The first Polynesians were from the Marquesas, an island group well below the equator, 2,400 miles to the southeast of Kaua'i and due south of California. What caused these Marquesans to take to the sea is not known, but their navigational skills remain a marvel of mythical proportions. The myth extends to the Americas, where some anthropologists suggest that early American peoples, those people known as the Anasazi, who pre-dated other tribal cultures in the Southwest, may have been of Polynesian descent.

The first Polynesians, perhaps coming in a series of migrations over the next several centuries, brought with them domestic animals, plants and seed stock to make a go of it in their new world. They became skilled stone workers, constructing many of the water ditches, agricultural terraces, fish ponds and heiaus—temples—that are in evidence today. Legend say these feats were accomplished by a mythical race of primitive engineers, tiny people, called the Menehunes.

The best guess now is that these Menehunes were actually the Marquesans, smaller in stature than the second wave of Polynesian settlers, who came from Tahiti as much as 1,000 years after the Marquesans. In the Tahitian language, the word for slave, or lower class worker is very close to today's "Menehune," giving credence to the theory that the Marquesans were subjugated and conquered by the Tahitians. The Marquesans who survived the Tahitian migration did so by retreating into river valleys, and, as recently as the late 1800s, the U.S. Census Bureau counted 65 "Menehunes" living in Wainiha Valley.

The Tahitian migrations are thought to have taken place in waves until the 1400s, perhaps including back-and-forth voyages on their double-hulled sailing canoes. Then, for reasons unclear, the migrations ceased and, like their predecessors, these Polynesian were on Kaua'i for good and without outside influence.

The second wave of Polynesians also brought with them domesticated animals, such as pigs, goats and dogs, as well as taro, breadfruit and other plants that were to sustain them over the next 400 years. Over the generations, the Hawaiians developed a way of life based on family communities sharing a self-sufficient plot of land, called an ahupua'a. The ahupua'a was usually a wedge-shaped plot, with an inland point encompassing a river or stream valley, and then fanning out over terraced agricultural lands to a seacoast.

From this ahupua'a, fruits, vegetables, livestock and sea foods—all that was needed to sustain the community—were cultivated by the members of the community, called the ohana. Today's aloha spirit has its roots in the ohana. Working together was a virtue among the Hawaiians, and all turned hands toward productivity. A person who was selfish and without friends did not survive in times of famine or natural calamity.

Hula Dancers

Aloha Nui

from a far away
friend here the mid-
Pacific
Angela H. Wright
Waimea, Kauai.

HAWAIIAN ISLANDS

Early Kauaians lived in harmony with their surround for centuries, developing a philosophy called the Huna. The Huna is an evolving belief system that includes both their spiritual views and the accumulation of practical knowledge. Many concepts of the Huna foreshadowed, or paralleled, concepts in Western schools of thought. The Huna—and the islanders' social fabric—was held in check by a system of rules—the kapu—governing behaviors among individuals as well as their interactions with their natural world. Kapu violations of the severest nature were dealt with by swift capital punishment.

The Kauaian culture was transmitted over the generations by the hula—a dance performed by men and women, accompanied by chants and percussion—which kept alive both history and mythology. This ancient dance is alive today. The hula supplanted textbooks, for the Hawaiians had no written word. The Hawaiian alphabet of 12 letters and the spelling of all words were developed by academics.

To the Kauaians, place names, which sound similar and comically run-together to the Western ear, are very precise and descriptive. Each place on this complicated island was described in terms of its attributes and relation with all other places. Each place was part of an ahupua'a, which sustained the ohana, and all this fit together to make Kaua'i.

Hawaiian culture not only survived, it also thrived, and by the time of Captain Cook's arrival in 1778, the population of Hawai'i was about 300,000. Cook, an accomplished navigator and captain, had been leading an exploration of the South Pacific for a dozen years, searching for the theoretical Southern Continent. Ironically, he had been sailing right over it—Oceania, the Polynesian civilization of islands cast about the sea. Giving up on the Southern Continent, Cook set sail northward, this time in search of the illusive Northwest Passage.

Cook was on the furthest edge of the known world when his ships, the *Discovery* and *Resolution*, raised three islands, Oahu, Kaua'i and Ni'ihau. The ships dropped anchor in Waimea, staying not much longer than a vacation—about three weeks— making cursory notes and provisioning before resuming their quest. An officer with Cook was William Bligh, who was to lose the *Bounty* to mutiny, ten years later.

A year later, Cook returned from North America, this time putting in at Kealakehua Bay on the Kona coast of the Big Island. He arrived during the Makahiki—a yearly time of celebration honoring the god of peace and fertility, Lono. His timely landing led local chiefs to proclaim that Cook himself was Lono. Cook's status as deity quickly wore thin, however, as his sea-weary men made increasingly greedy demands for women and food. After a few weeks, Cook and his men sailed from Kealakehua, but a storm damaged a ship's mast and they were forced to return.

Cook's return to Kona was as poorly timed as his arrival had been good. The Makahiki was over. While in harbor, local warriors stole one of Cook's cutters, a small boat. One thing led to another, a confrontation escalated. Cook was clubbed to death on the rocks of the bay, several Hawaiians were shot and Cook's ships skedaddled. Hawai'i was not visited by Western ships again for six years. Cook's arrival was coincident with the emergence of King Kamehameha the Great, nephew of an ali'i on the Big Island. Kamehameha was an intelligent, large man—over six-foot-six and north of three hundred pounds—whose political skills were matched by those as a warrior. By 1795 Kamehameha I, as he was later called, had unified all the islands under his rule, except for the island of Kaua'i.

Attempts to conquer Kaua'i were thwarted twice—once by the fierce waters on the Kaua'i Channel that separates it from Oahu, and a second time when the invading force was depleted by an illness that had been brought by Europeans. Kauaian warriors kept lookout for the invading ships for a dozen years, but the assault did not happen. Kaua'i did not come under Kamehameha's rule until Kaua'i's last ali'i, Kaumuali'i, voluntarily signed a treaty in 1810. The treaty was due in part to both kings' recognition that outside forces, represented by both American and Russian trading ships, were a part of the near future and it behooved the Hawaiians to be a unified people.

Kamehameha the Great ruled until 1819, during a time when whaling ships and other vessels traded with the Hawaiians to replenish their ships' stocks. The word out on these abundant islands, and spreading fast. Sandalwood trade also flourished during the early 1800s, when forests of this fragrant wood on Kaua'i were denuded. Significantly, one year after Kamehameha's death, when his son, Liholiho or Kamehameha II, ascended the throne, the kapu system was abolished and the first New England Protestant missionaries arrived in Waimea. The onset of the missionaries left an American imprint on the islands, and dispelled any last hopes the Russians—who had built two forts on Kauaian soil—had of making Hawai'i a Russian territory.

Kamehameha's sons and grandsons, two of each, ruled the islands until 1872. During this time American influence came not just directly from the missionaries. The Gold Rush in California created a demand for Hawaiian sugar, meat and vegetables, and a decade later, the Civil War increased the demand for sugar, since the Union was cut off from Southern sugar supplies and had no other source to satisfy its sweet tooth. The development of the sugar industry—the first mill on Kaua'i was built in Koloa in 1835—also brought in workers from China, Japan and the Philippines to meet the labor demand. On Kaua'i, since then, no ethnic majority has existed, and therefore no minority. The blending of different races sharing an island is also part of the Aloha spirit, compatible with the concept of the ohana.

Another influence stemming from the mid-nineteenth century evident today is land ownership. About 41 percent of Kaua'i's land is owned by six private corporations and families who trace their purchases back to the 1800s. Owning land was not a concept in Polynesian culture.

The end of the Hawaiian monarchy came in 1893, the last year of the reign of its first woman leader—Queen Liliuokalani. Part of the monarchy's downfall was due to the excesses and economic foibles of the two kings after Kamehameha IV, Queen Liliuokalani's predecessors. A power struggle between the queen and her rivals—during which Queen Liliuokalani was betrayed—ended in a bloodless revolution. In 1898, about five hundred years after the Tahitians took over from the Marquesans, the U.S. Congress annexed Hawai'i as a U.S. Territory. In 1900, Sanford B. Dole, a leader among plantation owners and industrialists and one of Queen Liliuokalani's adversaries, became Hawai'i's first governor.

Hawai'i's agriculture trade dominated development in the early 1900s, as more and more workers were brought in to meet demand. Most workers were from Japan, accounting for 40 percent of the island's population in 1930. U.S. Immigration put restrictions on Japanese immigration and workers from other Pacific locales were recruited. Tensions came to a head in 1941 when Pearl Harbor was attacked by Japanese planes. Midway Island, at the north of the Hawaiian Archipelago, became the strategic piece of real estate for American forces to defend.

In 1959, Hawai'i became America's fiftieth state, and thus the far north of Polynesia was linked with the way south of North America. Hawai'i is central to America's interests, both as a military force and an economic player with the Pacific Rim countries—the place where the Far East meets the West. In spite of this international context, visitors to Kaua'i will see that Hawaiian culture has endured. Hawai'i is the only state where the culture of its native peoples has retained such vitality, still the overriding influence on the island.

Driving Tours

Four drives feature the island's scenic, cultural and historical points of interest, taking you on back roads as well as to major tourist attractions. The four tours together cover the whole island. Use the trailhead descriptions to explore more thoroughly the places mentioned in the tours.

Each tour can be driven from half-day to a day, but to see all the listed attractions takes well over a day—be selective. Some eateries and shops are mentioned in the text. Check *Resource Links* for other recommedned places along the way.

top left going clockwise:
Haena
Hanapepe taro
Waioli Mission House
Wailua Coast
Lihue Lutheran Church
Poipu resort

DRIVING TOUR ONE

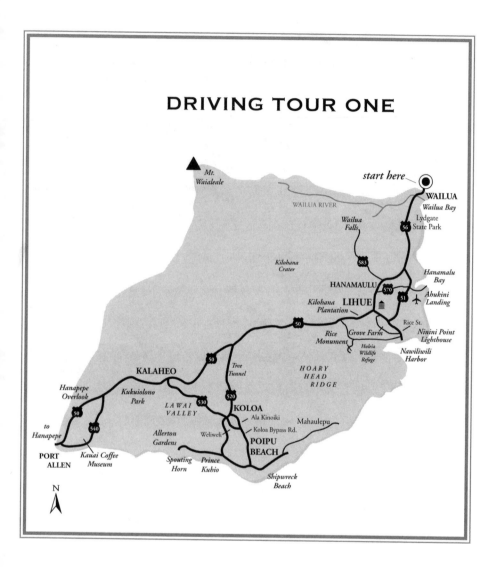

start here

WAILUA
Wailua Bay
Lydgate
State Park
56

WAILUA RIVER

Wailua
Falls

583

Kilohana
Crater

HANAMAULU
570

Hanamalu
Bay

Kilohana
Plantation
LIHUE

51
Ahukini
Landing

Rice St.

50

Rice
Monument
Grove Farm

Huleia
Wildlife
Refuge

Ninini Point
Lighthouse

Nawiliwili
Harbor

KALAHEO

50

Tree
Tunnel

H O A R Y
H E A D
R I D G E

Hanapepe
Overlook

Kukuiolono
Park

530

520

L A W A I
V A L L E Y

KOLOA

Ala Kinoiki

Mahaulepu

50

to
Hanapepe

540

Allerton
Gardens

Weliweli

Koloa Bypass Rd.

PORT
ALLEN

Kauai Coffee
Museum

Spouting
Horn

Prince
Kuhio

POIPU
BEACH

Shipwreck
Beach

Mt.
Waialeale

N

TOUR *one*

Waimea Falls, Hanamaulu Bay, Koloa Town, Poipu Beach, Allerton Garden, Spouting Horn, Kalaheo and Kaua'i Coffee plantation. A good tour for a rainy day or for those wishing to see Kaua'i's museums, historical buildings, and seaport.

START DRIVING TOWARD LIHUE ON HWY. 56. **TURN RIGHT** ON HWY. 583.

Wailua Falls is 4 miles up Hwy. 583, which is Ma'alo Road. Rainbows sometimes appear above the falls, especially in morning light when waters are brimming with storm runoff and mist roils from below. More often, twin cascades make the 80-foot plunge, which you may recognize as one of the shots for the opening of the television program, *Fantasy Island*. In ancient times, Kauaian chiefs would dive over the edge to prove their love and courage to chosen sweethearts.

BACKTRACK ON HWY. 583. **TURN RIGHT** ON HWY. 56.

Just after the turn, on the right you'll see **Kapaia Stitchery**, a must-stop for those interested in Hawaiian fabrics and quilts. Guys' bench outside.

CONTINUE ON HWY. 56 AND **TURN LEFT** ON HWY. 570 WHICH IS AHUKINI ROAD. **CONTINUE** ON AHUKINI TOWARD AIRPORT, **VEER LEFT** AND TAKE AHUKINI ROAD 2 MILES TO END.

Ahukini Recreation Pier State Park, with its dilapidated labyrinth of a concrete pier, was the major port for the sugar industry until Nawiliwili Harbor was developed. Meaning "altar for many blessings," Ahukini today is where locals fish and talk story. The view inland is of Hanamaulu Bay, once the community of Portuguese cane workers. Above the bay, inland, is Kalepa Ridge, where Kauaian warriors kept a lookout for Kamehameha's invading army in the early 1800s, and U.S. servicemen kept a lookout for invading Japanese in the 1940s. Driving back out Ahukini Road you will notice the offices and take-off pads for many of the island's tour helicopter companies.

BACKTRACK ON AHUKINI ROAD AND **TURN LEFT** ON HWY. 51, KAPULE HWY. GO 1.25 MILE ON HWY. 51 AND **TURN RIGHT** ON RICE STREET. **CONTINUE** 1 MILE ON RICE STREET AND **PARK** NEAR UMI STREET.

Lihue was not much of a settlement until recent Kauaian history, the late 1830s, when Kamehameha III's high chief was ordered to plant cane. Prior to that date, the high chief resided in Waimea and the major routes from there to Wailua bypassed Lihue. The chief chose Lihue—meaning "gooseflesh" or "cold chill"—for its wetter clime.

Now the county seat, Lihue still has a number of buildings dating back to the 1800s—check out Kress Street which is two blocks down from Umi Street. If you're hungry, try the Barbecue Inn for local-style fare, or the **Hanamura Saimin Hut**. The **Kaua'i Museum** is the lava rock building on Rice Street one block up from Umi on Eiwa Street. Opened in 1960, the museum features displays on volcanoes, Polynesian migrations, missionaries and sugar plantations, among its wealth of material. The best stuff is in the annex building, just out back. Across Eiwa Street from the

Kauai Museum, Lihue

museum, the County Building, which stood alone when it was built in 1915, is a good place to take a breather under huge shade trees at the park in front of it.

CONTINUE UP RICE STREET PAST MUSEUM. TURN LEFT ON HALEKO ROAD. LOOK FOR LEFT-HAND TURN LANE, THE BLOCK BEFORE YOU GET TO THE STOP LIGHT.

Haleko Road takes you down a gully and through the business end of the **Lihue Sugar Mill**, founded in 1849 and in operation until 2000. Most of Lihue's shopping areas, including Kukui Grove Shopping Center, were cane fields well into the 1900s.

CONTINUE ON HALEKO ROAD TO NAWILIWILI ROAD, WHICH IS HWY. 58. TURN LEFT ON NAWILIWILI ROAD, HEADING DOWNHILL TOWARD HARBOR.

On the left, almost 1 mile down and just past Aheahe Street, is **Grove Farm Homestead Museum**. Docent-led ours of the George Wilcox estate—the home, cottages and gardens of the Grove Farm sugar plantation, founded in 1864—are by reservation only. They've managed to preserve a place in time, close to neighborhoods. To call Grove Farm Homestead, see *Resource Links*.

Grove Farm Homestead

CONTINUE ON NAWILI-WILI ROAD FOR ABOUT .75-MILE AND VEER LEFT ON LALA ROAD.

Lala Road, which passes Kaua'i High School, is the back road down to **Nawiliwili Harbor**. For a good view of Nawiliwili Harbor, veer right just past the school and drive up to Kalapaki Memorial Park at the top of the hill.

AT THE BOTTOM OF THE HILL, **TURN LEFT,** AND GO SHORT DISTANCE AND PARK AT ANCHOR COVE SHOPPING CENTER OR NAWILIWILI BEACH PARK.

Nawiliwili Harbor is the main port for Kaua'i, both for glitzy cruise ships and get-down cargo freighters. A number of big gift shops cater to the wandering cruise ship passengers. Little do they know, that during World War II, on New Year's Eve 1941, this harbor was shelled 15 times by a Japanese submarine but sustained only slight damage, since most shells were duds. Economic downturns do more damage to these cruise-ship shops.

The **Kaua'i Marriott,** a world-class resort sitting above Kalapaki Bay, offers entertainment and Hawaiiana displays, including Prince Kuhio's vintage outrigger, *The Princess.* Both the lagoon at the resort's entrance and its poolside architecture are worth a visit. Then you can walk or drive out Nawiliwili Jetty for a view of the harbor, looking across the jetty to the Kuki'i Point light sitting at the edge of the golf course, and out to the mouth of the bay to Ninini Point Lighthouse.

CONTINUE, DRIVING AWAY FROM THE BAY ALONG THE HARBOR, ON WA'APA ROAD. **TURN LEFT** ON WILCOX ROAD, PASS MATSON. **TURN LEFT** AT THE BOAT HARBOR.

Nawiliwili Small Boat Harbor, a nook in the bay sitting below majestic Hoary Head Ridge, is an anchorage for cruising sailboats—offering an up-close look for those who have fantasized about this life-style. You can take a short walk out the harbor's jetty to heighten the effect, and also check out the Huleia Stream, a popular kayaking spot.

BACKTRACK AND **TURN LEFT** AND THEN **VEER LEFT** ON HALEMALU ROAD.

In a short distance you'll come to the turnout on the left for the Alakoko, or **Menehune Fish Pond,** a pool alongside the stream built by the Menehunes more than

Kauai Marriott

1,000 years ago. The Menehunes, several thousand workers, are said to have passed the stones from hand-to-hand from 25 miles away in Makaweli. The turnout also affords a view of the **Huleia National Wildlife Refuge**. The refuge is closed to people, but you can get a closer look by taking a side-trip down Haiku Road. You can also rent a kayak and see the refuge from the water.

Menehune Fish Pond

CONTINUE ON HALEMALU ROAD FOR SEVERAL MILES, TURN LEFT ON KIPU ROAD AND FOLLOW TO END.

At the end of Kipu Road is the **Rice Memorial**, erected by Japanese workers after the plantation owner's death. The memorial is at the start of Rice's Norfolk pine-lined drive, heading on private property to Hoary Head Ridge.

BACKTRACK ON KIPU ROAD AND TURN LEFT AT JUNCTION WITH HALEMALU ROAD, DRIVING .5-MILE OUT TO HWY. 50. TURN LEFT ON HWY. 50, GO 3 MILES AND TURN LEFT TOWARD POIPU BEACH ON HWY. 520.

Highway 520 is known as the **Tree Tunnel**, named for the shaded corridor formed by the eucalyptus trees that border the road. The trees were damaged by direct blasts from hurricanes—Iwa in 1982, and Iniki in 1992—but have recovered.

CONTINUE TO KOLOA ON HWY. 520. TURN LEFT AT STOP SIGN AND THEN TURN RIGHT ON WELIWELI ROAD.

Koloa Town

Koloa, which means "long cane," was the bustling center of Kaua'i from when the first sugar mill was built here in 1835 to the later part of that century. An early mission was established here also, in 1835, by the Gulick family. Today, Koloa's town square and shops make it one of the better places on the island to walk around amid fragments of another time. Grab a cone and get lost in the small historical courtyard or stop at the Snack Shop outdoor

Koloa Snack Shop walk-up window

counter for a local-style plate lunch of mahi-mahi, some Portugese soup, or a hot-off-the-grill teriyaki burger. Poke around the back streets, since there's more than meets the eye here.

CONTINUE ON WELIWELI ROAD.

Note a right turn for **St. Raphael's Catholic Church**, a short distance off the road. St. Raphael's is the oldest Catholic Church on Kaua'i, built in 1854.

CONTINUE ON WELIWELI, FOLLOWING SIGNS FOR POIPU—TURN RIGHT ON ALA KINAIKI, THE BYPASS ROAD.

Just as you near the bottom of the grade, look to your left for a glimpse of the crater, called **Pu'u Wanawana**, left by the island's last volcanic activity. Only a few lava spires stick up from cacti and brush.

TURN LEFT AT STOP SIGN

On your right will be the **Grand Hyatt Kaua'i**, one of the world's best tropical resorts, and definitely worth a walk-through and perhaps a lunch or beverage at the Ilima Terrace restaurant. The resort is situated on **Shipwreck Beach**, even though the wrecks are now gone.

Grand Hyatt lagoon pool

CONTINUE PAST HYATT ON WELIWELI ROAD. ROAD BECOMES DIRT, BUT GRADED. PASS ROAD TO STABLES, AND FOLLOW SIGNS TO KAWAILOA BAY. IF YOU DON'T

Koloa Sugar Mill

WANT TO DRIVE ON DIRT ROADS, OR WANT TO SPEND TIME ELSEWHERE, SKIP TO BACKTRACK BELOW.

Mahaulepu Beach at Kawailoa Bay was the site of a 13th century battle in which a Kauaian king outfoxed an invading armada of ships led by a king from the Big Island, who had already subjugated the rest of Hawai'i. This was 400 years before Kamehameha the Great failed twice to invade the island with consolidated forces. From Mahaulepu are rugged seascapes and a view of the other side of Hoary Head Ridge—which you drive past on Kipu Road.

For a side-trip from the gated entrance to Kawailoa Bay, go straight on the cane road to the **Koloa Mill**, on the site of the original mill of 1835. Sugar production ceased in the late 1990s, and tropical foliage is creeping up the sprawling structure. (This road may be restricted.)

BACKTRACK TO THE HYATT. CONTINUE TO STOP SIGN ON WELIWELI ROAD AND TURN LEFT ON PE'E ROAD. PE'E ROAD CONNECTS WITH HO'ONE ROAD.

Pe'e Road takes you over a bluff, through beachside condos and homes and down to **Brennecke's Beach**, a popular surfing spot next **Poipu Beach County Park**. You can walk several sandy coves of Poipu, a sunny beach fronted by resorts. The park is the site for various weekend cultural events and fairs.

CONTINUE ON HO'ONE ROAD AND TURN RIGHT AT BEACH PARK ON HO'OWILI ROAD. THEN TURN LEFT AT STOP SIGN ON POIPU ROAD.

Mahaulepu

Poipu Road bypasses the resorts, but is next to **Poipu Village**, a shopping mall with well known eateries (Roy's, Keoki's) and the site of a free Tahitian hula show, normally Tuesdays and Thursdays at 5. To get a look at Poipu resorts, turn past the village toward the Sheraton on Kapili Road. Kapili Road quickly joins

Ho'onani Road, at the **Sheraton**. Also worth seeing are the **Moir Gardens** at the Outrigger Kiahuna Plantation across from the Sheraton. Going away from the Sheraton on Ho'onani—or to your right as you come down—in about .5-mile you come to Koloa Landing at Whalers Cove. This little cove was in the glory, gory days of whaling the third most-used port in Hawai'i, behind only Honolulu and Lahaina.

Poipu Beach

CONTINUE ON POIPU ROAD, TURN LEFT ON THE ROUNDABOUT TOWARD SPOUTING HORN ON LAWAI ROAD.

In less than a mile on Lawai Road, you come to **Prince Kuhio Park**, with its monument marking the 1871 birthplace of the prince who was the Territory of Hawai'i's congressional delegate until 1922. The park features remains of a home site and heiau. Not far beyond Kuhio Park, on your right, is the visitors center for the **National Tropical Botanical Garden**. At the center are a gift shop and interpretive displays, and also a self-guided walk of the center's gardens. The center is also where you sign up for tours of **Allerton Garden** and **McBryde Garden**. The nearby gardens, once the favorite of Queen Emma, are now devoted to horticultural research and saving tropical plants.

Across the street from the visitors center is **Spouting Horn**, where wave-pressurized sea foam shoots geyser-like into the air from a hole in the lava reef. The gushing white water is accompanied by the plaintive groan of escaping air.

BACKTRACK ON LAWAI ROAD, TURN LEFT IN THE ROUNDABOUT ON ALA KA-LANIKAUMAKI RD. A SHORT DISTANCE.

Kukuiula Village offers 50 circa-2009 specialty shops and restaurants designed to be like an old sugar cane town. Touristy, yes, but they pulled it off. Dining ranges from Bubba's Burgers to gourmet Merriman's, as well as island-organic **Living Foods**. A courtyard curves through palms and gardens of heliconia, ferns, and bananas. Tommy Bahama, Quiksilver, and art galleries add to a tropical shopping experience.

McBryde Garden

CONTINUE UP ALA KALANIKAUMAKI RD. AND THEN TURN LEFT ON HWY 530, WHICH IS KOLOA ROAD.

Allerton Gardens

Koloa Road takes you up through pastoral **Lawai Valley**, flanking the grounds of the tropical gardens. At the junction with Highway 50, on the right, at Highway 50 is **Hawaiian Trading Post**, a longtime souvenir shop known for its large collection of museum-quality Niʻihau shell necklaces—the best deal in Hawaii.

TURN LEFT ON HIGHWAY 50

Immediatley on your left is small Wawae Road, entrance to the **88 Holy Places of Kobo Daishi**, a revered Buddhist shrine. Drive in and park at a gate for the Lawai International Center. The shrines are just beyond the gate, to your right. Each minature shrine is named for a Buddhist saint, and under each are sacred sands brought from the original 88 Holy Places in Japan, which date back a thousand years. The number 88 signifies the 88 sins committed by man, and it is believed that pilgrims worshiping here will be released from the sins. Might as well give it a try. Please tred lightly at this place of worship. Just past the shrines on Highway 50 is another spiritual place. Heads up and turn right near mm11 at Anuhea Place. Drive in up the hill to see the low-tech factory that cooks **Kukui jams**, made from guava and other tropical fruits. Inside (tours are unofficial, so ask someone) is the sacred spot where Jimmy the Jar Man tightened lids for 25 years.

CONTINUE ON HIGHWAY 50, 2 MILES TO KALAHEO. TURN LEFT AT LIGHT ON PAPALINA ROAD. CONTINUE ON PAPALINA 1 MILE AND TURN RIGHT ON PUʻU ROAD AND ENTER KUKUI-OLONO PARK.

From the pavilion on the large knoll in **Kukuiolono Park** is a commanding view of the south and west coasts, as well as of Niʻihau offshore and the Lawai Valley sweeping below. On the grounds are small Japanese and Hawaiian gardens, as well as a collection of stones carved on by the Menehunes. Kukui-olono—which means "Lono's

88 Holy Places of Kobo Daishi

light," after the god of peace and fertility—was once the site of several heiaus and later the estate of sugar magnate Walter McBryde. McBryde, who is buried here, beautified the grounds in honor of his mother.

BACKTRACK TO HWY. 50. TURN LEFT ON HWY. 50. PASS THROUGH KALAHEO.CONTINUE ON HWY. 50, PASSING THE JUNCTION WITH HWY. 540, FOR 2 MILES. STOP AT HANAPEPE OVERLOOK.

Hanapepe Overlook is a preview for the beginning of Tour Four. From the rim of the canyon is a view of the lush river agricultural fields hemmed by red-and-green cliffs. The acreage across the highway from the overlook, now a coffee orchard, has a history of its own. In 1824, the last battle on Kaua'i took place here, a failed revolt led by Prince Humehume, the son of Kaua'i's last king—or ali'i. Prince Humehume would not accept his father's treaty with Kamehameha's forces.

CONTINUE DOWN HWY. 50. TURN LEFT BEFORE PORT ALLEN ON HWY. 540, WHICH IS HALEWILI ROAD. CONTINUE 1.5 MILES ON HWY. 540 TO KAUA'I COFFEE MU-SEUM ON RIGHT.

In addition to offering free samples of the local brew, **Kaua'i Coffee Visitors Center and Museum** exhibits plantation artifacts and shows a video detailing coffee production from the tree to the mug. In recent years, the Alexander & Baldwin sugar cane fields have been converted

Kukuilono Park entrance, Kauai Coffee, Hanapepe

to the beans, and Kaua'i now surpasses Kona as the largest coffee grower in the islands. You can work off the coffee high by taking a self-guided tour on a paved path next to the center.

CONTINUE UP HWY. 540 BACK TOWARD HWY. 50 AT KALAHEO.

To your right as you head up Highway 540 is **Numila**, or "New Mill," with its row of classic sugar shacks. On the coast below Numila, which is private property, are two ancient fishing shrines and Nomilu Pond, a crater filled with brackish green seawater, where the fire goddess Pele made her last attempt to make a home on Kaua'i before leaving for the Big Island.

TURN RIGHT AT HWY. 50, HEADING BACK TOWARD START OF TOUR.

Kilohana Plantation

Just after passing Kipu Road, look on the right for **Kaua'i Nursery & Landscaping**. Though set up to service landscapers, the nursery's many acres include a huge covered area (great rainy day stop) that is one of Kaua'i's best places to commune with thousands of exotic and native plants and trees. Take your own free botanical tour. The nursery is certified to ship orchids and varities of native plants.

A little farther on the highway—after passing the community college —you'll want to check out **Kilohana Plantation Estate**, one of the top attractions in Kaua'i. Built in the 1930s, Kilohana is a 16,000-square-foot Tudor mansion, once home to the island's prominent Wilcox family. Wagon tours are available around the estate's 35 acres of manicured gardens and cane fields. Inside are top-rated Gaylord's restaurant, fine art shops, locally crafted giftware, and history exhibits. A popular Sunday buffet features a history talk. In 2007, Kilohana launched its **Kaua'i Plantation Railway**, a tour of surrounding agriculture fields aboard beautiful mahongany cars that are exact replicas of King David Kalakaua's Oahu Railroad. Kids will love the stop to feed wild pigs.

DRIVING TOUR TWO

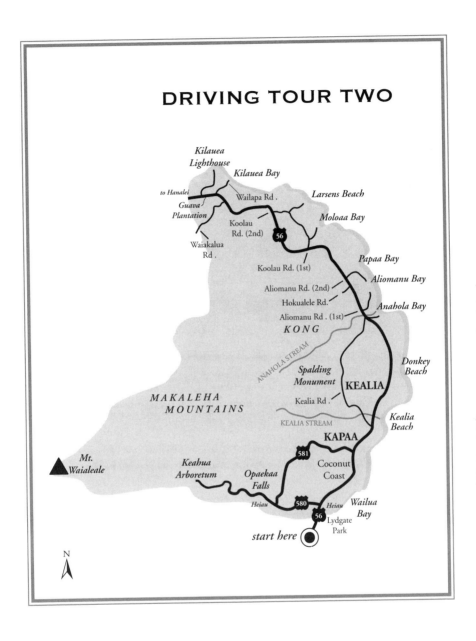

TOUR Two

Heiaus of Wailua Bay, Opaeka'a Falls, Kamokila Village, Keahua Arboretum, Kapa'a Town, Royal Coconut Coast, Sleeping Giant, Kong and Anahola Mountains, Larsens Beach, and Kilauea Lighthouse and Wildlife Refuge. A tour that blends scenery with shops, and beachcombing with resort beaches.

START DRIVING FROM LIHUE TOWARD WAILUA ON HWY. 56. TURN RIGHT ON LEHO DRIVE, BEFORE REACHING WAILUA RIVER. FOLLOW SIGNS TO LYDGATE PARK.

The mouth of the **Wailua River**, at today's **Lydgate Park**, is the cradle of Hawaiian civilization, where the royal ali'i built the first of seven sacred heiaus that led from here inland, following the Wailua River up to its source at Mount Waialeale. At a site on the grassy slope up from the river mouth are the remains of Hikina'akala Heiau. This area was also the site of **Hauola City of Refuge**, where miscreants and vanquished enemies could do time or escape punishment for having violated the kapu.

CONTINUE, TAKING LEHO ROAD OUT TO HWY. 56. TURN RIGHT ON HWY. 56, AND TURN LEFT IMMEDIATELY TOWARD SMITHS TROPICAL PARADISE.

Across Highway 56 from the resort is the largely intact, but hard-to-find, **Malae Heiau**. **Smiths Tropical Paradise** features luau hula shows and its own (excellent) tropical garden, and nearby are boat rides to **Fern Grotto** up the Wailua River. The genuine, family-run gardens are one of Hawaii's top attractions and best tourist values. At Wailua State Park Marina is a postcard view of the river and Sleeping Giant.

BACKTRACK AND TURN LEFT ON HWY. 56, CROSS RIVER AND TURN LEFT ON HWY. 580, WHICH IS KUAMO'O ROAD. CONTINUE .25-MILE AND PARK ON LEFT AT WAILUA RIVER STATE PARK POLIAHU AREA.

Smith's Tropocal Paradise

Located here are **Pohaku Hoʻoanau— Royal Birthstones**—on which the after-birth of royal babies were ceremoniously placed. The attributes of the animal which ate the afterbirth foretold the fortune of the child. This was also the site of the third heiau from the sea, Holoholoku Heiau, said to be used for human sacri-fices. Across the street is another king's sacred site—the now-defunct **Coco Palms Resort**, where Elvis filmed *Blue Hawaii*. The Coco Palms will be remembered by many Kauaʻi visitors for its nightly torch-lighting ceremony, enacted to the sound of drum beats and an exotic narration. The

Coco Palms lagoon

lagoon predates the resort, built for Queen Emma in the 1800s. Behind the resort is the **Royal Coconut Grove**, for which this area is also well-known. The resort was closed by Hurricane Iniki in 1992, and plans to rebuild have floundered.

CONTINUE UP HWY. 580.

In less than 2 miles, look on the left for **Poliahu Heiau**, formerly the residence of kings—the aliʻi. The Bell Stone, a short walk down a nearby trail, was used to ring in a royal birth. Great views of the river are to be had from this heiau.

CONTINUE UP HWY. 580.

Opaekaʻa Falls

On the right not far from the heiau is **Opaekaʻa Falls**, only 40 feet in height, but with a thunderous flow, especially during storms. Be sure to take the crosswalk to the other side of the highway to catch a pan-orama of the confuence of the Wailua River. Just beyond the falls on the highway, a steep road veers to the left to **Kamokila Village**, a recreated folk village showing the ancient Ha-waiian way of life. The riverside village, once a set for the movie *Outbreak*, is a quick-take on the ancient Hawaiian ways. Admission is cheap. Their tranquil docks are a good place to rent kayaks for a quick paddle. For different cultural respite, drive farther up the road to the **Kauaʻi Hindu Monastery** (turn left near mm. 4.5 on Kaholalele Road).

Keahua Arboretum

CONTINUE up Hwy. 580 for 5 miles, passing the junction with Hwy. 581, to END OF ROAD at Keahua Arboretum. To bypass the arboretum, turn right on Hwy. 581, and skip paragraph below.

A spillway marks the end of the road for most rental car drivers, and to take a short walk around the **Keahua Forestry Arboretum** you may have to get your feet wet. If the water is low, drive across the spillway and park. The nearby University of Hawai'i station has set up an educational walk among native and exotic trees. The arboretum is also the taking-off point for a number of hikes, including one toward the Mount Waialeale basin.

BACKTRACK on Hwy. 580. TURN LEFT on Hwy. 581, which is Kamalu Road.

The wide, green valley above the sea was where royal families made their homes and cultivated crops. This stretch takes you along the mountain-side of the Sleeping Giant, so readily visible from Kapa'a and many places on the island. The **Sleeping Giant** is part of **Nounou Forest Reserve**, featuring a wide variety of species planted in the 1930s.

CONTINUE on Hwy. 581 and TURN RIGHT on Olohena Road, which is a continuation of Hwy. 581. CONTINUE on Olohena to Kapa'a. PARK before reaching stoplight.

Kapa'a coastal bike path

Funky **Kapaʻa Town** is the capital of local-style living, a seamless blend of Kauaʻi's ethnic groups in a beachside community that is part falling-down and part brand new, and all local kine. Kapaʻa is conveniently located, but most people live here for the coral-and-coconut coast and the aloha spirit. Kapaʻa was once the pineapple center of the island and fell on hard times when the industry subsided in the mid-1900s. Several beach parks border cottages along the coast, and the town's triangular

Kapaʻa police station

"downtown" section. You'll discover a lot just poking around. Hemp kids hang around for the veggie stuff at Mermaids Cafe. To tour the town —and Kapaʻa's fabulous coast bike path—on two wheels, head for Coconut Coasters, a premier bike shop.

CONTINUE TO HWY. 56. TURN LEFT ON HWY. 56, AND CONTINUE TO KEALIA.

In 1877, the hills around **Kealia** were planted in sugar cane by Captain James Makeʻe. The cane road along the coast from the popular surfer's and stroller's beach also leads to a pier, used when Kapaʻa's pineapple cannery was thriving. Just beyond the pier on the dirt road is Donkey Beach. Just past the beach on the highway, turn right on Kamole Road and drive to the end for the ultimate scenic view.

TURN LEFT ON KEALIA ROAD, ACROSS FROM MAIN GATE AT KEALIA BEACH.

Keep to your right on Kealia Road. On Sundays, the open field becomes an artisans' market, with plenty of island fruit and veggies. Hours normally are 11 to 4. Next, the road climbs to the left , heading toward the two rows of tall Norfolk pines at **Spalding Monument**. The stone edifice marks the former estate of Colonel Zephaniah Spalding, son-in-law of Makeʻe, who eventually sold most of the properties to Lihue Plantation.

TURN RIGHT AT SPALDING MONUMENT.

This portion takes you on an up-close look of **Kong**, a.k.a. Kalalea, the sharp peak in the

Kong

Anahola Mountains. On top of Kong is a ruined heiau of three terraces. At the base of Kong was the **Hole in the Mountain**, which, legends told, was formed when a visiting king from the Big Island threw his spear clean through the ridge. After centuries as a landmark, the opening almost completely caved in during the late 1990s.

Anahola Beach Park   CONTINUE DOWN KEALIA ROAD TO HWY. 56. TURN LEFT ON HWY. 56 AND TURN RIGHT IMMEDIATELY ON ANAHOLA ROAD. CONTINUE .25-MILE ON ANAHOLA ROAD AND VEER LEFT AT BEACH PARK ON KAMANE ROAD.

The valley around **Anahola** was designated by the Land Act of 1895 as a settlement in which Hawaiians could acquire lands on 999-year leases. The Act was augmented in 1956 by the Hawaiian Homelands project, which allowed Hawaiians to finance homes on formerly government-leased sugar cane fields.

BACKTRACK TO HWY. 56 AND TURN RIGHT. CROSS OVER BRIDGE, PASSING STORE AND POST OFFICE AND TURN RIGHT ON ALIOMANU ROAD (FIRST). FOLLOW ALIOMANU DOWN TO THE RIVER MOUTH.

Anahola Bay, all of it a beach park, is split in two by the **Anahola Stream**—you can look across the bay to the other side of the park. Aliomanu Bay is to your left as you face the water. When you get back out to the highway, follow your nose across the street to the photogenic Ahahola Baptist Church (formerly Hongwanji Mission). The Anahola Mountains provide the scenic backdrop.

CONTINUE ON NORTH HWY. 56 TO JUST PAST MILE MARKER 14 AND TURN LEFT ON HOKUALELE ROAD.

This road, a dead end after less than one mile, gets you as close to **Kong** as you can get in a car. Along the way, you may see self-serve stands for gardenias and other flowers, as well as local produce.

BACKTRACK ON HOKUALELE ROAD TO HWY. 56 AND TURN LEFT. CONTINUE ON HWY. 56 AND TURN RIGHT ON

Moloa'a Bay

KOʻOLAU ROAD (FIRST), WHICH IS PAST MILE MARKER 16. AFTER ABOUT 2 MILES ON KOʻOLAU, **TURN RIGHT** ON MOLOAʻA ROAD. FOLLOW MOLOAʻA ABOUT 1 MILE DOWN TO BAY.

On the left before Koʻolau Road are roadside stands offering local produce, leis, and perhaps huli huli chicken fresh off the grill. At the highway turnoff to Koʻolau Road is Moloaʻa Sunrise Fruit Stand, where you can indulge in one of their smoothies while enjoying and open-air look at the mountains. Beyond the fruit stand, the paved road takes you down a lush tropical valley to scenic **Moloaʻa Bay**—made only slightly less so by a few houses that crowd the shore. Fans of *Gilligan's Island* will like to know the television program was shot here.

Anahola

Moloaʻa, meaning "tangled roots," was the island's main region for producing tapa, the paperlike cloth made from mulberry bushes.

BACKTRACK ON MOLOAʻA ROAD AND **TURN RIGHT** ON KOʻOLAU ROAD. CONTINUE ON KOʻOLAU A LITTLE MORE THAN ONE MILE AND **TURN SHARPLY RIGHT** AT WHITE BEACH ACCESS POLE.

This road takes you one mile out to **Larsens Beach**, a pristine coral-reef beach perfect for strolling. You look down on the beach from the parking lot, an easy .25-mile walk. But don't forget to look seaward: whales and dolphins have been known to breach offshore, and seabirds, such as albatrosses and tropicbirds, might be winging about.

Larsen's Beach

BACKTRACK TO KOʻOLAU ROAD, **TURN RIGHT**, AND CONTINUE TO HWY. 56. **TURN RIGHT** ON HWY. 56 AND CONTINUE TO MILE MARKER 21 AND **TURN LEFT** ON WAIAKALUA ROAD.

This one-mile dead-end road is part of **Kilauea Farms**. Many of the island's organic fruit and vegetable growers reside up this pastoral drive. Waiakalua Road gives you a look at the open, grassy upslopes along this part of Kauaʻi.

Na Aina Kai BotanicalGardens, Christ Memorial Episcopal Church

BACKTRACK TO HWY. 56 AND TURN LEFT. CONTINUE ON HWY. 56 AND TURN RIGHT ON WAILAPA ROAD, WHICH IS BEFORE YOU GET TO MILE MARKER 22. GO ALMOST .5-MILE AND VEER LEFT, DOWN A DIRT ROAD THAT ENDS AFTER .5-MILE.

Kilauea Bay has a large sandy beach and scenic stream, which borders the bluffs of the Kilauea Wildlife Refuge. At the end of Wailapa Road are the fanciful grounds of the Na Aina Kai botanical gardens—a must for green-thumbers and families with kids, who will like the village re-creation. Guided tours whiz through arboretum gardens, highlighted by a forest of bronze statues in lifelike settings.

BACKTRACK TO HWY. 56 AND TURN RIGHT. AT MM22.5 TURN LEFT ON KUAWA ROAD.

At the end of Kuawa Road is **Common Ground** an organic garden, restaurant, and gathering place for developing sustainable living concepts on Kauai. Founder Chris Jaeb took over the acreage of the former Guava Kai Plantation in 2006. Tours are offered, and you are also free to walk paths through the garden and around a large pond.

Mokuaeae Island

BACKTRACK TO HWY. 56 AND TURN-LEFT. NEAR MM23 TURN RIGHT TOWARD KILAUEA.

Kilauea was shaken by the 1971 closure of the Kilauea Sugar Mill, but has since reinvented itself as a tourist stopover and bedroom community for both the north shore and Kapa'a. Helping attract tourists is **Christ Memorial Episcopal Church**—located on Kolo Road as you make the left turn toward the lighthouse on Kilauea Road—a small edifice built of lava rock and featuring detailed stained-glass windows. Just down Kolo from this church is St. Sylvester's Church, an octagonal building of lava rock, glass and wood, whose walls are adorned with frescoes by Jean Charlot.

Nene

TURN LEFT ON KILAUEA ROAD AND CONTINUE TWO MILES TO END, AT LIGHTHOUSE.

On the way to the lighthouse, browsers will want to stop at **Kong Lung**, a classy gift store. The shopping area also has an upscale restaurant and a bakery cafe. In back, Island Soap & Candle Works is a particularly illuminating stop. **Kilauea Natonal Wildlife Refuge and Lighthouse** is the northern-most part of the populated Hawaiian Islands. This is one of Hawaii's top attractions. From the tip of the bluff you look down on tiny, wave-washed Mokuaeae Island. Among the birds soaring and flitting about are Laysan albatrosses, the B-1 bombers of the bird world, able to fly thousands of miles

over oceans; great frigatebirds, with wingspans of seven-to-eight feet; tropicbirds; nene, or Hawaiian goose, the state bird; plovers; red-footed boobies; and wedge-tailed shearwaters, which nest around the visitor's center near the lighthouse. A small admission is charged. The **lighthouse** was built in 1913, featuring a French-made, 12-foot high Fresnel lens, the tallest in the world. The lens was replaced by a light beacon in 1974, and four years later the lighthouse was placed on the National Register of Historic Places.

BACKTRACK ON HWY. 56 AND TURN LEFT, RETURNING TO WAILUA. *Note: Hwy. 56 at Kilauea is where Tour Two connects with Tour Three.*
A mile or two past Kapa'a is **Kaua'i Village** on your right noted by the green Safeway and whale

Laysan albatross and chick

murals. If you're hungry, try the very organic Papaya's, where you can hang with the health food set. For an afternoon buzz, there's a Starbuck's. A little farther down the highway from the village on the left is the **Coconut Marketplace**. Surrounding an inside square are a number of places to find a Kauai souvenir for someone waiting back home or chill out with a creamy double-scooped Lappert's cone. The Marketplace also has free hula shows, where aloha-shirted onlookers are snagged to demonstrate their Polynesian wiggles. Art lovers will want to

Kapa'a, artist Fred Tangalin, hula at the Marketplace

stop by **Ship Store Galleries,** featuring the work of a host of other local artists. If leaving Wailua for Lihue, keep a mauka eye peeled for **Bambulei**—it's before reaching the Coco Palms. The shop is a restored plantation house that is chockablock with vintage and aloha wear, jewelry, and antiques, all uniting to say, *Bambulei!* (C'mon, say it.) In the same jungled nook is **Cafe Coco**, an island-hip bistro where local musicians may arrive incognito to serenade the moonlight.

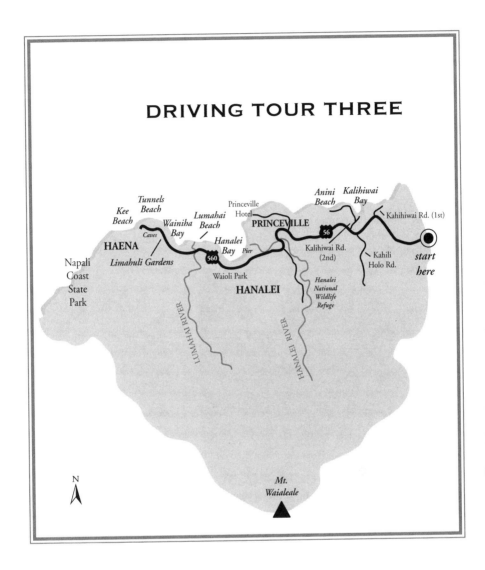

DRIVING TOUR THREE

Tunnels
Beach

Kee
Beach

Wainiha
Bay

Caves

Lumahai
Beach

Princeville
Hotel

Anini
Beach

Kalihiwai
Bay

Kahihiwai Rd. (1st)

PRINCEVILLE

56

Hanalei
Bay

HAENA

Limahuli Gardens

Pier

Kalihiwai Rd.
(2nd)

Kahili
Holo Rd.

*start
here*

Napali
Coast
State
Park

Waioli Park

HANALEI

Hanalei
National
Wildlife
Refuge

LUMAHAI RIVER

HANALEI RIVER

N

Mt.
Waialeale

TOUR *Three*

Anini Beach, Kalihiwai Bay, Princeville, Hanalei Town and Wildlife Refuge, caves, hula temple, and all the beaches along the tropical paradise of the north coast. Start early, especially on sunny days, when road's end attracts many visitors.

START ON HWY. 56 IN KILAUEA AND PROCEED TOWARD HANALEI. AFTER MILE MARKER 24, TURN LEFT ON KAHILIHOLO ROAD.

Get the tour started right with a banana-mango smoothie (eats like ice cream) at **Banana Joe's**, which is on the left just past Kilauea. Behind Joe's is is **Garden Ponds Nursery**, home to floating ecosystems in a huge array large pots. Next door is a tropical putt-putt golf course. Then head up **Kahiliholo Road** a few miles through the "Beverly Hills of Kaua'i," with rolling gardens separating opulent estates, and some more

modest homes. Among local notables are Pearce Brosnon, Bette Midler, and Ben Stiller. The main attraction in these uplands are the trail rides at **Silver Falls Ranch** in lush forests below Kalihiwai Ridge.

BACKTRACK ON KAHILI-HOLO ROAD TO HWY. 56 AND TURN LEFT. CONTINUE ON HWY. 56, CROSSING BRIDGE, AND TURN RIGHT ON KALIHIWAI ROAD (SECOND), ON THE UPHILL PAST MILE MARKER 25. VEER RIGHT AT FIRST OPPORTUNITY AND FOLLOW ROAD ABOUT 1 MILE DOWN TO THE END.

Kalihiwai Bay is a locals' beach, for picnicking and surfing. To access the beach park, across the river, you turn on Kalihiwai Road (first), which is just past Kilauea. Kalihiwai Bay was twice devastated by tidal waves, in 1946 and 1957. This bay historically was a favorite spot for a hukilau—when people of the ohana would gather and haul in a huge fishing net, reaping a bounty of fish, while shouting in unison, "Huki!"

Silver Falls Ranch, Kalihiwai Bay

Anini Beach

BACKTRACK ON THE ROAD. **TURN RIGHT** BEFORE THE HIGHWAY ON **ANINI ROAD** TO **ANINI BEACH PARK**.

Along **Anini Beach** is the longest coral reef in Hawai'i. Windsurfers, kite-boarders, snorkelers, campers, and even polo players enjoy the pleasant park space that borders a two-mile beach. You can spot old-timers on Kaua'i if they call this place "Wanini Beach," its name before the "W" fell off a highway sign that no one bothered to fix. When leaving Anini for Princeville, look on the right at a large turnout for the **Coconut Experience**, an excellent fruit stand set in a trailor with and awning. It's priced right and full of organic goodies from the north shore.

BACKTRACK OUT TO HWY. 56 AND **TURN RIGHT**. **CONTINUE** PAST MILE MARKER 27 AND **TURN RIGHT** ON KA HAKU ROAD, THE MAIN ENTRANCE TO PRINCEVILLE MARKED BY LARGE FOUNTAIN. **CONTINUE** ON MAIN ROAD FOR TWO MILES TO ST. REGIS PRINCEVILLE RESORT.

Both of Princeville's golf courses are championship quality, and the **St. Regis Princeville Resort**, with its splashy view of Hanalei Bay, Wainiha Pali, and the tip of Bali Hai, is rated among the world's top tropical resorts. Prior to becoming a manicured resort community, Princeville was a cattle ranch. Before that, in 1853, the lands were owned by British Resident Minister R.C. Wyllie. Wyllie, who made his fortune in Scotland in 1845, came here to find a new career as King Kamehameha IV's foreign minister, working for 20 years to get Hawai'i recognized a sovereign nation. But Wyllie's personal dream was

St. Regis Princeville Hotel

of a grand plantation on this bluff above Hanalei Bay to be named for Kamehameha's son, Albert—thus the name Princeville. Unfortunately, little Albert died at age four; Wyllie died three years later and the plantation was auctioned off in 1867.

Pu'u Poa Beach

Prior to being Wyllie's plantation, the Princeville bluff was the site of **Russian Fort Alexander**. An interpretive kiosk to the right of the hotel marks the spot, and provides an excellent viewpoint of Hanalei Bay and north coast. The Russians, under the leadership of Dr. Anton Schaffer, retreated here from Fort Elizabeth in Waimea after being banished by Kauaian chiefs. For several days they considered making a stand for the Russian Empire—Schaffer had proclaimed his country would claim Hawai'i at all cost—but they soon realized their predicament and left the islands for good.

BACKTRACK TO HWY. 56 AND TURN RIGHT. CONTINUE BEYOND THE PRINCEVILLE SHOPPING CENTER, TURN LEFT INTO THE HANALEI OVERLOOK.

The valley, like all such valleys with streams or rivers, was an ahupua'a—a division of land that provided the entire needs of a community. From this viewpoint, you can easily imagine how these fertile lands could be cultivated. Taro is the prominent crop today, taking over from rice. Across the street, the **Princeville Shopping Center** is dedicated mainly to local and touristcommerce. A few of the shops are worthy of a walk through, notably the whimsical **Magic Dragon Toy & Art Supply**.

CONTINUE ON HWY. 56 AND CROSS ONE-LANE BRIDGE OVER HANALEI RIVER. TURN LEFT IMMEDIATELY AFTER BRIDGE AND CONTINUE TWO MILES ON OHIKI ROAD. *Note: Hwy. 56 becomes Hwy. 560 after Princeville.*

Waterfowl and shorebirds streak over the taro fields as you drive

Hanalei Wildlife Refuge

Mission School of Waioli Hui'i Church

though **Hanalei National Wildlife Refuge**. About a mile in on your right is the restored (perhaps unsigned) Haraguchi Rice Mill, a remnant of large-scale rice production that took place alongside the taro from 1912 through the 1950s. During prohibition, bootleggers made a fiery spirit, called okolehao, from ti plants harvested in the hills above the mill.

BACKTRACK OUT TO HWY. 560 AND **TURN LEFT. CONTINUE** TO **HANALEI TOWN**. *Note: You may want to drive through to the end of the road and catch town on the rebound.*

You could easily spend the day—some people spend years—wandering around **Hanalei Town**, with its long bay, beachside bungalows, historic buildings, and quirky shops. **Hanalei Pier**, at **Black Pot Beach** near the river mouth, was the link to civilization and commerce after it was built in 1912, and later became a set piece for a number of Hollywood movies.

Several churches draw visitors, including St. William's Church, a longhouse-style building with sliding doors as sides, and St. Thomas Episcopal Church, of Asian design. But the town's postcard is green-shingled **Waioli Hui'ia Church**. Near Waioli church is

the **Waioli Mission House**, built in 1841. The mission was established several years earlier by Bostonians Abner and Lucy Wilcox. Take the short walk across the line to behold the mission's 'back yard,' one of the fairest views in Hawaii.

Rising inland from the town are the ridges of **Waioli Valley**, called the "birthplace of rainbows." Numerous waterfalls appear in the dark green walls after rains. Much of Hanalei's walk-around shopping charm lies at the base of this valley, with the **Hanalei Center** set in the old elementary school. (Though don't overlook the places on the way into town, especially Ola's for art glass and fine woodworking, and Kayak Kaua'i, which has lots of outdoor stuff,

Surfer swap meet, Hanalei Center

along with being ground-zero for north shore adventuring. Crystals & Gemstones, on Aku Road, has a real-deal, world-class collection.) At the Center, the Hanalei Surf Company buzzes to local tunes amid a breaking wave of surf wear and gear. But don't spend all your clamshells before heading out back to **Yellowfish Trading Company** to see its esoteric collectibles, and Havaiki, a trove of oceanic tribal art. In the center of the center is **Hanalei Coffee Roasters (Java Kai)**, where you can buy beans roasted on-site and embrace a coffee beverage amid the local hipsters. At **Ching Young Village** (across the street), you'll find good old Village Variety, crammed with cheap stuff and **Pedal 'n Paddle**, *the* place to go prior to getting wet, muddy, or sandy.

One of Hanalei's ultra-charms is **Ki Hoalu Slack Key Guitar**—in the **Hanalei Community Center**—where Doug and Sandy McMaster give low-key concerts and talk story, usually on Friday and Sunday afternoons; see *Resource Links,* page 242.

CONTINUE ON HWY. 560.

Leaving Hanalei, you cross Waioli Stream and pass **Waikoko Beach**, which forms the far side of the bay. Then around the point is **Lumahai Beach** and River, after mile marker 5. Lumahai is best known for its treacherous combers, able to snatch a stroller from the shore, and for being where Mitzi Gaynor wanted to "wash that man right out of her hair," in *South Pacific*. Prior to that, in the mid-1800s, Lumahai gained a reputation of being a spot where robbers would waylay travelers.

CONTINUE ON HWY. 560.

Lumahai Valley

At mile marker 7 is **Wainiha**—the town, valley and river. Spanning the river are quaint, one-lane bridges. Much of the island's power is generated from the perpetual cascades deep up the Wainiha Valley. The Wainiha Pali—cliffs—rise nearly 4,000 feet from the river valley. They appear to be a ridge, but in actuality the other side of the pali is the Alakai Swamp, resting on a horizontal plane at the same elevation as the top.

The last of the Kaua'i's Menehune, 65 of them, lived in Wainiha, according to a late 19th century U.S. Census. Even prior to the Menehune, the valley, according to legend, was also home to tiny people, refugees from the Lost Continent of Mu. The Hawaiians would try to lure them from the jungle with traps set with tasty foods, but the Mu people were too swift, taking the food and fleeing in the night. Some Hawaiian families currently living in Wainiha trace their heritage back several hundred years.

CONTINUE ON HWY. 560.

Haena Beach

Rounding the turn from Wainiha, past mile marker 8, you reach **Haena Beach Park** and **Tunnels Beach**, popular among campers and surfers, and also a premier snorkeling destination. From the beach are views of **Bali Hai Ridge**—correctly called **Makana** or "Fire Cliff." In pre-missionary times, specially trained men would hurl flaming logs from the summit to the sea, creating a shower of sparks that Kauaians would come to see, in canoes and on foot, from all parts of the island. The fire fall was not only for entertainment, but also to honor the sacred hula temple below.

On your left just past the spillway is **Maniniholo Dry Cave**, the end of a lava tube that extends several hundred yards under the cliff and finally, as a narrow opening, pokes out the top of the mountain. Legend tells that this cave was dug by Menehune, who used it to trap demigods who were stealing their fish. Beyond the dry cave, look to the mountains to spot Pohakuokane—the Rock of Kane—a large boulder sitting atop a rounded peak. It is said that when this rock falls, Kaua'i will sink beneath the sea. A sister rock, perched near the beach, was washed away in a tidal wave of 1946.

Haena Beach Park

CONTINUE ON HWY. 560.

On your left past mile 9 is **Limahuli Garden, a National Tropical Botanical Garden**, and one of the few spots on the north shore where you can get into one of the lush valleys. Limahuli specializes in native plants, providing a historical as well as horticultural experience. The garden tour is self-guided along stream terraces and hillside forests. Included is a plant booklet that alone is worth the price of admission.

On the left just beyond the garden entrance are **Waikapalae Wet Cave** and, a short hike up beyond the first cave, **Waikanaloa Wet Cave**. The volcano goddess Pele is said to have dug these caverns, in search of a fiery home for herself and her lover, Lohiau, but, alas, she came up wet, prompting her to flee Kaua'i and head south through the island chain. In the 19th century, Hawaiian boys would make sport of climbing the walls of the cave and diving 30 feet into its chilling waters.

Alula
Brighamia insignis
An endangered species native to Kaua'i and Ni'ihau presently being reintroduced into the protected wild habitat of Limahuli Garden

CONTINUE TO END OF HWY. 560 AT MILE MARKER 10.

The end of the road is better known as the beginning of the **Kalalau Trail**, a rugged path along 11 miles of the roadless Napali Coast. You can see down the coast from about .5-mile on the difficult trail—or by walking a short distance to your right down **Ke'e Beach**. In the winter, huge waves explode against the buttresses that stick out to the sea. During calm conditions, during the summer and also frequently in the winter, Ke'e is an excellent snorkeling pool.

Approach to Hankapiai Beach, Kalalau Trail

Napali

A short trail from Keʻe Beach leads to the **Kauluolaka Heiau, Lohiau's hula temple**. The sacred heiau, the passionate meeting place for Pele and her lover, Lohiau, is the only dancing platform in Hawaiʻi dating back to mythological times.

Among Hawaiians studying the ancient dance, this site was the equivalent of the most prestigious university. The best young pupils from Hawaiʻi came, camping nearby, and were taught the traditions, chants and dances of their ancient heritage. The graduation ceremony included a swim out the channel from Keʻe Beach, said to be guarded by a large shark.

The hula temple is in use today—treat it like a church. Just below the dance platform are the remaining ramparts of another heiau, Kaulupaoa Heiau, dedicated to seafaring and navigation.

Kauluolaka Hula Heiau

DRIVING TOUR FOUR

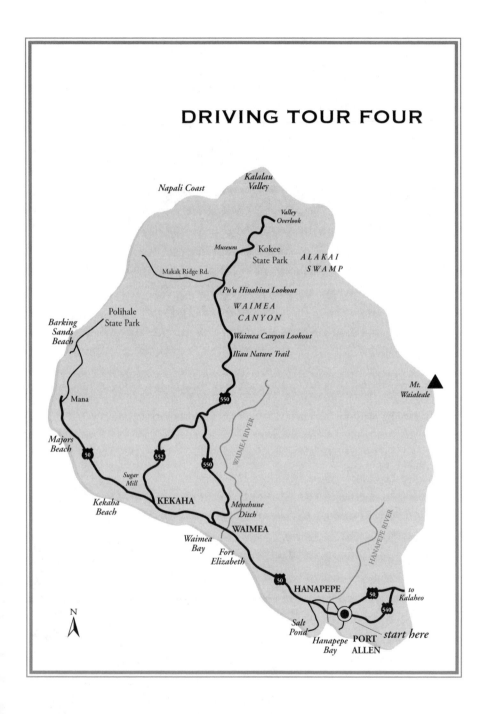

Kalalau Valley

Napali Coast

Valley Overlook

Museum

Kokee State Park

ALAKAI SWAMP

Makak Ridge Rd.

Pu'u Hinahina Lookout

WAIMEA CANYON

Polihale State Park

Barking Sands Beach

Waimea Canyon Lookout

Iliau Nature Trail

Mt. Waialeale

Mana

WAIMEA RIVER

Majors Beach

550

552

550

Sugar Mill

Kekaha Beach

KEKAHA

Menehune Ditch

WAIMEA

Waimea Bay

Fort Elizabeth

HANAPEPE RIVER

50

HANAPEPE

50

to Kalaheo

540

Salt Pond

Hanapepe Bay

PORT ALLEN

start here

N

TOUR *four*

Port Allen, Hanapepe and Waimea towns, Waimea Canyon, Koke'e State Park, Kalalau Valley overlook, Kekaha Beach and Barking Sands Beach. Take the Waimea Canyon portion on a clear day.

START AT SECOND JUNCTION OF HWYS. 50 AND 540. **TURN LEFT** TOWARD PORT ALLEN AT MILE MARKER 16/50 ON WAIALO ROAD. **CONTINUE** .5-MILE DOWN TO DOCK AREA.

Port Allen, on Hanapepe Bay, is Kaua'i's most active port for sportfishing, sightseeing and whale-watching excursions. Its breakwater and docks provide a glimpse of bustling harbor life, as does the small boat harbor down a road on the right from the larger dock. Napali Coast cruises, which used to begin in Hanalei, now depart from Port Allen. Some cruisers, like HoloHolo and Captain Andy's, take you offshore of **Ni'ihau**.

BACKTRACK OUT TO HWY. 50 AND **TURN LEFT.** AFTER A SHORT DISTANCE ON HWY. 50 **VEER RIGHT** TOWARD HANAPEPE ON HANAPEPE ROAD. **PARK** AFTER .5-MILE AT SWINGING BRIDGE.

Hanapepe, Kaua'i's "biggest little town," is known for its bougainvillea and an eclectic assemblage of old-style buildings, some being converted into galleries and shops, all strewn along the banks of the Hanapepe River. The town's historic markers tell the story. You'll want to take a walk across the **Swinging Bridge** and poke into a gallery or three. Hanapepe has a history that befits its Wild West look: In 1924, 20 people died here in a riot between police and striking sugar cane workers. And just up the road is where Prince Humehume, son of Kaua'i's last king, staged an unsuccessful revolt against the forces of Kamehameha the Great. If you want to get wild these days in Hanapepe, try Art Night (usually Fridays from sundown to maybe 9 p.m.) when the town is all prettied up. A hot dinner ticket is **Hanapepe Cafe**, which has its own gallery and sits besides one of the town's better art nooks, the **Dawn M. Traina Gallery**. Not far away is the

Robin McCoy Gallery and **Kama'aina Cabinets**, with koa tables. Across the street at the Banana Patch Studio you can watch them make colorful ceramics, and at **JJ Ohana** you can get a bead on reasonably priced Ni'ihau shell jewelry and lots of other stuff.

CONTINUE THROUGH HANAPEPE, CROSSING THE RIVER ON ONE-LANE BRIDGE AND REACHING HWY. 50. **TURN RIGHT** ON HWY. 50.

Hanapepe Town

On the way to Waimea Town are three side trips. The first is immediately after Hanapepe on your left, the turnoff on Hwy. 543 to **Salt Pond Beach Park.** This is a good snorkeling and picnicking spot you might want to try on the return leg of the tour. The park includes salt ponds, dating back to the 1700s— they may look like puddles,

Salt Pond Beach Park

but the salt was highly valued by seafaring vessels, and remains in use to this day.

At mile marker 19, turn makai on Kaumakani Avenue and you'll be transported immediately to main street of a 19th century sugar mill town a real one that leads to the former **Gay & Robinson Plantation.** The mill ran its last harvest in 2009, and they no longer offer tours, but you can catch a look at the plant from the end of the road. Ownership and use of the land is in limbo.

Gaye & Robinson Plantation

The third side trip, off Highway 50 after mile marker 22, is **Russian Fort Elizabeth Historical Park.** Due to its location, the fort is a popular attraction, but you'll have to use your imagination to see a fort amid the remnants, dating from 1817. The Russians, along with the Americans, established a trading presence on Kaua'i during the early 1800s. But, not long after the fort was built, Kauaian chiefs decided to boot the Russians from the island, distrusting them and feeling the Yankees were the stronger ally.

CONTINUE ON HWY. 50 TO WAIMEA TOWN.

Along the weathered streets of **Waimea Town** are layers of the past that echo a diverse history. Captain James Cook made the first European landing here in 1778, and for nearly the next century, Waimea was the capital of Kauaʻi—a favorite harbor and provisioning port for early whalers and traders. The red-dirt fields around town were well-suited for crops and livestock, in great demand by seafarers. The destructive sandalwood trade of the early 1800s, Hawaii's first commerce with the outside world, was also centered here.

In the 1820s, the first missionaries landed in Waimea, not branching out to other parts of the island until 1835, and Waimea then was the major settlement for whites. In 1850, the town was named the port of entry for all foreign ships, on par with Honolulu. Japanese, Chinese and Portuguese grew rice and taro in surrounding fields, their presence evidenced by the churches tucked away on back streets. These

Captain Cook Monument, Waimea

historical strands, and other local lore, is on display at the drably-named-but-really-cool **West Kauaʻi Technology & Visitor Center** (at the Highway 550 junction); they offer walking tours and talk story. On the way out of town are the **Waimea Plantation Cottages** and the Waimea Sugar Museum, which is located inside the lobby of the resort. Long before any of this, Waimea was a principal settlement for the Menehunes, who built heiaus and an ambitious water-conveyance ditch, extending 25 miles up the canyon. You can drive one mile up **Menehune Road** to see a fragment of the ditch and walk a footbridge that spans the river.

Waimea Plantation Cottages

CONTINUE THROUGH WAIMEA TOWN ON HWY. 50 AND **TURN RIGHT** TOWARD WAIMEA CANYON ON HWY. 550, JUST AT THE EDGE OF TOWN.

Views of the canyon begin not long after starting up highway 550, and you could spend many days exploring the trails and viewpoints along the way to the top. On the other hand, for the first-time visitor to the "Grand Canyon of the Pacific," a drive to the top can deliver what seems like weeks' worth of experience in a few

hours. **Waimea Canyon** is an eroded gorge of the **Alakai Swamp**—the swamp itself is the transition of a 60-square-mile ancient caldera that was Hawai'i's origin and which lies at almost 4,000 foot elevation on the side of the canyon opposite the road. The canyon is about one-mile wide, ten-miles long, and 3,700-feet deep, with other canyons branching off it. Several developed lookouts adorn the road, part of **Waimea Canyon State Park**. The first, after mile marker 7, is the **Kukui Lookout**, which features a nature walk. After mile marker 10 look for **Waimea Canyon Lookout** and after mile marker 13 look for **Pu'u Hinahina Lookout**, which inncludes another viewing area for **Ni'ihau**

Kalalau Valley, Alakai Swamp

island. Note also, as you drive this stretch, on your left are a series of trails that head out onto ridges of the west Napali.

TURN LEFT ON MAKAHA RIDGE ROAD, JUST PAST PU'U HINAHINA LOOKOUT, BEFORE MILE MARKER 14.

This road takes you four miles out on **Makaha Ridge**, where Kaua'i's strongest winds were recorded during Hurricane Iniki—227 mph. Although a military installation prevents you from getting to the very end, you do get looks at steep valleys and ridges to either side on this lesser-known part of the Napali Coast.

BACKTRACK OUT TO HWY. 550 AND **TURN LEFT. CONTINUE** TO KOKE'E STATE PARK MUSEUM.

The boundary for **Koke'e State Park** is just after Makaha Ridge Road, and where Halemanu Valley Trailhead offers a series of trails to canyon viewpoints. **Koke'e Natural History Museum**, at the edge of the park's spacious lawn and towering trees, is a wealth of information about the natural and cultural history of the area. No trip to the canyon should exclude a stop here. Then wade your way through the wild chickens to the **Koke'e Lodge** next door, for a restful lunch and a browse of their giftstore. Short and long trails network the park. Some trails, east of the park, are forested and others, the Nualolo and Awa'awapuhi west of the park, lead out to spiny ridges far above the wild shores of Napali Coast State Park. Many Kauaians have cabins in the Koke'e area, and church and community organizations maintain camps along the many unpaved roads.

Kokee Museum

CONTINUE UP HWY. 550

Two miles beyond Koke'e's lawn area is **Kalalau Lookout**, a viewpoint of the fabled valley, 4,000 feet below steeply diving, rippling green walls. As recently as the early 1900s, 500 Hawaiians lived in the valley. Garden terraces rise above the beach. Now only adventuresome backpackers make the 11-mile hike down the Kalalau Trail, that begins at Ke'e Beach on the north shore. Kalalau means "the straying."

A mile beyond this first lookout is **Pu'uokila Lookout**, providing another don't-miss view of the valley. Listen and watch for goats on tangled perches of the valley's

Kokee Museum, Napali Coast

Ni'ihau shoreline

bowl. The **Pihea Trail** begins at this overlook, providing not only a walk along the valley rim, but also entrance to the **Alakai Swamp** and, at the edge of the swamp, a high-altitude look from the Wainiha Pali down to Hanalei Bay—a hike more than any other that underscores the island's peculiar and spectacular topography.

BACKTRACK DOWN HWY. 550. CONTINUE PAST MILE MARKER 7 AND VEER RIGHT ON HWY. 552, WHICH IS KOKEE ROAD, TOWARD KEKAHA.

From Highway 552 to Kekaha are dramatic views of **Ni'ihau**, lying less than 20 miles offshore—the so-called Forbidden Island where only those of the purest Hawaiian blood are allowed to live. The 100-square-mile island remains in the hands of the Robinson family, whose ancestors bought it in 1864 for $10,000. A ferry each month brings Ni'ihau residents, who are known for intricate shell necklaces, to Waimea. Ni'ihau's two, tiny satellite islands, both uninhabited, also can be seen on the clearest of days—Lehua, a mile to the right, and Kaula, 19 miles to the left of Ni'ihau.

The only Japanese fatality on land during the Pearl Harbor attack took place on Ni'ihau, on December 8, 1941. After a Japanese pilot had crash-landed, he terrorized the locals with a pistol, searching for the persons who had taken his papers from the wreckage when he had been unconscious. The pilot threatened the wife of one Hawaiian, and the husband charged, taking three shots before he was able to get hold of the pilot and smash him, with one fatal toss, against the lava wall of his house. Since then, there has been a saying in the islands: "Don't shoot a Hawaiian more than twice. The third time he gets mad!"

AT THE BOTTOM ON THE GRADE IN KEKAHA, **TURN LEFT** ON KEKAHA ROAD.

If in need of libation, stop by the Waimea Canyon General Store at the junction. Then drive past the old Kekaha sugar mill, a red-dirt stained, gargantuan structure that washed and chewed tons of cane. The mill ceased operation in 2000.

TURN RIGHT ON PUEO ROAD, OR ANY ROAD THROUGH THE NEIGHBORHOOD. MAKE YOUR WAY SEVERAL BLOCKS BACK OUT TO HWY. 50. **TURN RIGHT** ON HWY. 50.

You drive along **Kekaha Beach**, playground for surfers, fishermen, strollers and horseback riders. Although it's hard to imagine, the area inland along this drive, surrounding the bygone village of **Mana**, used to be swamplands, created by water seepage from the ridges fanning down from the Alakai Plateau. A canal ran through the lower part of the bog, allowing the Hawaiians to canoe all the way to Kekaha. Water development for cane and seed crops have drastically altered the horticultural landscape. Also on these sloping lands was the Holua slide, a long chute paved with lava rock and padded with pili grass. In February, at the end of the Makahiki—a four-month festival during which work and war were prohibited—young Hawaiian athletes would fashion sleds from logs and ride the slide with abandon.

Road to Polihale Beach

CONTINUE ON HWY. 50 TO ITS TERMINUS. FOLLOW SIGNS SEVERAL MILES TO POLIHALE. *Note: The road to Polihale rough, often muddy, and subject to closures.*

The beach at **Polihale State Park**, including **Barking Sands**, is part of the longest sand beach in Hawai'i. A massive dune abuts the northwest section of the Napali Coast—the ridges loom over the beach—and fans all the way around Mana Point to Kekaha, although the Naval base makes some of the beach inaccessible. Surfers dare the waves at Polihale, but the only spot for swimmers, except during rare calms, is **Queens Pond**. Barking Sands, a fine mixture of coral and lava particles, gets its name from the "woofing" sound the sliding dunes make when settling or being trod upon. Legend says these are the barks of an ancient fisherman's beloved pets, directing him ashore after being lost at sea.

Polihale was the heiau on the island from which the etheral spirits of the deceased escaped their mortal coils and went to the next world. Two heiaus are in the area, Kapaula Heiau, inland from the camping area, and Polihale Heiau, also the site of Sacred Springs, located beyond where the beach meets the cliffs.

Polihale

free advice & opinion

SAFETY TIPS THAT CAN SAVE YOUR LIFE
AND RECREATIONAL FACTOIDS OF MARGINAL USE.

HIKING

People have been walking here for centuries: If there is no trail already, you can't get there ... That nice green embankment may be tangled grass and air: stay back from drop-offs ... Carry an equipped day pack on hikes more than a mile or two ... Drink plenty of water ... Don't trust rocks with footing: they break free ... Use a hiking stick ... Never walk downhill with your hands in your pockets ... Boink! Be aware of falling coconuts ... At hike-to beaches, make sure to memorize where you enter the sand: finding the trail on the return trip can be difficult ...

Use hunting trails on weekdays and wear bright colored clothes ... If you see hunters, don't hide behind bushes and snort or squeal ... Even bloodhounds get lost on Kaua'i: follow the trail, not your nose ... Backtrack the moment you get lost or lose the trail ... Don't hike alone ... Give right-of-way to a 400-pound pig ... If the sun rises on a clear Waialeale, head for Waimea Canyon ... Bring something warm when hiking Koke'e ... Go south and west to look for sun in the winter ... You're in the tropics: protect your skin ... Drink more water ...

Loose rocks fall with waterfalls; don't dawdle beneath one ... On black rock beach trails: follow the mud and sand left by the flip-flops of your predecessors ... Flash floods happen on sunny days too, when it's raining inland: stay alert in stream beds ... A high stream will subside, so wait a couple hours rather than make a dangerous crossing ... Know the halfway point of your hike, and plan for enough time to get back ... Heed No Trespassing signs ... Public right of way on the coast is all land and rocks below the vegetation line, as a rule of thumb ... Let someone know if you're taking a long hike ... You need a permit to camp anywhere or to sleep on any beach ... Hikes on Kaua'i take longer than you expect, due to tough conditions and astounding scenery; add an hour for every four hours you think it will take.

WATER SAFETY

Good judgment beats the most dangerous conditions ... Throw a stick in the water before entering to see which way it floats ... Float face-down when you first get in to see which way the current takes you ... Observe the water for fifteen minutes before getting in ... Outgoing current is like a river, carrying out the surf surge: look for blue channels, riffles, and places in a wall of surf offshore where the waves aren't curling: that's where water is going out ... Wave for help if you're in trouble ... Be extra cautious at remote beaches ... High surf means stronger rip current ... Stay out of rocky areas with surge ... If possible, view swimming place from above to observe current ... Waves coming in means current is going out someplace ... Water isn't safe just because some tourist like you is in it ... Aloha Survival: Locals will be glad to tell you about water safety: ask a surfer or swimmer who knows ... Start your swim against a mild current, so you can swim with it when returning ... Get out of a current too strong to swim against ... Swim with fins ... Waves are like thugs: don't turn your back on them ... Every beach is both safe and unsafe, depending on the day ... If you get swept out, go with it and then swim parallel to shore once the current has taken you out and released you ... Don't panic and wear yourself out by swimming against a current you can't beat; it will release you ... Surfers offshore are a safety net, but don't count on them ...

Shore break can break you ... High surf rolls in on nice days from storms unseen far offshore ... Local surfers will be safe in water that is dangerous for you ... Tilted sand means deep water ... But drop-offs can occur on flat beaches, too ... Don't dive into unknown waters ... Swim with a buddy, always ... Go to the opposite side of the island from a high-surf beach: it should be calmer in the lee ... Safest swimming is near a lifeguard ... If you get stung by a jellyfish, put meat tenderizer on the wound ... You don't need to fear the ocean; fear your bad judgment ... When in doubt, stay out ... All beaches are public places: keep your pants on.

BICYCLING

Bust a helmet, not your head ... Lower your seat going downhill ... Dismount for horses and speak so they know this helmeted thing is a person ... Look: It's a vehicle! No, it's a pedestrian! Biking is the best of both worlds ... Most of the backroads on Kaua'i are places rental cars can't go ... Leaving bikes unlocked is a sign of a local ... But why take the chance? ... You can't take bikes on buses ... A bike is the fastest wasy to get through Kapa'a ...

You can continue past gates unless a sign tells you not to ... Respect private property ... Stay on trails to avoid erosion ... Exception: Swerve onto grass on paved paths to avoid pedestrians ... Dismount if you see hunters with dogs ... Never ride down a road you can't get back up ... Hard dirt becomes greasy slick after a few drops of rain ... Add extra lube: rust grows here fast ... Carry an extra tube ... Don't assume cars see you: drivers are looking at scenery.

KAYAKING

It may be raining inland: watch for flash floods ... Don't venture offshore without a local's advice ... Paddling upstream, branches usually stop you before shallow water does ... Remember your way back ... Some of the island's best streams have no people on them ... Ask a local if authorities ever found the anaconda in the Wailua River ... Rivers were Kaua'i's first roads: you'll see the island on them like no other way ... Don't paddle into mangroves ... Keep open wounds out of stagnate fresh water: bacteria danger.

DRIVING AROUND

Driving is the most dangerous sport ... Wear a seatbelt or get a ticket ... Aloha driving: allow merges and turns ... Speeding tickets are likely souvenirs ... Park it or drive it: rubbernecking is dangerous ... Hanging beads or a shell necklace from your rearview mirror will give your rental a local look ... A box of baby wipes in the glove box provides an instant relief from red-dirt sweat ... Signs that beckon: Dead End, No Outlet ... On weekends, try to leave locals' beaches to the locals ... Littering carries a stiff $1,000 fine.

GEAR

Hiking poles are a third leg and you'll need one ... Bring a waterproof shell jacket ... Spitting in your swim mask will clear fog ... Muddy puddles make for great dye-your-own red dirt shirt dunking ... It's cheaper to rent snorkeling gear for a few days, cheaper to buy for a week or more ... It's cheaper to rent a bicycle for a couple days, cheaper to ship if biking for more than that ... You can rent a bike rack for the rental car ... Or hang the bikes out the trunk ... It's cheaper to rent kayaks and surfboards ... Call rental places first to make sure expert advice comes with the rental ... See *Packlist* for what to bring ... When mountain hiking, bring a plastic bag to put your shoes in after hike ... Clothes are gear: No nudity on any Hawaiian beach ... Attend to skin with antibacterial and fungicide: This is the Garden Island and everything grows here ... Carry water, but if you do use a water pump, use iodine to go along with the filter ... Most-common island footwear: bare feet ... Bring lightweight hiking shoes that you can hose off.

DISCLAIMER

Think of this book as you would any other piece of outdoor gear: It will help you do what you want to do, but it depends solely upon you to supply responsible judgment and common sense. Weather and new rules may alter the condition of trails and beach access; please let us know. The publisher and authors are not responsible for injury, damage, trespassing, or legal violations that occur when someone is using our books. Furthermore, the publisher and authors hope that none of these bad things happen and that you have a great time.

ALOHA AUTHORS
Excerpts from some better known writers

"*The far end of Kalalau Valley had been well chosen as a refuge. A sea of vegetation laved the landscape, pouring its green billows from wall to wall, dripping from the cliff lips in great vine masses, and flinging a spray of ferns and airy plants into its multitudinous crevices. Koolau had fought with this vegetable sea. The choking jungle, with its riot of blossoms, had been driven back from the bananas, oranges and mangoes that grew wild, and in every open space where the sunshine penetrated papaya trees were burdened with their golden fruit.*"

—Jack London,
Koolau The Leper

"*The Pacific is inconstant and uncertain like the soul of a man. Sometimes it is grey like the English Channel, with a heavy swell, and sometimes it is rough, capped with white crests, and boisterous. When it is calm and blue, the blue is arrogant. The sun shines fiercely from an unclouded sky. The trade wind gets into your blood and you are filled with an impatience for the unknown, and you forget vanished youth with its memories, cruel and sweet, in a restless, intolerable desire for life.*

—W. Somerset Maugham,
The Pacific

"No alien land in all the world has any deep strong charm for me but that one, no other land could so longingly and beseechingly haunt me, sleeping and waking, through half a lifetime, as that one has done. For me, its balmy airs are always blowing, its summer seas flashing in the sun; the pulsing of its surfbeat is in my ear, I can see its garlanded crags, its leaping cascades, its plumy palms drowsing by the shore. I can hear the splash of its brooks and in my nostrils still lives the breath of flowers that perished twenty years ago."

—Mark Twain,
Roughing It in the Sandwich Islands

"I wish I could tell you about the Pacific. The endless ocean. Reefs upon which waves broke into spray, and inner lagoons, lovely beyond description. I wish I could tell you about the sweating jungle, the full moon rising behind an ancient volcano."

—James A. Michner,
Tales of the South Pacific

"The sea was smooth under the lee of the island; it was warm besides, and Keola has his sailor's knife, so he had no fear of sharks. A little way before him the trees stopped; there was a break in the line of the land like the mouth of a harbor; and the tide, which was then flowing, took him up and carried him through. The next minute he was within, floated there in a wide shallow water, bright with ten thousand stars, and all about him was the ring of land, with its string of palms trees."

—Robert Louis Stevenson,
The Isle of Voices

HAWAIIWOOD

Take a self-guided tour to the locations of some of the more recent among 50-plus major motion pictures that have been filmed in Kaua'i. The first was *White Heat* in 1934. TH = Trailhead, DT = Driving Tour.

Ke'e Beach, TH1 — *Lord of the Flies, Throw Momma From the Train, Thorn Birds*
Haena Beach Park, TH2 — *North*
Kepuhi Point, TH3 — *Body Heat*
Wainiha Beach, TH4 — *Pagan Love Song*
Lumahai Beach, TH5 — *South Pacific, Pirates of the Caribbean*
Lumahai Valley, TH5 — *Uncommon Valor, Dragonfly*
Hanalei Bay, TH7 — *South Pacific, Wackiest Ship in the Army, Miss Sadie Thompson*
Hanalei Valley, TH8 — *Uncommon Valor, The Time Machine*
Anini Beach, TH13 — *Honeymoon in Vegas*
Kalihiwai Bay, TH14 — *Soul Surfer*
Pila'a Beach, TH16 — *None But the Brave*
Moloa'a Bay, TH21 — *Gilligan's Island, Castaway Cowboy*
Papa'a Bay, TH22 — *Six Days, Seven Nights*
Anahola Mountains/Kong, TH23 — *Raiders of the Lost Ark, Dragonfly, Avatar*
Kamokila Village, DT2 — *Outbreak, Tropic Thunder*
Kapa'a Town, TH28 — *Honeymoon in Vegas*
Coco Palms, TH33, DT2 — *Blue Hawaii, South Pacific*
Lydgate Park, TH34 — *Blue Hawaii*
Waialeale Basin, TH32 — *Jurassic Park, Flight of the Intruder, Jurassic Park III*
Wailua River, TH33 — *The Hawaiians, Islands in the Stream, Donovan's Reef, Outbreak*
Wailua Falls, TH36 — *Fantasy Island*
Ahukini Landing, TH39 — *Donovan's Reef, Pagan Love Song*
Nawiliwili, TH41 — *Diamond Head, The Lost World: Jurassic Park, Throw Momma from the Train*
Kalapaki Beach, TH41 — *Hawaiian Eye*
Huleia Stream, TH41 — *Raiders of the Lost Ark, Tropic Thunder*
Mahaulepu, TH42 — *Six Days, Seven Nights; Islands in the Stream, Hook*
Kukuiula Harbor, TH45 — *The Thorn Birds, Islands in the Stream*
Allerton Garden, TH46 — *Jurassic Park, Acapulco Gold, Last Flight of Noah's Ark, Honeymoon in Vegas, Mighty Joe Young*
Hanapepe Town, TH51 — *The Thorn Birds, Jurassic Park, George of the Jungle*
Waimea Canyon, TH34 — *Wackiest Ship in the Army, Fantasy Island*
Barking Sands, TH57 — *South Pacific*
Kalalau Valley, DT4, TH1 — *King Kong*

KAUAIAN TIMELINE

5,000,000 BC	Lava pokes above water; Kaua'i is born.
200 AD	First Polynesians arrive from Marquesas; the Menehunes.
1100	Second Polynesian migration, from Tahiti.
1700	600,000 Hawaiians living on eight islands.
1778	British Captain James Cook arrives at Waimea; Hawai'i is discovered by the rest of the world.
1795	King Kamehameha unifies islands into one kingdom, except Kaua'i. Two attempts to conquer Kaua'i fail.
1810	Kauaian King Kaumuali'i signs peace treaty with Kamehameha.
1816	Russian traders erect fort in Waimea.
1817	Russians driven from the island; their attempt at empire over.
1819	Kamehameha the Great dies.
1820	First New England missionaries arrive in Waimea. Kapu system of laws abolished by Kamehameha II.
1835	First sugar mill, Koloa; worker emigration from China, Japan, Portugal, Philippines and Korea over next decades as sugar becomes king. During Civil War and Gold Rush, Kaua'i becomes major sugar supplier to U.S.
1842	United States recognizes Hawai'i as independent nation.
1864	Eliza Sinclair, ancestor of today's Gay & Robinson Corporation, buys island of Ni'ihau for $10,000.
1874	Rule of Kamehameha's two sons and two grandsons ends.
1893	Queen Liliuokalani betrayed and overthrown; end of monarchy. First hotel opened in Lihue.
1898	United States annexes Hawai'i as territory; Marines occupy Honolulu.
1912	Duke Kahanamoku wins Olympic gold medal. Goes on to win 5 more medals in swimming, ending with silver in 1932.
1930	U.S. restricts Japanese emigration to Hawai'i. Japanese comprise 40 percent of population.
1941	Nawiliwili Harbor shelled during World War II.
1958	*South Pacific* movie released.
1959	Hawai'i becomes 50th state.
1967	One million people visit Hawaiian islands.
1982	Hurricane Iwa.
1992	Hurricane Iniki.
1993	United States formally apologizes for overthrow of Hawaiian kingdom.
2005	Kaua'i most popular island for outdoor recreation.
2006	40-day rains cause fatal floods in Kilauea.
2007	Flotilla of activists block inter-island Hawaii Superferry.
2009	Gay & Robinson harvests last sugar cane crop.
2011	Vog (volcanic fog) from the Big Island reaches the north shore.

A GLOSSARY OF HAWAIIAN WORDS AND PHRASES

The Hawaiian alphabet consists of 12 letters: A, E, I, O, U, H, K, L, M, N, P, W.

The Polynesians transmitted their knowledge and culture through speaking, dance and chants; they had no written language. Missionary scholars in the 1800s derived word spellings from the Polynesian phonetics.

Kaua'i is pronounced: kow-WAH-ee

The apostrophe-like doohickey that goes between double vowels is called an okina. For instance, "a'a" is pronounced, "ah-ah."

Selected Hawaiian place name suffixes and prefixes, to give you an idea of how places were named and interconnected by their attributes:

A'a, rough lava
Ahi, land
Aina, land
Akau, north
Ala, road
Ana, cave
Anu, cool
Hana or *hono*, bay
Hema, south
Hikina, east
Haole, foreigner
Hau, spreading tree
Holo, run
Hono, bay
Hou, new
Hua, fruit, seed
Iki, small
Kaha, place
Kahawai, stream
Kai, sea
Kea or *keo*, white, clear
Koa, rocky, coral
Koko, blood
Komo, enter
Komohana, west
Kua, black
La, sun

Lani, heaven
Lau, leaf
Lena, yellow
Lolo, stupid
Lohi, slow
Lua, crater
Lulu, sheltered
Luna, high
Mala, garden
Malu, shelter
Maka, point
Mana, power or divide
Mano, shark or many
Manu, bird
Mau, moist
Mauka, toward the mountains
Mauna, mountain
Mele, merry or song
Mo'o, water spirit
Moi, king
Moku, island
Nalu, surf, wave
Nani, pretty
Niu, coconut
Nui, large
Ohu, fog
Olo, hill

Omao, green
Oluolu, please
One, sand
Papa, flat
Pau, finished
Pele, goddess of fire
Pono, harmony
Puna, water spring
Pu'u, hill
Tutu, aunt
Ua, rain
Uka, inland
Ula, red
Ulu, breadfruit
Uma, curve
Waa, canoe
Wai, water
Wailele, waterfall
Waimea, reddish waters
Walu, many
Wili, twist

SOME HAWAIIAN WORDS

Ahi, albacore or yellow tuna
Ahupua'a, land and coast segment that
        supported a community
'Aina, land, earth
Ali'i, king, royalty of highest nobility
Aloha, love, affection, welcome, hello,
        good-bye
Hale, house or building
Hana, work or activity
Haole, caucasian, originally any foreigner
He'enalu, surfing
Heiau, ancient temple or place of worship
Hoku, star
Huki, pull
Hukilau, hawaiian method of
        group net-fishing
Hula, the art of hawaiian dance
Ilio, dog
Kahuna, an expert, priest or
        religious leader
Kai, the ocean
Kama'aina, citizen of long standing,
Kanaka, human being, the Hawaiians
Kane, male
Kapu, prohibited, keep out
Keiki, child
Kona, leeward
La, sun
Lanai, porch or balcony
Lei, necklace made of flowers
Luau, Hawaiian feast
Mahalo, thank you
Mahina, moon
Makahiki, annual harvest and
        peace festival
Makai, toward the ocean
Mana, power
Mauka, toward the mountains.
Mauna, mountain
Moana, ocean
Mu'umu'u, mother hubbard dress

Na Ala Hele, trails for walking
Ohana, the people of the community
Pali, cliff
Paniolo, hawaiian cowboy
Pele, goddess of volcanoes
Po, night
Poi, dish of mashed taro root
Popoki, cat
Pupu, hors d'oeurve
Spam, a traditional pork dish
Ua, rain
Wahine, female
Wikiwiki, fast, quickly

GREETINGS, TOASTS AND PHRASES

Aloha Nui, A Big Aloha!
Hau'oli La Hanau, Happy Birthday
Hau'oli Makahiki Hou,
        Happy New Year
Hiki, Okay
Honi Kaua Wikiwiki, Kiss Me Quick
Kamau, Here's To Your Health
Kipa Mai, Welcome
Komo, Enter
Mahalo Nui, Many Thanks
Me Ke Aloha, With Love
Mele Kalikimaka, Merry Christmas
Nani Wahine, To a Beautiful Woman
Okole Maluna, Bottom's Up

PIDGIN EXPRESSIONS

Pidgin is a form of English spoken by kamaʻaina. It is more a dialect and intonation of speech—flowing like a babbling brook—than a collection of phrases. Pidgin's origin is not Polynesian, but rather the rainbow of ethnicity that meld together as Hawaiian. Hang around places where locals shop or surf and you may hear snippets.

ʻAss awri, That's alright
ʻAss why hard, That's why it's hard, life is tough
Auntie, Kids' word for all adult women in the calabash
Boddah you? You like to start something?
Brah, Brother
Bumbye, In the future; by and by, soon
Bummahs, Too bad
Bus laugh, Laugh out loud
Bus nose, Reaction to bad smell
Calabash, Friends and family, extended family
Calabash cousin, Not blood relation, but close friend
Chicken skin, Chills, goosebumps
Coast haole, Caucasian from the Mainland
Cockroach, To steal
Cool head main ting, Keep calm, don't panic
Da Kine, thingamajig, whatever speaker wants it to mean
Eh, Brah, Hey, you
Garans, Guaranteed
Grind, To eat
Grinds, Food
He been go, He went

Hey, Bruddah, Hey, Brother
Howzit?, How are you? Pidgin for Aloha
Huhu, to be upset
I shame, I'm embarrassed
J.O.J., Just off the Jet (tourist)
Junks, small personal things
Lesgo, let's do it
Local style, Hawaiian way of doing things
Lolo, Dumb-dumb
Moke, Local tough guy
Mo' bettah, Better
No boddah, Don't bother
No can, Cannot
No mention, Don't mention it, you're welcome
Not, No can be, You got to be kidding
Moah betta, More better
Plate lunch, Rice, meat or Spam and veggies, a fast counter lunch
Poi dog, Local mix of many breeds, small canine
Shaka, Right on, brah' (hand sign: fist with thumb and pinky out.)
Shave ice, Snow cones
Slack key, Hawaiian folk-blues played on loose-string guitar
Stick, Surfboard
Stink-eye, Dirty look
Stuffs, see Junks
Talk story, Tell stories, conversation
T'anks, Thank you, mahalo
Tita, Local tough girl
Uncle, Kids' word for all adult men in the calabash
Whack 'em, Eat up
Whatevahs, Whatever
Yeah?, Put anywhere in sentence

SURFER'S DICTIONARY

AIR: The invisible stuff that's on top of waves. Also, a gaseous substance necessary for a surfer to surf.

BAD: That which has nothing to do with surfing.

CAR: A disposable device used to transport a surfer and surfboard to the surf.

CRUELTY: Taking a surfer's surfboard.

FEET: Things that allow a surfer to stand on a surfboard.

FOOD: A substance that surfers swallow in order to go surfing.

GOD: An entity that created waves and surfboards.

JOB: An activity by which a surfer acquires money in order to go surfing.

LIFE: Surfing.

KAUA'I PACKLIST
For two weeks, staying in hotel.

BASICS
Long pants/dress for airplane
Swimming suit (can buy here)
Rash guard (optional, for water sports)
Hat, sunglasses
Rain-proof shell (pants optional)
Aloha or polo shirt/dress for dress-up
2 pair hiking/riding shorts
1 pair dress shorts
7 T-shirts, one for every two days
1 or 2 lightweight long sleeve tops
(Dri-fit or polyester equivalent)
Waterproof watch

FOOTWEAR
2 pair lightweight hiking socks
1 pair flip-flops, a.k.a., zories, slippers
    (for driving, beach walking, shopping)
1 pair lightweight, washable
  hiking shoes; your mud shoe
1 pair tennis shoes—*can be hiking shoe*
1 pair hotel/airport/dress shoes
Optional boat shoes, sandals

KNAPSACK/DAYPACK:
Water, energy bar/emergency food
Flashlight
Swiss Army Knife
First aid, sunscreen
Water treatment tabs or pump
Rain shell
Sunglasses/hat
Mosquito repellant
Camera

GEAR:
Hiking pole *(retractable, bring with you)*
Mask, snorkel, fins *(Bring or rent here. Cheaper to buy if you'll use for more than 5 or 6 days. Cost here about $30.)*
Surfboard *(Ship if you will use more than 5 days; otherwise rent. Contact airlines and outfitters to compare prices.)*
Bicycle helmet
Bicycle *(Contact airlines and outfitters to compare prices. Usually cheaper to rent here.)*
Kayak *(Rent, about $20 per day.)*

FACTSHEET

TEMPERATURES
Average, year around, day and night: 75 degrees

Extremes:	Record High	Record Low
Kilauea	87	50
Lihue	90	50
Poipu	92	40
Kokee	90	29

WIND
Summer:	Trades and Kona winds from south
Winter:	Trade winds generally from north

RAINFALL YEARLY AVERAGE IN INCHES
Waimea Town	28
Poipu	35
Koloa	65
Lihue	38
Kapa‘a	56
Princeville	98
Waialeale	460 (most in the world)

ETHNIC MAKEUP:
Hawaiian: 23%
Filipino: 23%
Japanese: 22%
White: 19%
Other: 13%

MAJOR HURRICANES
	average wind speed m.p.h.	maximum m.p.h.
1950 ‘Hiki	68	93
1957 Nina	92	111
1959 Dot	81	103
1982 Iwa	65	117
1992 Iniki	145	227

HIGHEST PEAKS: Kawaikini, 5,243 ft.; Waialeale, 5,148 ft.
MILES OF COASTLINE: 110
SQUARE MILES: 550
AVERAGE DIAMETER, MI.: 28

LAND OWNERSHIP: (397,000 acres)
Six largest corporations: 41 percent
State of Hawaii: 39 percent
Small private landowners: 13 percent
Hawaiian Homelands: 6 percent
Federal government: 1 percent

POPULATION
Locals: 65,000
Visitors (average daily): 15,000
Total: 80,000

SUNSHINE MARKETS

County-licensed outdoor markets offering home-grown produce. Times may vary, call 241-6390 for more information. Bring dollar bills, plastic bags, and be on time!

Monday:	Koloa Ballpark, Maluhia Road, Koloa, 12 noon.
Tuesday:	Kalaheo Neighborhood Center, 3:30 p.m.
	Hanalei-Waikoko, 2 p.m.
Wednesday:	Kapa'a New Town Center, near Armory, 3 p.m.
Thursday:	Kilauea Neighborhood Center, 4:30 p.m.
	Hanapepe Park, behind fire station, 4:30 p.m.
Friday:	Lihue, Vidinha Stadium, Ho'olako St., 3 p.m.
Saturday:	Kekaha Neighborhood Center, 9 a.m.
	Hanalei Town Center, 9:30 a.m.
Sunday:	Kealia (across from beach), 11 a.m. to 4 p.m.

(Driving tours note the location of fruit stands.)

FREE HULA SHOWS

Call to verify times and inquire about other cultural events.

Coconut Marketplace, Saturday noon, 822-3641

Kaua'i Coconut Beach Resort, nightly 7 p.m., 822-3455

Hyatt Regency Kaua'i Resort, nightly 6 to 8 p.m., also torch-lighting ceremony daily at sunset, except Tuesday, 742-1234

Kaua'i Marriott Resort, Wednesday and Saturday at sunset; also torch-lighting ceremony Monday and Thursday, 245-5050

Kukui Grove Shopping Center, Fridays, 6 p.m., 245-7784

Poipu Shopping Village, Tuesday and Thursday, 5 p.m., 742-2831

***Queen Emma Polynesian Festival**, October, Koke'e Park, 335-6466

THE MEANING OF *Aloha*

as adopted by a resolution of the State Legislature:

A is for Akahai. Kindness, to be expressed with tenderness.

L is for Lokahi. Unity, to be expressed with harmony.

O is for Oluolu. Agreeable, to be expressed with pleasantness.

H is for Ha'aha'a. Humility, to be expressed with modesty.

A is for Ahonui. Patience, to be expressed with perseverance.

The meaning of ALOHA not yet considered by the State Legislature:

A is for Attire. It's hard to be uptight or uppity in a place where nobody wears pantyhose or neckties, and "dressing up" is colorful prints and flip-flops.

L is for Latitude. In the temperate tropics, with a lack of snow and boiling heat, everyone stays mellow.

O is for a Circle. On an island there's no point in rushing just to get where you've already been. Even the dogs don't chase their tails here.

H is for Healthy. With papayas, bananas, guava, mangos and spam, everyone enjoys the serenity of a healthy diet.

A is for Alone. The opposite of island fever is island euphoria; everyone is alone and isolated in the ocean, pitching in together to help out their neighbors. You don't outrun a bad reputation on a small island.

got aloha?

KIDS

The Hawaiian word keiki (KAY-key) means both 'child' and also the green shoot of a new banana plant. Bananas are plants, not trees, and each year a new generation must be nurtured to maturity—just like children. By caring for each generation, the arts and skills of village life flourished for centuries on this beautiful, but isolated, island of Kaua'i. Your kids can see many of these arts practiced today. They can also do a lot of other fun stuff that will create life-long memories and bring the family together. The suggestions below will help you plan a day of family fun. Remember that trailhead numbers close together numerically will also be close geographically.

TH = trailhead. DT = driving tour. Activities are listed by ascending trailhead number. See *Resource Links* for telephone numbers.

KEIKI SWIMMING
Ke'e Beach, TH1, page 32
A reef-protected oval pool rests under the jagged Napali ridges. High surf, mainly in winter, makes for strong current.
Mola'a Baths, TH2, page 65
Drive down a lush valley and then walk the beach to a palm-shaded shore with natural pools in the coral reef.

Baby Beach, Kapa'a, TH28, page 78
This wading pool is popular among new moms. Beach cottage neighborhood setting.
Lydgate Park, TH34, page 99
Snorkeling is a sure thing year around at this big man-made lagoon.
Poipi Beach Park, TH44, page 120
A sand spit creates protected swim spots and Hawaiian sun graces this popular beach park, even when clouds frown elsewhere.

Waterhouse Beach, TH45, page 123
You'll have to look for this toddlers' beach, tucked away near Prince Kuhio Park. Bigger kids will like the snorkeling at Longhouse Beach.
Salt Pond Beach Park, TH52, page 140
West Kaua'i's best swimming beach. To the far right of the beach is a smaller splash area.
Queens Pond, TH57, page 150
Families with a sense of adventure will like this calm spot along the long Polihale Beach. High surf often makes conditions very unsafe. Bring your own shade and water to these open sand dunes.

FAMILY NATURE WALKS
Limahuli National Tropical Botanical Garden, TH1, page 31
You might expect dinosaurs to stride down the green ridges and onto the gar-

den terraces. Native and endangered plants abound, many unique to Kaua'i.
Okolehao Trail, TH8, page 40
Big views of Hanalei Valley and Bay are the payoff on this forested ridge hike. It's a bit of a workout, but you'll feel like you've been somewhere.
Sleeping Giant, TH30, page 81
You get a fantastic view of interior Kaua'i and the Coconut Coast from the top of the Giant (Nounou Mountain.) The Norfolk Pine forest on the way up will have everyone's interest. Kids will get a sense of accomplishment.
Keahua Arboretum, TH32, page 84
You've got many options at the arboretum, all beginning where the Wailua River crosses a spillway in the jungle. The Kuilau Ridge is green fantasy land—but make sure to stay on the trail on the steep parts.
Smiths Tropical Paradise, TH33, page 95
The little ones may shriek like the peacocks that float down from the treetops. Bridges span the lagoons of Kauai's best-value gardens and arboretum.
Kukui Trails-Iliau Loop, TH58, page 152
Make this commanding overlook your first stop on the way up Waimea Canyon. Bigger kids in active families can make the trek to the bottom of the canyon.
Koke'e State Park, TH66, page 163
With all the trails and overlooks around Waimea Canyon, many families might miss these woodland, bird-lover's strolls.

BEACH PICNICS
Haena Beach Park, TH2, page 33
Stop by on the way back from Ke'e Beach. Surfers and a play stream add interest to this developed park. The cool caves are across the road.

Pine Trees Beach, TH7, page 37
Large ironwood trees cast shade on a few tables, about midway around Hanalei Bay. Surfers and joggers pass by. (Access via Ama'ama Road, down from the City Pavilion on Weke Road.)

Anini Beach, TH13, page 49
Drop down to this long coral-reef park. Large trees shade camping and picnic areas. A polo field and windsurfers add to the charm.

Kilauea Bay-Kahili Beach, TH18, page 54
No facilities here, but you can take sand seats where Kilauea Stream emerges from a tropical valley at a big sand beach. The drive down is a mini-adventure.

Anahola Bay, TH23, page 66
The road to the beach curves down through a leafy canopy. This side of the bay is rustic, but you can get comfy along the sandy river bank.

Poipu Beach Park, TH44, page 121
You may have company at the pavilions, since sun and safe swimming make this Kaua'i's most-popular beach park.

Prince Kuhio Park, TH45, page 122
The scant-sand beaches nearby are great for snorkeling, but this is the place for a quiet family repast.

Salt Pond Beach Park, TH52, page 140
Palms shade the grassy shores, and swimming is normally safe. Pull off here if cruising West Kaua'i—the locals do.

Lucy Wright Beach Park, TH54, page 144
Water quality is not the greatest, as this is where the Waimea River enters the Pacific, but you can show the kids where Captain Cook landed and take a stroll down the beach to a long fishing pier.

SHORT WALKS TO BIG PLACES

Hula Platform, Ke'e Beach, TH1, page 30
The Kalalau Trail is well-known, but the short walk to the scenic terraces above crashing waves packs a punch. Tread lightly at this sacred Hawaiian site.

Hanalei Pier, TH7, page 37
Watch fishermen haul 'em in and surfers whiz by. The covered pier at Black Pot Beach is a short walk down past the surfer cars to where the Hanalei River enters the bay.

Aliomanu Beach, Anahola, TH22, page 66
Easily reached, this hike-to beach holds the promise of treasure found—shells, coral bits, or maybe a message in a bottle.
Kukui Point Light, TH41, page 107
A path curves from the posh grounds of the Marriott to the entrance to Nawili-wili Harbor. Pick a sunset when a cruise ship is leaving the harbor.

Mahaulepu, Poipu, TH42, page 115
A bumpy ride out sets the tone for a walk along sculpted bluffs and wild waves. You may see a Monk Seal (don't get closer than 100 feet if you do).
Kukuiolono Park, Kalaheo, TH48, page 127
A high green knoll provides a respite. Wild chickens flit about formal gardens and a path skirts the golf course to a pavilion with a big view.
Pihea Overlook-Alakai Swamp, Waimea Canyon, TH69, page 168
All the thrilling overlooks of the canyon on the way up are a prelude to the panorama of the Kalalau Valley. A trail skirts the rim. Trekking families can pile on the adventure by taking the boardwalk trail across the Alakai Swamp.

EASY & ENTERTAINING & EDUCATIONAL
Kilauea Lighthouse, Kilauea, TH17, page 53
Free binoculars aid in the bird-and-whale watching at this dramatic northerly spot.
Kaua'i Children's Discovery Museum, Kapa'a, DT2, page 197
Day-camp programs and walk-through exhibits delight the kids.
Lydgate Park Play Bridge, TH34, page 99
The ocean snorkeling pool here is the big draw, but you've also got Kamalani Play-ground and—just down the bike path—the awesome Play Bridge.

National Tropical Gardens-Spouting Horn, Koloa, TH46, page 124
Kaua'i's sea geyser gets the oohs and ahhs, but the garden visitors center across the street is an escape into remarkable flora.
Menehune Ditch Bridge, Waimea, TH54, page 144
Everyone over four will get a kick out of the suspension bridge that spans the river.
Koke'e Natural History Museum, Koke'e, TH67, page 164
Caps off a visit to the to Waimea Canyon. Hurricane and natural history exhibits are eye-openers.
Kauai Museum, page 180
The story of the island unfolds through photos and displays. Giftshop gets an A+.

GUIDED ADVENTURES
—see resource links for phone numbers
Get a View from Above
You won't believe the sights from the sky. Several helicopters tour the island.
Princeville Ranch Zipline
It's a perfectly safe thrill: Fly over the jungle gorge of a huge private ranch.
Fern Grotto Boat Ride
Kaua'i's classic since the 1950s. Family hula and ukulele performers enliven the ride up the river to the massive cave.

Pedal the Coconut Co[...]
A beach path winds alon[...] Kealia to the Wailua Rin[...] colorful Kapa'a Town. C[...] one place to rent wheels (or embark on a guided tour if you'd prefer).
Float through the Hanalei Wildlife Refuge
The lazy Hanalei River leads from the surf, through taro fields, and into Hanalei Valley. Several kayak places are in town.
Learn to Surf
Beginners may like Poipu, but many think Hanalei Bay is the best beginner's beach in the Hawaiian Islands. You can learn from one of the greats, Titus Kinimaka, or take your pick from many other skilled boarders. Hanalei Surf Company has advice to go with their gear.
Wailua River Paddle
The first Hawaiian kings chose to make their home along these banks. Wailua River Kayaks leads a tour to Secret Falls, which includes a short hike.
Na Aina Kai Botanical Gardens
Separate children's garden. A world of greenery where kids can be delightfully lost.
Kilohana Plantation
All aboard! Ride the vintage railway or hop on a horse-drawn carriage.

FUN PLACES TO EAT

Duke's Canoe Club, Kalapaki
Surfboards and other memorabilia adorn this special occasion resort restaurant right on Kalapaki Beach. Duke Kahanamoku was a surfing legend and Olympic medalist.

Wailua Marina Restaurant
Enjoy local-style eats with a river view, after a river boat cruise or before taking in an evening hula show.

Hamura Saimin Stand, Lihue
Enough noodles to reach the moon and back have been served up at the counter in Lihue's old-town. Spills okay, the counter is Formica. Chopsticks optional.

Koke'e Lodge
Stop in at the old building after a visit to Waimea Canyon and watch the chickens and roosters flit about outside plate glass windows that frame a green expanse of the park.

Banana Joe's, Kilauea
Joe jams frozen fruit through a juicer and it comes out like soft ice cream. A tropically themed putt-putt golf course is on the grounds. BJ's is not a sit down restaurant, but it's full of island goodies.

JoJo's Shave Ice, Waimea
One of these sweet coolers (a traditional Hawaiian treat) might save the day if the family got ornery after a little too much sun at Polihale. The funky joint is part of the fun.

Hanalei Dolphin, Hanalei
Tables are set along the river for lunch, making birds and kayakers part of the show. Their kids' menu is tops.

HULA SHOWS

With chants, dancing, and percussion, the hula tells the story of Polynesian culture. Performances vary from keiki dance clubs and resort performers to Hawaiian cultural groups from Ni'ihau and Kaua'i. A listing for free performances is on page 229. Smith's Tropical Garden also holds a Polynesian dance extravaganza, and traditional luaus also come with entertainment. (Princeville Resort and the Sheraton in Kapa'a are two popular feast sites.) Many performances include impromptu lessons by kids. If you're here in October, don't miss the **Queen Emma Festival** in Koke'e State Park.

Princeville Ranch Adventure zipline

CAMPING PERMITS AND INFORMATION

Try to call for permits a month ahead of your trip. Camping is by permit only in established campsites. Backpacking in the tropics is challenging, even for experienced hikers; be prepared. Car camping in Koke'e and forest reserves is often at unimproved sites; get specifics from agencies listed below. Beach park camping is on small sites on lawn areas near parking, pavilions and restrooms. Plan for rain: Consider bringing a car-camping tent rather than a backpack tent.

Koke'e, Polihale and Haena State Parks, 274-3444,274-3446, 335-8405
Kalalau Trail, Napali Coast, 274-3445
      Backpacking. Department of Land and Natural Resources, State Parks
Koke'e Forest Reserves, including Waimea Canyon, 274-3433
      Department of Land and Natural Resources, Forestry & Wildlife
County Beach Park Camping, 241-4463, 241-4460
      County of Kaua'i. Including these beach parks: Haena, Anini, Hanamaulu, Salt Pond, Lydgate, Kekaha, and Lucy Wright; see Trailhead Maps.

OUTFITTERS/RENTAL GEAR

Each outfitter is listed once, under primary activity; ancillary services also noted for each outfitter.

HIKING

Most of the trails in Kaua'i, both coastal paths and mountain routes, were laid down centuries ago by native Hawaiians. In addition to these historic paths are forest reserve trails and four-wheel drive roads. Trails usually follow ridgelines up to higher elevations, since steep relief and thick flora doesn't allow for switchbacks. Treks in this book are for day hikers, but backpacking trailheads are included.

Kayak Kaua'i, Hanalei, 800-437-3507, 826-9844
Kaua'i Nature Tours, Poipu, 742-8305, 888-233-8365, *natural history and ecology*
Native Hawaiian Hiking Expeditions, 652-0478, *Charlie Cobb-Adams will take you
      to the wild places out of Waimea Canyon and the Napali. True adventure.*
Pedal 'n Paddle, Hanalei, *camping gear, clothes, maps,* 826-9069
Princeville Ranch Adventures, 826-7669, *guided tours, equipment included. 2,500-
acre ranch, also has cross-valley zipline rides and kayak tours.*

SNORKELING, SCUBA & CRUISES

Kaua'i has 110 miles of coastline, with waters supporting 650 different kinds of fish. Generally speaking, calmer waters and better snorkeling will be found during the winter months on south and east side beaches. During the summer months, calmer waters will generally be on north and west shore. East and west shore beaches are the least predictable. However, on any given day, any beach can be calm—or turbulent—throughout the year.

all area codes are 808 unless otherwise noted

BEACHES WITH FULL OR PART-TIME LIFEGUARDS:
Wailua Bay, Lydgate Park, Anahola Beach Park, Poipu Beach, Hanalei, Kealia, Haena Ke'e, Kekaha, and Salt Pond Beach Park.

Captain Andy's, Port Allen, 800-335-6833, *south coast specialists, ranging from Kipu Kai Beach to the Napali. Large to smaller vessels, great crews.*
Blue Doplphin Charters, Port Allen, 335-5553
HoloHolo Charters, Port Allen, 800-848-6130, 335-0815, *daily excursions, boat tours to Ni'ihau, Napali*
Kalapaki Beach Boys (True Blue), Kalapaki Beach, 246-6333, *rentals, tours, lessons, also surfing, windsurfing, kayak, hiking.*
Kayak Kaua'i, Hanalei, 800-437-3507, 826-9844
Liko Kaua'i Cruises, Waimea, 338-0333
Napali Explorer, Waimea, 877-335-9909, 338-9999
Smiths Fern Grotto Cruise, Wailua, 821-6892
Snorkel Bob's, Kapa'a, 823-9433; Koloa, 742-2206, *rentals*

BICYCLING
With miles of forest reserve roads and trails, resort bike paths, disused cane roads and quiet rural roads, Kaua'i is made for biking. The paved Kapa'a Coasta Path is a great family ride of one of Hawaii's top outdoor attractions. On the down side, highway bike lanes could be better, and it's too bad buses aren't equipped to take cyclists over one or two highway stretches that are unsafe. Rentals are about $25 a day. You may want to inquire with your air carrier about shipping your own bike.

Bicycle John, Lihue, 245-7579, *sales, service*
Bicycle Downhill, Waimea, 742-7421, *tours, Waimea Canyon*
Bike Doktor, Hanalei, 826-7799, *rentals, sales, service*
Coconut Coasters, Kapa'a, 822-7368, *Sparks & Melissa Costales can set you up with first-class cruiser; centrally located on the Kapaa Coastal Path. Top pick.*
Kaua'i Cycle and Tour, Kapa'a, 821-2115, *rentals, tours, sales, service*
Pedal 'n Paddle, Hanalei, 826-9069, *rentals; also kayaks, snorkeling, boogie boards, camping*

KAYAKING
Kaua'i has the only navigable waters in Hawaii, including six rivers and as many streams that are wide enough to be called rivers in most states. Rivers and streams can rise fast after storms, but more often river kayaking on the island is on quiet lagoons that curve inland. Coral reefs and bays also provide dozens of places for sea kayaking, under calm conditions.

Aloha Canoes and Kayaks, Nawiliwili, 246-6804, *tours, rentals*
Kamokila Village, Wailua, 823-0559, *their docks are upriver and out of the wind*
Kayak Hanalei (summer and fall only) 826-1881
Kayak Kaua'i, Hanalei, 826-9844, 800-437-3507
        tours, rentals; also bikes, snorkeling, surfboards, camping
Napali Kayak Tours, Hanalei, 826-6900, *specialize in coast camping*
Outfitters Kaua'i, Nawiliwili and Poipu, 742-9667, *tours; also bicycles, hikes*
Pedal 'n Paddle, Hanalai, *north shore's best adventure store*, 826-9069
Princeville Ranch Adventures, also hikes and zipline, 826-7669
True Blue, Kalapaki-Nawiliwi, *Family lagoon paddles, paddle-hike tours*, 246-6333
Wailua River Kayak, Wailua, 822-5795, 639-6332
        rentals and paddle-hike tours to Secret Falls on Wailua River.
        Smaller groups and special requests.

SURFING AND WINDSURFING

Surfing originated here, and is called the sport of kings, since Hawaiian royalty began riding the waves centuries ago. Winter months usually bring the biggest surf to north shore and west side beaches. During the summer, look for the biggest surf on the south and east sides of the island.

Garden Island Surf School, Poipu, 652-4965, 652-5330
Hanalei Surf Company, 826-9000, *rentals, lesson referrals, and the island's*
        best surf shop; also snorkeling
Kaua'i Beach Boys, Kalapaki-Nawiliwili, 246-6333
Learn To Surf, 826-7612, *lessons, rentals, island-wide*
Nukomoi Surf Company, Poipu, 742-8019, *rentals, surf shop, known world-wide*
Tamba Surf Company, Kapa'a, 823-6942, *rentals, surf shop, lesssons*
Titus Kinimaka, Hawaiian School of Surfing, 652-1116 *one of Hawaii's greatest*
        surfers; will teach from novice on up.
Dr. Ding's Westside Surf Shop, Hanapepe, 335-3805, *custom boards*

HELICOPTERS

Beautiful Kaua'i has been 5 million years in the making, nuanced by numerous river valleys, seacliffs, and ragged ridges, all of it adorned with a tangle of life that would put Darwin in a tizzy. The sure way to see how it all folds together is by heli-copter. Recent economic hard times have brought the demise of several companies, including Air Kauai, but several good choices remain.

Blue Hawaiian, 245-5800, *has respected operations on all the islands. This is your best*
        bet. Features quiet Eco-star choppers.
Safari Helicopters, 246-0136
Sunshine (Will Squyres) Helicopters, 245-8881

HORSEBACK RIDING
CJM Country Stables,
    Poipu, 742-6096
Esprit De Corps Riding Academy,
    Kapaʻa, 822-4688
Princeville Ranch Stables, 826-6777
Silver Falls Ranch, Kilauea, 828-6718, *Rides on a private ranch take in a huge palm aboretum, the falls, and an ancient caldera which is now a lush bog.*

GOLF
Kauaʻi Lagoons Golf Club, Kalapaki Bay, 800-634-6400
Grove Farm Golf Course at Puakea,
    245-8756
Kiahuna Golf Club, Poipu, 742-9595
Kukuiolono Golf Course, Kalaheo, 332-9151
Poipu Bay Resort Golf Course, 800-858-6300
Princeville Golf Club, 800-826-1105
Wailua Golf Club, 241-6666

MAPS
Kauaʻi Trailblazer's maps and descriptions are all you need for recreating on the island. However, you may want a supplemental map. Generally speaking, the trick to hiking in Kauaʻi—whether coastal or inland—is knowing where to go and finding the trailhead; and then following the trail, not a map.

Border's Books and Music, 246-0862, 245-3041 *carries most maps*
Full Color Topographic Map of Kauaʻi, The Garden Isle.
    Best overall for use with this book; indexed place names, widely available, inexpensive. By University of Hawaii Press.
Northwestern Kauaʻi Recreation Map, 800-828-MAPS
    Best by far for Kalalau Trail, very good for Kokeʻe area; only includes half of island. By Earthwalk Press
Na Ala Hele State Recreation Map, 274-3433
    Very good for state park and forest reserve trails. Mile markers on map don't match highway. Perhaps out of print.
Basically Books, 800-903-6277. *Bookstore on Big Island that does credit card phone orders; handles USGS and other maps.*
The Ready Mapbook of Kauaʻi, 935-0092. *Handy companion street atlas.*
Kokeʻe Trails, 335-9975. *Inexpensive map for hiking woodland trails of Kokeʻe State Park. Available at museum at the park.*
USGS Topographic Maps, 888-ASK-USGS. *Because of jungle growth, steep relief and other factors, topo maps are not as useful in hiking Kauaʻi as other places. They do not show roads and familiar place names, as a rule.*

MUSEUMS, HISTORICAL ATTRACTIONS, CHURCHES
Grove Farm Homestead, Lihue, 245-3202
Kamanawa Foundation (Polynesian Festival), 335-6466
Kaua'i Coffee Company Visitors Center, Port Allen, 800-545-8605, 335-5497
Kaua'i Hindu Monastery, Kapa'a, 822-3012, 822-3152
Kaua'i Museum, Lihue, 245-6931
Kilohana Plantation, Lihue, 245-5608, Plantaton Railway 245-7245
Koke'e Natural History Museum, Kokee, 335-9975
Lawai International Center (88 Holy Places of Kobo Diashi),
    Kalaheo, 639-4300, 652-0447
St. Raphaels Church, Koloa, 742-1845
Waioli Mission House, Hanalei, 245-3202
Waioli Hui'ia Church, 826-6253
West Kaua'i Technology & Visitor Center, Waimea, 338-1332

GARDENS AND OUTDOOR ATTRACTIONS
Allerton/McBryde National Tropical Botanical Gardens, 742-2623, 742-2433
Common Ground, Kilauea, 828-2194 (off.), 639-8158 (tours)
Fort Elizabeth State Park, Waimea, 245-4444
Garden Ponds Nursery, Kilauea, 828-6400
Kamokila Hawaiian Village, Wailua, 823-0559
Kaua'i Nursery & Landscaping, Lihue, 888-345-7747, 245-7747
Kaua'i Products Fair, Kapa'a, 246-0988
Kilauea Point National Wildlife Refuge, 828-1413, 828-0383, 246-2860
Limahuli National Tropical Botanical Garden, Haena, 826-1053
Moir Gardens, Kiahuna Plantation, Poipu, 742-6411
Na Aina Kai Botanical Gardens, Kilauea, 828-0525
Orchid Alley, Kapa'a, 822-0486
Smith's Tropical Paradise, Wailua, 821-6895
Smith's Fern Grotto Cruise, Wailua, 821-6892, *a Hawaiian tradition.*
Taro Patch (John & Suzanne Pia), Anahola, 822-9563, 245-8101

CULTURAL CONTACTS
Anahola Ancient Cultural Exchange, 822-9563, 245-8101
Kahea, The Hawaiian Environmental Alliance, 524-8220
Kamanawa Foundation (Hula), 335-6466
Kaua'i Heritage Center of Hawaiian Culture & Arts, 821-2070
Ki Hoalu Slack Key Guitar, 826-1469
Garden Island Arts Council, Lihue 246-4561
Ka'ie'ie Foundation, perpetuating Hawaiian culture, 821-2070
Kateo Club International, dance, 338-0265
Kikiaola Foundation (plantation heritage), Waimea, 337-1005
West Kauai Main Street, Waimea, 338-9957

HAWAIIANA SHOPS & GALLERIES
Banana Patch Studio, Hanapepe, 335-5944
Bambulei, Wailua, chic antiques, 823-8641
Crystals & Gemstones Gallery, Hanalei, 826-9304
Dawn M. Traina Gallery, Hanapepe, 335-3993
The Glass Shack, Kapa'a, 822-2236
Hanalei Surf Company, Hanalei, 826-9000
Hawaii Express Flowers & Gifts, Lihue 888-345-7747, 245-7747
Hawaiian Trading Post, Lawai, 332-7404
Haviki Oceanic Tribal Art, Hanalei, 826-7606, 635-7404
Island Soap & Candle, Kilauea, 828-1955. Koloa, 742-1945
JJ Ohana, Hanapepe, 335-0366
Jungle Girl, Kapa'a 823-9351, Koloa, 742-9649
Kapaia Stitchery, Hanamaulu, 245-2281
Kaua'i Fine Arts, Hanapepe, 335-3778
Kaua'i Products Store, Lihue, Kukui Grove, 246-6753
Kaua'i Museum Gift Shop, Lihue, 246-2470
Kilohana Galleries, Lihue 245-2452
Kong Lung, Kilauea, 828-1822
Kukuiula Village, Poipu, 742-9545
Magic Dragon Toy & Art, Princeville, 826-9144
Ola's, Hanalei, 826-6937
Pineapples & Palms, Koloa, 742-1199
Robin McCoy Gallery, Hanapepe, 839-7569, 335-3705
Robin Savage Gift & Gourmet, Hanalei, 826-7500
Ship Shore Galleries, Coconut Marketplace, 800-877-1948, 822-7758
Village Variety, Hanalei, 826-6077
Whalers General Store, Poipu, 742-9431 Coconut Marketplace, 822-9921
Yellowfish Trading Company, Hanalei, 826-1227

LOCAL INFORMATION
Chamber of Commerce, 245-7363
County of Kaua'i Transportation (public buses), 241-6410
Hawai'i Visitor and Conventions Bureau, 800-464-2924
Kaua'i Visitors Bureau, 245-3971, 800-262-1400
Matson Shipping, 800-628-7661, 245-6701
Public Libraries, 800-390-3611, Lihue, 241-3222
Weather, 245-6001, 961-5582
Wind and Surf Conditions, 245-3564, 245-6001
Hawaiian Waters **report**, 245-3564, 335-3720

Where to eat

A calabash of island-style eats, ranging from take-out plates to Pacific Rim gourmet. Some have views and all have Kauai character. Not all serve dinner; call ahead to ask about menu specifics, prices, and ambience. All are recommended; special selections are boldfaced. Area codes are 808.

(C) Cheap or take-out (under $10)
(M) Moderate, family ($10-$20)
(P) Pricey, special occasion (over $20)

KILAUEA
PRINCEVILLE
HANALEI

Bar Acuda, Hanalei (M) 826-7081
Banana Joe's, Kilauea (C) 828-1092
Bubba's Hanalei (C) 826-7839
Common Ground, Kilauea (C) 828-1041
Hanalei Dolphin (M-P) 826-6113
Hanalei Coffee Roasters
  (Java Kai), (C) 826-6717
Healthy Hut Natural Foods (M) 828-6626
Kilauea Bakery-Pau Pizza (M) 828-2020
Moloa'a Sunrise (C) 822-1441
Ono Char Burger, Anahola (C) 822-9181
Panda's Kitchen (C) 826-7388
Postcards Café, Hanalei (M) 826-1191
Tahiti Nui, Hanalei (M) 826-6277

KAPA'A
COCONUT COAST

Bubba's, Kapa'a (C) 823-006
Caffe Coco, Wailua (C-M) 822-799
East Side Grill & Bar (M-P) 823-950
Island Palm Grill, Kapa'a (C-M) 823-8828
Kauai Pasta (M) 822-7447
Lemongrass Grill, Kapa'a (M) 821-2888
Mermaids Café, Kapa'a (C) 821-2026
Olympic Cafe, Kapa'a (C-M) 822-582
Papaya's, Wailua (C) 823-0190
Pau Hana Grill, Waipouli (M) 821-2900
Restaurant Kintaro (M) 822-3341
Wailua Marina (C-M) 822-4311

LIHUE
NAWILIWILI

Barbecue Inn	(C-M) 245-2921
Cafe Portofino, Marriott	(P) 245-2121
Dani's Restaurant	(C-M) 245-4991
Duke's Canoe Club, Kalapaki	(M-P) 246-9599
Garden Island Barbecue	(C) 245-8868

Local style plates are tops

Hamura Saimin Stand	(C) 245-3271
JJ's Broiler, Kalapaki	(M) 246-4422
Kauai Pasta	(M) 245-2227
Rob's Good Times Grill	(C-M) 246-0311

KOLOA
POIPU

Beach House	(P) 742-1424
Casablanca, Poipu	(M-P) 742-2929
Dali Deli & Cafe, Koloa	(C) 742-8824
Gaylord's, Kilohana Plantation	(P) 245-9593
Ilima Terrace Grand Hyatt Poipu	(M-P) 742-1234
Living Foods, Kukuiula	(M) 742-2323
Merriman's, Kukuiula Village	(P) 742-8385
Poipu Tropical Burgers	(C-P) 742-1808
Roy's Poipu Bar & Grill	(M-P) 742-5000
Sueoka's Snack Shop, Koloa	(C) 742-1112
Keoki's Paradise, Poipu	(M) 742-7534
Plantation Garden, Poipu	(M-P) 742-2121

HANAPEPE
WAIMEA

Brick Oven Pizza, Kalaheo	(M)332-8561
Grinds Cafe, Port Allen	(C) 335-6027
Hanapepe Cafe	(M-P) 335-5011
Jo Jo's Shave Ice, Waimea	(C) 635-7615
Kalaheo Steak House	(M-P) 332-4444
Koke'e Lodge, Koke'e	

Try their homemade chili

	(C-M) 335-6061
Waimea Brewing Co.	

At lovely Plantation Cottages resort

	(M) 338-9733
Wrangler's Steakhouse, Waimea	
	(M) 338-1218

Where To Stay

Hyatt Regency

Give these places a call to inquire about amenities and location. Be sure to ask if you're getting the lowest rate, including weekly offerings. Calling is also a good way to find out which places have Aloha. Also contact Kaua'i Visitors Bureau, 800-464-2924. For island-wide referrals, try *Hawaii's Best Bed & Breakfast* at 800-262-9912 or Hawaiian Beach Rentals, 808-262-6968.

Area code is 808 unless otherwise provided. All listings are recommended; special selections are boldfaced.

TYPE
(**Rustic**) Cabins, hostels
(**B&B**) Bed & Breakfasts, cottages, homes
(**Condos**) Condominium complex
(**Hotel**) Mid-range, mid-size hotels and motels
(**Resort**) High-end, larger, luxury
(**Agent**) Real estate broker for private residences

(C) Cheap ($60 to $100)   (M) Moderate (low-$100 to $200)   (P) Pricey ($200 & up)

NORTH SHORE — KILAUEA, PRINCEVILLE, HANALEI

Jagged green ridges, secret beaches, and waving palms on the North Shore will fulfill everyone's fantasy about what a tropical vacation should be. Hanalei is hip, funky, and beautiful, with walk-around sightseeing. Princeville is manicured condos and two hotels, set on a bluff and buffeted by golf courses and hike-to beaches. Anini Beach is a quieter, more remote beach community, and Kilauea has more of a pastoral feel. During the winter months, storms hit this shore, along with larger surf. During the summer, blue lagoons await. The North Shore is also a long haul to visit other parts of the island.

Aloha Sunrise Inn, Kilauea (cottages)   (**M**) 888-828-1008, 828-1100
Anini Aloha Properties (Agent)   (**M-P**) 800-323-4450
Hanalei Bay Resort, Princeville (Resort)   (**M-P**) 800-922-7866
Hanalei Colony Resort, Haena (Condos)   (**P**) 826-6235, 800-628-3004
    On the beach, the choice for families and groups.
Oceanfront Realty (Agent)   (**M-P**) 800-222-5541, 826-6585
Princeville Vacations (Agent)   (**M-P**) 800-800-3637, 828-6530
    Lori (652-2916, cell) has a wide-range of quality condos.
St. Regis Princeville Resort (Resort)   (**P**) 800-826-4400, 826-9644
Westin Princeville Resort Villas   (**P**) 827-8700

COCONUT COAST — KAPA'A, WAILUA

With palm groves and coral reef at the shore and mountainous forest reserves inland, the Coconut Coast is a place to visit, no matter where your room is on the island. Weather is decent year around, and the central location makes the rest of Kauai easily accessible.

Aloha BeachResort (Resort), Wailua   **(M-P)** 888-823-5111
Alohilani (B&B)   **(C)** 800-533-9316
B&B Kauai (Agent)   **(C-M)** 823-0128
Garden Island Properties (Agent)   **(C-P)** 800-801-0378
Islander on the Beach (Hotel)   **(M-P)** 800-847-7417
Courtyard Marriot Kaua'i (Resort)   **(M-P)** 877-622-2975, 822-3455
The place has aloha, and is the site of various community events.
Kaua'i International Hostel, Kapa'a (Rustic)   **(C)** 823-6142
Plantation Hale (Condos)   **(M)** 800-775-4253
Pono Kai (Condos)   **(M-P)** 800-535-0085
Rainbow's End (B&B cottage)   **(C-M)** 961-3833, 966-4663
Sleeping Giant Realty (Agent)   **(C-M)** 800-247-8831

LIHUE AND NAWILIWILI

Lihue is the county seat and business district, meaning fewer tourists stay here, except on cruise ships in the harbor. Central location is good for outings.

Garden Island Inn (Hotel)
    (C-M) 800-648-0154
Kauai'i Marriott Resort
    (P) 888-236-2427
    Grounds and pool are fabulous. On Kalapaki Beach. Rooms fairly small. (Nearby, Marriott's Kalanipu'u has big rooms, but no grounds or beach.)
Kaua'i Beach Resort (Resort)
    (M-P) 888-236-2427, 245-1955
    On miles of open beach. Well-run with nicely appointed (small) rooms. Nice pools.
Kaua'i Palms Hotel (C) 245-0908

Suite-Paradise.com, Poipu Beach

(C) Cheap ($60 to low-$100)   (M) Moderate (mid-$100 to $200)   (P) Pricey (mid-$200 & up)

POIPU AND KOLOA

Beach potatoes will like sunny Poipu, particularly in the winter when surf is lowest and the weather is approaching from the other side of the island. (Surf's up in the summer here.) The environs are arid, with low scrub on the coast, giving way to indigenous forests inland. Good snorkeling and coast walking, along with ready access to Waimea Canyon. Hanalei is a long haul, but reachable on a day trip. Rates vary from mid-range condos—which tend to be spaced fairly close—to the luxury rooms at the fabulous Hyatt Regency. In Koloa and inland communities, you can find low- to -mid-priced cottages in garden settings. Suite Paradise rents spacious condos at affordable prices.

Hale O Kapeka, Poipu B&B)	(M) 742-6806
Grand Hyatt Kaua'i (Resort)	(P) 800-233-1234, 742-1234
Kahili Mountain Park (Rustic)	(C) 742-9921
some restrictions, go to www.kahilipark.org for current info	
Kiahuna Plantation (Condos)	(M-P) 800-367-8020

> *Large greenspace opens up to the middle of Poipu Beach. Close to great dining.*

Koloa Landing Cottages (B&B)	(C-M) 800-779-8773
Kuhio Shores (Condos)	(C-M) 800-367-8022
Lawai Beach House (Guest Home)	(M-P) 800-325-5701
Nihi Kai Villas (Condos)	(M) 800-367-8020
Poipu Crater Resort (Condos)	(C) 800-367-8020
Poipu Kai Resort (Condos)	(C-P) 800-367-8020

> *Ocean views with easy walks to Poipu Beach and coastal trails.*

Poipu Shores (Condos)	(M-P) 800-367-8020
Sheraton Kauai (Resort)	(P) 888-847-0208
Suite Paradise (Agent)	(C-P) 800-367-8020

> *Selection, guest services, and extra amenities make them the first choice. A wide selection of reasonably priced, top-end condos, many located on a quiet walking path that connects Poipu with the Grand Hyatt and Shipwreck Beach. Beach gear available to guests and the staff are always ready to help.*

WEST SIDE — WAIMEA, KOKE'E, KALAHEO

The West Side is basically non-tourist, although during the day rental cars parade to Waimea Canyon and Barking Sands Beach. This is the arid side of Kauai, which means sun most-often graces its long beaches. Hanapepe and Waimea draw visitors looking for old-style rural settings. Poipu is close by, but the North Shore is a long day trip. Koke'e State Park is a few thousand feet up, so prepare for cool weather if that's your choice.

Camp Sloggett, Koke'e (Rustic, also campsites)	(C) 245-5959
Kauai Tree Houses, Kalaheo (B&B)	(C) 635-3945, 332-9045
Koke'e Lodge Cabins (Rustic)	(C) 335-6061
Waimea Plantation Cottages (Resort)	(P) 800-922-7860, 338-1625

> *Spruced-up authentic cottages set on huge, parklike grounds Oceanfront, but the water is often murky due to Waimea River runoff.*

surfin' da Web

INFORMATIONAL/CULTURAL
www.trailblazertravelbooks.com
www.alternative-hawaii.com
www.gohawaii.com
www.gohawaii.about.com/od/kauai/
    All_About_Kauai_Hawaii.htm
www.hawaii.com
www.hawaii.gov/dlnr/dsp/kauai.com
www.hawaii-nation.org
www.hawaiitrails.org
www.hawaiiweathertoday.com
www.hotspots.hawaii.com
www.pacificislandbooks.com
www.kauai-hawaii.com
www.kauaipolynesianfestival.org
www.kauaigov.org
www.kauai-hawaii.com/parks
www.hawaii-stuff.com
www.kauaimonkseal.com
www.kauainews.com
www.kauaivisitorsbureau.org
www.kauaiworld.com (weather)
www.mele.com
www.nativebooks.com
www.ntbg.com
www.oleo.hawaii.edu
www.planet-hawaii.com
www.thegardenisland.com
www.tripadvisor.com
www.thisweek.com
www.101things.com
www.islandergroup.com
http://en.wikipedia.org/wiki/Kauai

ACTIVITIES & SERVICES:
www.trailblazerhawaii.com
www.adventureskauai.com
    (Princeville Ranch Adventures)
www.bikehawaii.com
www.campingkauai.com
www.cjmstables.com
www.scuba.about.com
www.kauaiseatours.com
www.hawaiianair.com
www.hawaiioutside.com
www.hulasource.com
www.kauaiexplorer.com
www.kauaiwedding.com
www.kayakkauai.com
www.outfitterskauai.com
www.rainbowphoto.com
www.napali.com
www.uhpress.hawaii.edu

ACCOMMODATIONS:
www.wheretostay.com
www.bestplaces.com
www.bnb-kauai.com
www.hanaleisurf.com
www.kauai-bedandbreakfast.com
www.kauaivacationrentals.com
www.poipubeach.org
www.princeville-vacations.com
www.staykauai.com
www.suiteparadise.com
www.travel-kauai.com
www.tripadvisor.com
www.hawaiianbeachrentals.com
www.vrbo.com

Notes

For publisher-direct savings to individuals and groups, and for book-trade orders, please contact:

DIAMOND VALLEY COMPANY

89 Lower Manzanita Drive, Markleeville, CA 96120

Phone-fax 530-694-2740
www.trailblazertravelbooks.com
www.trailblazerhawaii.com (blog)
e-mail: trailblazertravelbooks@gmail.com

Check for eBook versions on Kindle, NookBook, and other devices.
Please contact us with comments, corrections, and suggestions.

DIAMOND VALLEY COMPANY'S
TRAILBLAZER TRAVEL BOOK SERIES

ALPINE SIERRA TRAILBLAZER
Where to Hike, Ski, Bike, Fish, Drive
From Tahoe to Yosemite
ISBN 0-9786371-0-0
ISBN 978-0-9786371-0-1
"A must-have guide. The best and most attractive guidebook for the Sierra. With you every step of the way."—Tahoe Action

GOLDEN GATE TRAILBLAZER
Where to Hike, Walk, Bike
In San Francisco and Marin
ISBN 0-9670072-7-5
ISBN 978-0-9670072-7-4
"Makes you want to strap on your boots and go!"—Sunset Magazine

KAUAI TRAILBLAZER
Where to Hike, Snorkel, Bike, Paddle, Surf
ISBN 0-9786371-4-3
ISBN 978-0-9786371-4-9
"Number one, world-wide among adventure guides."—Barnesandnoble.com

MAUI TRAILBLAZER
Where to Hike, Snorkel, Surf, Drive
ISBN 0-9670072-4-0
ISBN 978-0-9670072-4-3
"The best of them all."—Maui Weekly

HAWAII THE BIG ISLAND
TRAILBLAZER
Where to Hike, Snorkel, Surf, Bike, Drive
ISBN 0-9670072-5-9
ISBN 978-0-9670072-5-0
"Top three world-wide among adventure guides."—Barnesandnoble.com

OAHU TRAILBLAZER
Where to Hike, Snorkel, Surf
From Honolulu to the North Shore
ISBN 0-9786371-2-7
ISBN 978-0-9786371-2-5
"Marvelously flexible. A well-marked trail of tropical adventures."
—San Francisco Chronicle

NO WORRIES HAWAII
A Vacation Planning Guide for
Kauai, Oahu, Maui, and the Big Island
ISBN 0-9670072-9-1
ISBN 978-0-9670072-9-8
"Really a travel planning guide without peer. If only other travel destinations had someting this good."—Guide to Travel Guides

NO WORRIES PARIS
A Photographic Walking Guide
ISBN 10: 0-9786371-6-X
ISBN 13: 978-0-9786371-5-6

"Trailblazers are deserving of ongoing praise. You are guaranteed a unique experience that is high quality and perfect for independent travelers."—Midwest Book Review

"Trailblazers are the essential books to pack when planning a trip to Hawaii."—About.com

The one you'll want to have along. Kauai's most respected and best loved book.—TripAdvisor.com